THEATRE AND NATIONAL IDENTITY IN COLONIAL INDIA

Formation of a Community Through Cultural Practice

THEATRE AND NATIONAL IDENTITY IN COLONIAL INDIA

Formation of a Community Through Cultural Practice

Sharmistha Saha

AAKAR

Theatre and National Identity in Colonial India: Formation of a Community Through Cultural Practice
Sharmistha Saha

First Published 2018

ISBN 978-93-5002-523-9

Published by
AAKAR BOOKS
28 E Pocket IV, Mayur Vihar Phase I
Delhi 110 091 India
aakarbooks@gmail.com

Laser Typeset at
Arpit Printographers, Delhi 110 032

Printed at
Sapra Brothers, Delhi 110 092

Contents

Foreword

Sharmistha Saha's study *Theatre and National Indentity in Colonial India* marks a highly innovative addition to Indian theatre historiography. The first pages already testify to the fact that this book opens up a new perspective on history. Living up to its title, it begins with a critical re-examination of its two fundamental terms—"India" and "theatre". What do they mean? What parameters have been and continue to be used to define the Indian nation and Indian theatre? By looking at both as certain kinds of groups, Saha investigates how the emergence of an "Indian nation" and that of an "Indian theatre" are interrelated. Tracing the problems inherent in the term "theatre" when it comes to different performance genres from the Sanskrit plays to various religious and folk traditions, Saha wisely chooses to retain the term, albeit in inverted commas, thus continuously reminding the reader of its origin and limitations.

It speaks to this book's brilliant approach and completely novel take on historiography to tell the history of colonisation and the coming into being of an Indian nation by retracing the history of 'theatre' in India during this time – even if the focus lies exclusively on Bombay and Calcutta. This has never been attempted before and is accomplished here in an exemplary way. Theoretical reflections and historiographical case studies are closely interwoven. Obviously, the author succeeded in finding new and exciting material in the different archives she visited – material that allowed for a new view on the problem at hand. Among the case studies the one on the *swadeshijatra* in Barisal stands out as well as that on the history of the Indian People's Theatre Association (IPTA), founded in 1943. In these as in the other cases examined, the particular communities that came into being during the performances are explored along with the nature of the freedom that emerged, especially in the latter case: "freedom for all—an equal freedom or a freedom shared equally by all".

The book opens up a new perspective on the history of Indian 'theatre' as well as of the Indian nation. This is a challenging, gripping and, at the same time, highly rewarding read. It deserves a broad readership and will hopefully trigger a number of stimulating debates and discussions.

Berlin, March 2017 **Erika Fischer-Lichte**

Preface

Sharmistha Saha has, in the book, tried to explore the problems of formation of theatre community in the context of colonialism and then of the early years of nation-building exercise in post-colonial India. For this purpose, she has focussed mainly on two important sites of modern Indian theatre, Bengal and Maharashtra. During the period analysed by her, the multiple and contradictory processes of theatre formation happened in response to the challenges of contemporary history. Existing literature on this subject is mostly lacking in focus, precision and depth as it is based on lopsided information, inappropriate conceptual tools and superficial conclusions. Ms Saha's work has avoided this beaten track by combining cogent argument, theoretical perspicacity and well-researched empirical data of texts and contexts.

At the very outset, Ms Saha interrogates the two terms-Indian and theatre, which are normally taken for granted. What constitutes the collective entity called India? How appropriate is the word theatre, which, thanks to colonial intervention, became shorthand for apposite phenomena that had a totally different nomenclature in Indian traditions? The semantic indeterminacies of these terms are kept in mind throughout this book. She invokes and employs critically two concepts, *groupuscule* and *communitas,* borrowed from Sartre and Victor Turner to theorize the cohesive aspect of both nation and theatre. How such voluntarily formed structures freeze into oppressive structures foregoing the initial foundation of freedom is the theme of her narrative.

The formation of collective identity, she points out, was not born out of dialogue between the colonizer and the colonized, but of a compromise between elites in both the groups.

The new concept of 'theatre' without any antecedent in pre-colonial Indian consciousness was identified with the Indian synonym-*nataka* following William Jones' suggestions. Also, the reduction of Indian dramatic tradition to Hindu/Sanskrit tradition happened as a result of orientalist delimitation and by writing off multiple strands of people's performative traditions denominated by synonyms of *khel or lila* (play). This problem of nomenclature is also hinted at. It is commendable that Ms Saha recognizes this problem ignored in most literature on the subject. This recognition also informs her tracing of two forms of dramatic activity: the colonialism-inspired imitative theatre of playhouses and local forms like *jatra*, which were also responding to throes of change in different ways. Because the setting of both these processes was part of a socio-political situation based on unequal exchange, the state later imposed acts inhibiting the freedom of theatre.

There were other types of *groupuscules* in theatre of these times. Ms Saha hints at one of them when she discusses, Tagore's radically different view on theatre as expressed in his essay 'On Stage.' She also mentions his dance dramas based on different principles. This assumes significance in pan-Indian context not just because of Tagore's domineering presence in modern Indian culture but considering the fact that what can be called 'poets' theatre' initiated by Tagore's counterparts in other regions of India had a potential completely unexplored in Indian theatre histories.

The most impressive part of her account is the well-researched analysis of the birth, growth and decay of IPTA due to the contradictions it developed in relation to Left and later to the new Indian state.

The dramatic reversal consequent upon the setting up of state-funded institutions like SNA hijacked the management of theatre and related arts is the culminating point of this theatre history. This sealed the possibility of voluntary participation with a certain kind of bureaucratic control. The sequel of this story, which is the takeover of culture by corporate forces in a world where state has withered away in a way never predicted by Karl Marx, is of course outside the purview of this research.

The main merits of this work are the cogency of arguments, a passionate engagement with the complexity of situations, richness of empirical data and well-structured narrative. A refusal to fall prey to the facile shibboleths of Performance Theory is also commendable. Theoretical tools are used cautiously not to cover up gaps in data but as tools to understand the same. I consider this book which has evolved from her Phd-dissertation as a path-breaker among works on Indian theatre.

I recommend it strongly to all students, teachers and practitioners of Indian theatre. It is of particular value to students and scholars from other related areas of culture interested in progressive and feminist dimensions.

New Delhi, June 2017 **H.S. Shiva Prakash**

Acknowledgement

This acknowledgment is of a deferred nature. There have been at least a few written before this final one and every time as the author I realized more people joined in to make this book possible. In that sense this book, in its very process from being written to now being published has been a collective effort. However the responsibility of possible errors are entirely mine. To begin with, this book has resulted from my doctoral thesis that was submitted to the Institut für Theaterwissenschaft at the Freie Universität in Berlin, Germany in 2014. It would not have been possible without the encouragement and support of my supervisor Prof. Erika Fischer-Lichte who as my Doktormütter walked me through the restrained-ness of cold German weather to active thinking and writing. The extensive archival work that supports this work has been possible because of the financial help that I got from Erasmus Mundus and Deutsche Forschungsgemeinschaft (DFG) . DFG also made the research possible at Internationales Graduiertenkolleg 'InterArt'. During the course of my research, I received continuous support from the visiting fellows of the International Research Center "Interweaving Performance Cultures" like Prof. Rustom Bharucha, Prof. Vasudha Dalmia, Prof. Aparna Dharwadkar and Prof. Sudipto Chatterjee with whom I discussed my dissertation. Prof. Christoph Wulf, my second supervisor and Samik Bandhopadhyay also helped me think through important debates which was otherwise a solitary affair of writing a dissertation. Here I must also mention the immense support of Prof. H.S. Shivaprakash with whom I spent several dusks in discussion over issues of theatre, literature, music, art and most importantly life. Prof. Soumyabrata Choudhury's critical inputs to my work remained valuable. In India, the staff at the West Bengal State Archives, Natya Shodh (Kolkata), National Library of Kolkata, Maharashtra State Archives in Bombay, Library of Mumbai University, National Archives in New Delhi and P.C. Joshi Archives at New Delhi helped me dig into the history of the colonial period.

I found equal support in the staff of the British Library in London and the South Asia Institute in Universität Heidelberg. Old friends like Farah Noor, Ramya Swayamprakash, Sarah Niazi, Preema John, Anoushka Gupta, Ananya Parikh, Tarique Hameed, Ipsita Sahu, Amita Rana, Prabhat Raghunandan, Gourab Ghosh and my sister Sushmita Saha helped with scanning, couriering material, buying books not often immediately available to me and sending them wherever I was, allowing me to just crash at their places during my research trips, formatting my bibliography last minute or just giving me moral support. I am immensely grateful to my family in Germany, Brigitte Hamburger and Paula Wörteler without whom life in Berlin would not have been easy. Nisha and Lavinia continued to be there whenever I needed them. I had very many meaningful discussions with Michael Dusche and Julia Kansok, the ever so joyful couple. My colleagues at Interart especially my several conversations with Andrea, Anu, and Anne were extremely stimulating. The editor Mr. M.V. Kannan arduously went through the several corrections that required to be made to the dissertation and the publisher Mr. K.K. Saxena gave it the form of a book. Rinu Koshi, a research scholar at Indian Institute of Technology Bombay, where I am presently employed gave the citations a last minute nudge. I must add here that Ashish Ranjan's insistence made the completion of this book possible. Lastly, I thank my parents for having patiently struggled with me as I continue to do so with myself. This book is for you!

Mumbai, December 2017 **Sharmistha Saha**

List of Images

depicting the mood of 'terror' (*People's Age*, January 6, 1946).

11. Holi: The popular harvest dance in the villages of the United Provinces (*People's Age*, January 6, 1946).
12. India Immortal: Ballet depicting the story of our country and our people from early times to the present days, the background of our rich cultural heritage and the growing unity of our people to end foreign rule (*People's Age*, January 6, 1946).

Introduction

I. A Matter of Conjuncture

We, the People of Europe? – A big question mark, a question mark that Eteinne Balibar in his book *'We, the People of Europe? Reflections on Transnational Citizenship'* can afford. His concern here becomes a wide variety of socio-political questions that include questions of unification of Europe, sovereignty and citizenship in the age of globalization. This leads him to the interrogation of the 'nation-form' and 'nationalism' and the relation between the two, which he studies in the light of (a) historicity of nations and of nationalisms, (b) national identities and (c) structural violence. My concern is not his study by itself, which of course is an important contribution in political philosophy in the given historical conjuncture, but rather my interest lies in the question mark. What he questions here is a certain socio-political congregation, which in reality, exists. When I say, *We, the people of India*—this very speech-act entitles me not only to my existence as an Indian alone but also to the 'We' as 'Us' the 'Indians' who exist—is it not a matter of fact? Can I question—do we Indians exist? If in political philosophy as Balibar also points out, borders and territories, state, community and 'public' structures, citizenship and sovereignty, rights and norms, violence and civility are considered to be speculative categories, then what is that *force* which makes these theoretically speculative structures inherent in terms of existence? Can 'seriality' of being whereby Sartre meant a loose congregation under vigilance of power and institutionalized groups become so forceful as to not allow any threat of breakage? Or do we simply call this 'state violence'? I think here lies the difference between Balibar's question mark and mine. I arrive at this conclusion not because of any structural causality that is inherent to each of these questions but because certain unpredictable events, and dialectic evolutions nourished the idea of 'Indianness' in a way that the idea of being 'European' did not experience. What I mean by this is a shared experience of a colonial past that functioned as an adhesive and initiated the effort of assembled individuals to dissolve the 'seriality'[1] in them to create this certain 'group' in the Sartrean sense[2]—I quote 'we are free together; therefore the ensemble is free'. One could evaluate this free-ness in the Indian context and to engage with that evaluation would lead me to a different direction altogether but what I am interested in is to see how *We, the people of India* came together. Within what kind of discursive matrix does such an identity lie? To engage with the material of *inert determination of the future* and go backward in tracing the moments of such congregations into the groupuscules that led to a massive movement against colonial power. Having said that, I limit this project and I will explain how.

Now this group, whose inherent will is to become free from the 'seriality' and the 'practico-inert'[3] is not only bound together by performative gestures like the oath as Sartre elucidates but also belongs to each individual praxis as an interiorized unity of multiplicity. This element of reciprocity finds manifestation not only in terms of resisting power but also in representing each of the selves creating a 'group'- for all who belong. Now that such forms ultimately take the shape of coercive institutionalized bodies is not being questioned here, but what becomes important to see is what works as cohesive agents whereby each belongs, by his or her own will. Especially in the present historical juncture to see it entirely as a coercive institution with complete lack of keen participation and no political will would be naive given that India has continuously been hailed in the recent times as the largest democracy of the world which at least votes to maintain such a body. Hence, rather than staying in denial, it is important to see what really brought the 'Indians' together. How has such a *truth of being* been achieved? What historical experiences did confer on this community such a 'matter of fact' identity without any essential basis? What is that *force*? Or was it an invented narrative that the 'Indians' would rather cling on to? In the 2014 Lok Sabha (lower house) elections, after the Bharatiya Janata Party was voted in, *The Hindu*, a major English daily published an article as a reminder/warning, apparently to the elected Prime Minister Narendra Modi and the country called 'Preserve the idea of India'[4], highlighting the fact that plurality was what added to such an idea. If nationalism is a rather homogenizing concept, then how does plurality still hold such an idea? Sudipta Kaviraj's essay gives us some insight about such narrativization. In his essay *The Imaginary Institution of India*, Kaviraj sees that such narrative persuasion had begun from the early stages of colonialism in India, although at that stage it could not have been called fully nationalist, if one is to understand nationalism as 'the presence of an idea of a determinate nation with clear boundaries, unambiguous principles of inclusion, established by a clear act of choice'[5]. He at the same time warns against any kind of anachronistic view by which he means the understanding that earlier periods and cultures were structured like the present day in their institutions, practices, discourses, meanings and significations of concepts. Such a view, he argues would lead us to believe that the earlier stages of nationalism were a paler version of patriotism. He sees no such connection between being patriotic and being Indian. He writes—

> ...historically speaking, this configuration of consciousness becomes nationalist before it becomes Indian. Happily, Indianness is not entirely an afterthought, this Indianness would have been a mere insubstantial pretense and a large historical movement and a constitutional democratic state after independence could not be hung on that wispy thread.[6]

Borrowing from Gramsci's argument about Italian nationalism, he sees unilinear national hagiography impossible; however within this fragmentedness, he finds the roots of nationalist thinking. In the early stages, it remained an unnamed community. He argues therefore 'the resposibility, the role, the character of nationalism emerges earlier in history than the community'. The reponsibility being born before the agent. He sees this responsibility, this politics born in earlier generations, within a colonial society in 'a world of performatives. In a colonial society, utterance itself becomes political given many a time that faces restrictions. He sees in the earlier stage an anti-colonial consciousness/discourse that is genetically related to 'mature nationalism'. For Kaviraj anti-colonialism as he is using it here is 'merely an oppositional attitude towards colonialism, and if we gather up all its historical characteristics, it is more a cultural critique, a resentment against ignominy rather than a political economic rejection'. The other useful insight that one comes across in Kaviraj's study is that nationalism can be seen as a 'thought-form which is by definition collective'. He uses the Foucauldian trope of *enonciation* by which he means the context within which utterance takes place. The process—in case of nationalism, which Kaviraj argues is always collective. However, he sees it as a 'fuzzy' one that is yet to discover its reasons of coming together. Although for the British it was a map that defined India, the colonized 'Indians' needed more reasons than one to internally justify themselves. Especially in case of India, earlier distinctions that were socially normativized were according to caste groups without any clarity of geographical location as such. Kaviraj writes, if asked about one's community (*samaj*) the answer would invariably be the name of the village or neighbourhood or caste or religious denominations, and never the linguistic group.[7] The plurality, a 'narrative-contract' was achieved when the English educated intellectuals could no more justify colonialism in rationalist utilitarian arguments. Initiated by the Bengali bourgeoisie or *babu* as they came to be known, started by being concerned about the *bangali jati* or Bengali race, and later within this consciousness were incorporated other linguistic regions and races. History-writing was put to use in 'gerrymandering the boundaries of their collective self' argues Kaviraj. He further adds that enlightenment and its social epistemics that were used to develop consciously this 'thought-form' were historically more conscious than earlier patriotism against English 'invaders'. He writes that 'The telling of a story brings into immediate play some strong conventions invoking a narrative community', a narrative which is an abstract universe of ideal consensus. In the process, as the fuzziness is removed, they get enumerated, knowing their strength in terms of numbers as it were. In the earlier phase, the colonial government used utilitarian social theory as a justification for their stay but by the twentieth century, such a need was no more felt by the colonized educated class who had imbibed the same ideological principles creating a process of distinction from the British—an image of the other. To understand broadly colonialism, Kaviraj points at the need to understand anti-colonialism. He writes—

> Unless the people who are subjected to colonialism are seen to engage in such an enterprise which—despite evident internal differences between periods, between high and folk culture, between the great tradition and the small, between the anti-colonialists and the nationalists, between the radicals and the conservatives—is still seen as one—as a single whole historical enterprise—its history cannot be written.[8]

He ends with a word of caution. He points at the 'colligatory element in history' by which 'historical accounts join incidents (accounts of facts) or processes in a sequence: a->b->c->d and so on'. He suggests that there is a requirement to be aware of such a sequencing that is not self-evident. Hence a 'justifiability' of such a colligation can be argued for but not its 'finality'.

Kaviraj's insights are largely useful for this research which begins by posing a simple question 'What is Indian Theatre?' What does it essentially mean when a claim about a certain form being 'Indian Theatre' is made? The question really begins with the word 'Indian', an identity that as we have already argued appears as an unquestionable matter of fact today. The moment such a question is posed, it brings to the fore as Kaviraj points out, its *enonciation* i.e. it came to be what it is as it is not historically self-evident. What constitutes this community which we have borrowing from Sartre, called a 'group'? Interestingly, the perspective from which we are looking at it—the theatre, like nationalism itself is ontologically based on the 'group'. The theatre director Peter Brook wrote—

> I can take any empty space and call it a bare stage. A man walks

> across this empty space whilst someone else is watching him, and this is all that is needed for an act of theatre to be engaged.[9]

What does this imply for a definition of theatre? It brings us to the bare truth about theatre. It is not the stage, the lights, mise-en-scène but two people within a given spatio-temporal reality. It is the act of one, in Brook's example walking across and the observation of the other, it is doing things together and it is a communion. So we can say the modality of existence for theatre is communion, something that in reality happens—theatre hence is not a 'thought form' but rather something that has material existence. Let us call it a 'material-form'. Then what would a study of 'Indian Theatre' imply when the modality of *enonciation* for both Indian and Theatre is the community? What do we mean by a study of 'Indian Theatre' when one is a 'thought-form' and the other a 'material-form'? The utterance of the word Indian implies a matter-of-factness of an indissoluble identity that naturally points at a community of Indians. (Is a singular Indian being possible? Possibly not.) However theatre always already implies dissolution. To use Maurice Blanchot's words, the community of the theatre is an unavowable community. It explicitly produces its own impossibility. It always ends. What would then be the consequences of studying two communities that are both indissoluble and unavowable at the same time? Theatre always ends for its spectators with uncertainty. But as Sudipta Kaviraj points out, even the fuzziness of the nation finds concrete forms, whatever might be its reasons of concreteness. However this research works with a hypothesis that an agent does not always necessarily remove the fuzziness although Kaviraj points at the 'Western educated' as the agents of nationalist thought. They might have been the storytellers but the ones who heard the story did not necessarily perceive it the way it was meant to be perceived. At least in case of theatre, which was used as a platform of disseminating such stories, the space where nationalist discourses were *play*-ed (*khel*), left communities that remained ever indeterminate although affected, transformed which often coagulated into a singular mass but was never constructed in the sense of an external agent facilitating its becoming. I would like to extend this argument even to the performers. This means that theatre is a volatile space and always remains so, precisely, because of which it also remains a political one.

II. Coagulating Communities—Towards a Methodology

The interest of this work is to locate *Coagulating Communities*. What do we mean by that? The fact that congregations or tiniest of groups, even of only two as in the case of Peter Brook's definition of the theatre, which borrowing from Sartre could be called the 'groupuscule' that was indeterminate in a certain historical juncture, only to become determinate later, taking the shape of an institutionalized body i.e. the nation whose unbecoming then becomes an impossibility, is the subject of our study. One of the fundamental problems of such a study in conjuncture i.e. the idea that such a study struggles with questions that are provoked and determined by economic, social and political conflict, —remains always within conjuncture. Here I mean that neither the study nor the researcher can go beyond the 'here and now' (jetztzeit). Therefore a study of a linear genealogical sort becomes impossible. However it remains overtly historical. Because ultimately to arrive at any theoretical proposition about the national being i.e. the 'Indian' or a philosophical doctrine about theatre and the so called 'Indian Theatre'—a category that rightfully requires thorough questioning,—such a methodology becomes imperative.

At a methodological level, what I am trying to do is create citations.[10] The method of picking on citations, helps create an understanding of historical processes that have manifold impact, sometimes even beyond the purview of the repercussions certain historical events are said to have had. Walter Benjamin in his beautiful piece *Theses on The Philosophy of History*, that appears as though it were a poetic allusion about history, unfolds history as the view of the past. However, this past has a 'secret agreement' with the present generations. He writes—'Our coming was expected on earth'. He calls this link 'a weak Messianic power'. As a retroactive force, it comes back as nothing should be counted as lost for history, he writes. It appears as an image that flashes up at an instant and then disappears making every moment citable. But it is not recognition of that past historically 'the way it really was'; rather it's like grabbing a memory that just came by in a flash. His concern in the essay is historical materialism and he argues for a dialectical process of history writing—narrative that is ever in a process of breaking away from conformism. He therefore makes the historical narrative a very private affair—it is private insofar as it belongs to a specific generation that always already carries the past. He uses the metaphor of Paul Klee's 'Angelus Novus' which shows an angel looking like he is moving away from something he is fixedly contemplating. 'His eyes are staring, his mouth is open, and his wings are spread. This is how one pictures the angel of history' he writes. He continues— 'This storm irresistibly propels him into the future to which his back is turned, while the pile of debris before him grows skyward.' Sudipta Kaviraj also acknowledges this fact of the ever-indomitable process of history. It is by keeping in mind this dialectical process of a dialogue that the past always engages in, with the present, that certain moments from the past have been chosen to serve the purpose of our narrative. The rationale behind such a selection is a very private one, by which I mean that its inherent logic lies within the present scenario where nationalities have come to be understood as indissoluble categories—Indianness in reality that has real economic—political—social consequences for those of our generation who hold this identity. However, the material for this research was selected or cited based on what I as the researcher thought best held through my research question. It is like the best berries I could get for my marmalade. It, at the same time has a certain logical progression insofar as it attempts to begin from the beginning of English trade and subsequent colonization of India. Unlike many other studies that see this interaction with the British, of the 'Indian' people as an 'encounter', this study refrains from such a substantive usage. The reason for that could be explained borrowing from Louis Althusser's *Philosophy of the Encounter: Later Writings, 1978- 87.* He argues that in the history of philosophy there exists apart from the rationalist traditions of materialism, another kind of materialism, which he calls the 'materialism of the encounter', or 'aleatory materialism'. To briefly explain what he proposes—he argues for a randomness of origins i.e. a 'non-necessary chance' from which the world is born. An Althusserian definition of an 'encounter' hence presupposes birth from vacuum—the coming of the new. Keeping in mind such a taxonomic appointment, it becomes necessary to take a divergent path from such a theorization by those who call British colonial rule in India an encounter. From the dates available, one of the first contacts with Europeans happened around 327-326 BC. If the logic of an encounter is to be solely understood as a first, then for the geographical mass that is India, the English were not the first 'external' culture that it came in contact with. Efforts of colonization began as early as the sixteenth century, which were led by clear economic-political agendas of the colonizing countries of Europe at home and in the colonies. These early experiences of colonization had socio-cultural along with political-economic consequences for the subcontinent. To call British colonial rule, an encounter of some sort only tends to overlook the causality of past events that led to colonization by the British. It was not aleatory in that sense i.e. not an encounter. The term that has been used for the purpose of the research is interaction—an interaction between two distinct cultural and distant geographical spaces that interacted mostly to the economic benefit of the colonizing power. It is this relationship of power that becomes the driving force from the very beginning of this research.

III. The Historical Context

Keeping in mind the above premise, the study of such an interaction has been limited in this research to the Bengal and the Bombay Presidency, very consciously especially because of their importance as trade centres and cities under British colonial rule. At the same time, these were some of the first areas to be annexed by the British. However, my personal familiarity with these two areas was also kept in mind, which is why Madras Presidency was kept out of the purview of this study, although it was one of the early possessions of the East India Company. The East India Company as we know was a British joint-stock company that took parts of the subcontinent in their own possession in the eighteenth century that set forth British colonial rule later on.

During chapter division, the political implications of the colonial rule were kept in mind, especially the anti-colonial movements, which were not necessarily always nationalist in the sense that we understand 'Indian', or 'India' today. A good example would be that of the 'Sepoy Mutiny' of 1857 that could be called anti-colonial and also patriotic but the fuzziness of nationalism was not done away with at that historical juncture. Historian Shireen Moosvi writes,

> Indeed it was a mutiny not of a small group, but one involving the vast bulk of soldiers of the largest modern army in all of Asia at the time. The Bengal Army comprised 132,000 native sepoys, out of whom barely 8,000 remained loyal to the English. The mutiny involved the troops stationed in the east, from Barrackpore near Calcutta, all the way to Peshawar on the north-west frontier of the subcontinent. The Revolt was nevertheless much more than a mutiny. In a large geographical region, whose population today amounts to nearly a quarter of the population of this country, the revolt took on the complexion of what Disraeli and Marx pronounced to be a 'national revolt'.[11]

The other significance that this event has for our study is that post 1857, 'India' became a Crown colony to be governed directly by the British Parliament, and thereafter the responsibility for Indian affairs fell upon a member of the British cabinet, the Secretary of State for India, while in India itself, the man at the helm of affairs continued to be the Governor-General, and later known in his capacity as the representative of the monarch, the Viceroy of India. This largely affected the mode of governance of the colony and at the same time the anti-colonial movement. One of the oblique consequences of the 'Mutiny' of 1857 was the censorship law called *The Dramatic Performance Act, 1876* which laid down the power to prohibit certain dramatic performances, power to serve order of prohibition, penalty for disobeying order, power to notify orders, penalty for disobeying prohibition, power to call for information, power to grant warrant to police to enter and arrest and seize, and the power to prohibit dramatic performance in any local area, except under licence.[12] Within the scope of this research, it has been possible to further the study till the final stages of the anti-colonial movement, which stretched to the mid-twentieth century.

Theatre in this research has been studied as an *archigenre*. We have tried to elaborate on the matter in Part I of this book. It has been seen as an all-encompassing performative mode. At the same time, the research takes note of the discourse around the theatre during the colonial period when 'theatre'[13] (note the inverted commas), a by-product of British colonial rule came to reside in India. Europe in the eighteenth century was moving on from the medieval theatre that was still concerned with divine intervention to a bourgeois theatre whose concern was to represent reason and nature.[14]

Richard Schechner[15] argues that in the West, the drama-script dyad was emphasized over the theatre-performance one unlike in the East letting go of the manifesting capacity of theatre-performance while focusing on communication. In India, the so-called coming of 'theatre' initiated a process of genre trouble during the colonial period. A nationalist discourse about the theatre got generated in this process which in turn created 'groupuscules' that participated in such discourse. These organized theatre/performance groupuscules which often were directly associated with socio-political societies or *samitis* or sabhas as they were known, like for example in Poona, the Poona Sarvajanik Sabha which was affiliated by Aurobindo Ghose and many such other 'groups' functioned as subsidiary organizations of the reformist/nationalist *samitis* or *sabhas* of the later anti-colonial phase. By the early mid-twentieth century this movement of the cultural societies on the one hand got nourished by nationalist-extremist thinking and on the other by nationalist-moderate thinking of the Indian National Congress (founded in 1885) brand and later by communist thinking as for example, groupuscules like the *Youth Cultural Institute* or *Friends of Soviet Russia*. The immediate concern of these groupuscules was socio-political and economic problems that mostly were guided by a reformist logic informed by the colonial educational system. In the work of *Youth Cultural Institute* and *Friends of Soviet Russia* and later *Progressive Writer's Association* and their affiliated performance groups mostly in urban regions like Bombay or Calcutta, not only social reform but also international issues became matters of concern. The idea of an 'Indian People' or *jati* slowly got carved out through a realization of difference not only within a national context as the colonial master vs. the colonial subject but at the same time as against an international ambit. This was also because many of these groupuscules were formed outside the national borders of British India. For example, Mulk Raj Anand, one of the founder members of the *Progressive Writer's Association* writes—

> PWA was founded in November 1935 in London when after the disillusionment and disintegration of years of suffering in India and conscious of the destruction of most of our values through the capitalist crisis of 1931, a few of us emerged from the slough of despond of the cafes and garrets of Bloomsbury (in London) and formed the nucleus of the Indian Progressive Writer's 'Association'.[16]

Throughout, the main concern remains the idea of the 'political' and the formation of the 'national' subject or identity formation[17] i.e. the *homo nationalis*. With the formation of the idea of an Indian 'people' came the idea of a national culture that was to ultimately become *free* from any colonial dominance. Now the notion of *free* or free-ness as I had earlier pointed out borrowing from Sartre is not a collective idea alone but what becomes important in Sartre's concept of the 'group' is the individual as free within the 'group'. However within a colonial context, the union takes place due to some divine intervention as it were. Rabindranath Tagore writes,

> He, who is one, who is above all colour distinctions, who dispenses the inherent needs of men of all colours, who comprehends all things from the beginning to the end, let Him unite us to one another with the wisdom which is the wisdom of goodness.[18]

In *On India*, Tagore's short piece on what was the idea of India to him or how he perceived that which was India, nation becomes almost a platonic ideal, to something that was yet to be—an artist's work, who combines *Satyam, Jnanam, Anantam Brahma*—truth, knowledge and an eternal being. This idea of the 'whole' and its 'being' as material existence opens us to one of the most 'continually confronted' questions which is, that of 'representation'. How can the nation be represented, a representation that incorporates 'all colour distinctions' holding in it the truth of 'being' from the 'beginning to the end' as is prescribed by the 'wisdom of goodness'. But in this, the artist is not the divine one but that divinity of expression is embedded in the 'people' who are to create that 'work of art'. So their being together is not only driven by freedom but also by an idea of the togetherness. Tagore's writings on art and theatre and his dance dramas become a reflection of this thought-form. Many of the groupuscules that functioned during this period were highly influenced by Tagore's work. His influence can be clearly seen in many of the works of the *Indian People's Theatre Association* (IPTA) as also of the IPTA Central Squad. In this chapter, I feel it necessary to talk about Puran Chandra Joshi who on the other hand believed art to be a tool in moulding the 'people'—art therefore goes beyond the capacity of aesthetics alone and becomes 'work'—'desher kaaj' or work for the nation. At the same time, Bankim Chandra Chatterjee, Bal Gangadhar Tilak, Aurobindo Ghosh, would like to believe in the nation where the sovereign is still God. Aurobindo Ghosh writes—

> For what is a nation? What is our mother country? It is not a piece of earth, nor a figure of speech, nor a fiction of the mind. It is a mighty *shakti*, composed of all the *shaktis* of all the millions of units that make up the nation...The *shakti* we call India, 'Bhawani Bharati' is the living unity of the *shaktis* of three hundred million people....[19]

In the dramatic works of Aurobindo Ghosh and many of the performances of his dramatic works, the almighty as the nation gets representation.

In order to understand that which was the *theatrum mundi* –a vision for the theatre of the world, it became necessary to place oneself as the 'national being' against the world; and at a conscious evaluation and re-evaluation of the 'nation-form', their ideas were used by the 'groups' in the conjunction of modernity.

IV. The Logic of Progression

This research hence looks at two different thought-forms,—that of a nationalist idea that gave birth to an identity called 'Indian' and that which has been called *theatre*. So far, we have discussed how 'Indian' has been understood as a thought-form. There has been some research in the social sciences regarding this idea, which is also often refered to as 'Indianness'. Especially with the growth of post-colonial critique of colonial modernity and questions of identity, such a study was on the rise. However, such research continued even after there was disillusionment regarding the post-colonial agenda.[20] We are leaving such a study solely focussing on the question of 'Indianness' out of our purview. However, our focus is on another subject, which also needs to be understood as a thought-form to begin with. It is that *thing* we have called *theatre*! The word theatre came to be used in Indian languages from its usage in English by the British colonizers during the nineteenth century. Initially there was enough speculation as to what it refers to when *theatre* is meant and on the other hand, the orientalist discourse was how India lacked *theatre*. This research begins with a study of the discourse around theatre and what relationship it developed with the other thought-form that is 'Indianness'. We move from the question of the thought-forms to the material-form they took. The investigation begins with the study of the colonial British population, their cultural practices and what relation that held to their identity. It then looks at the colonial native urban population, their cultural practices and emerging aspects of a new identity that was focussed on understanding *samaj* or society, *jati* or race, public etc. We also look at the interaction between the two and the shape that *theatre* took in this context. We move on in time with two other examples of the material-forms evolving through dialogue with the thought-forms, one from the early twentieth century, and the other from before independence when a more vivid imagery of the nation had taken shape.

This research henceforth has been divided into four main chapters apart from the *Introduction* and the *Epilogue*. The main thread of our argument, which we have discussed above i.e. an interaction, an anti-colonial consciousness and a nationalist movement, become the guiding principle throughout. The main focus has been to deal with distinct theatrical forms that in the anglophone world have often been put under the umbrella term performance maintaining although a difference with 'theatre', which is mainly defined by its use of drama and the auditorium space.[19] However, here I have largely refrained from using the term performance, as we would see in our first chapter the theatre/performance distinctions do not really fit right within the scenario of the subcontinent or even take different meanings than its anglophone use. The notion of the performative was always inherent in the early bearings of the word theatre as slowly theatre directors like Rabindranath Tagore, Vishnudas Bhave, Girish Chandra Ghosh and others had always already incorporated elements of the then existing performance forms within the idea of a drama based 'theatre'. Hence, the word 'performance' as is used especially in the anglophone countries does not quite fit in. In passing, I would like to highlight here rather reiterate that we probably cannot get rid of the debris of our past as Walter Benjamin highlighted. So Part I looks at these issues of genre identification and claims of non-existence of certain genres and what implications these debates had on an overall understanding of theatre. In most cases, the premise of such an understanding would be set on what comprises the theatre. At the same time, the premise would be set by the agent of such a question. The agent celebrated a discovery like the discovery of *Shakuntala* or shrugged its absence as was claimed about the medieval period. These were the orientalists. This discourse about the theatre constantly moved back and forth marking the checklists of a civilised subject. The haves and have-nots judged how much at par the colonized society was, at least in terms of cultural superiority, with the colonial master as every time they made anthropological revelations. This discourse was followed up within an anti-colonial and later nationalist consciousness. The chapter also explores how a hybrid category of the 'theatre' which was the 'same but not quite' in the sense of Homi Bhabha came into being.

The following three chapters of Part II are distinctive from the Chapter 1 in terms of being fixed to specific periods of history and the *theatre* discourse at that point. Chapter 2 deals with the idea of theatre being a space of sociability that we have introduced already here in the *Introduction*. Within an interactive, colonial atmosphere this space i.e. the colonial urban space and here in this case we are looking at the urban centres

Bombay and Calcutta, was used as just another tool of sociability apart from ball room dances, dinners etc. However, though the native and the English community interacted, they maintained their separate identities in these spaces. The spaces of sociability remained incommensurable. The 'theatre' of the colonial English population in the newly developing cities in the early nineteenth century became occasions for nostalgic articulations and merry-making, all in the name of the homeland. The 'foreign air' about it collided with the interests of the educated bourgeoisie of these cities. 'Theatre' evolved and found a new home in the *babu*'s cultural life. While the *babu* or the native elite became more and more self-determined in their grip over the technologies of a modern society, the English society became increasingly dispassionate about it. We see the same thing happening with the Parsi community, Gujaratis and Maharashtrians in Bombay. This was also the early phase of groupuscule formation in the colony that became aware of a national being that was distinct from earlier modes of communitarian life.

Chapter 3 is the study of theatre as the 'House of Satan'. This has been explained in the chapter. It deals with the social, moral and ethical transformations that happened with the so-called 'coming of the theatre' in the nineteenth century. Ideas of social rectification, conduct and censorship evolved in turn transforming the question of a national identity. Especially when the colonial government felt threatened with sedition, it brought into force the *Dramatic Performances Act of 1876*. The institutional validation of the theatre in this way, by a declaration of what were those genres that could be called 'performances', opened the debate to what the definition of performance could be. Here it needs to be highlighted that 'theatre', farces, pantomimes etc. were all initially put under this category with later additions to be made. This chapter explores how *jatra*, a performative form known to different parts of India was incorporated within such a vocabulary although there was initial hesitance. We deal with the *Swadeshi Jatra* that evolved in Barisal in present day Bangladesh which, at that time was part of the Bengal Presidency. This case study opens up the fact that the theatre discourse in India was not only something that in the early days the orientalists engaged in, and later was taken over by the

'Indians', but rather that it remained within the colonial official discourse, transforming the colonizer's perception of theatre as much as that of the colonized's as thought-forms started evolving as material ones.

The last chapter, Chapter 4 looks at the groupuscules of the urban centres once more. Here it takes a very specific case study for its purpose of evaluating how theatre and the nationalist discourse evolved late in the anti-colonial phase, that is the mid-twentieth century. In 1943, the *Indian People's Theatre Association* was formed, which was affiliated to the Communist Party of India. The IPTA had several regional wings but what were striking were the performances of the IPTA Central Squad, which functioned as a national unit, and were often distinct from the concerns of the regional wings. As a unit that had assigned itself the broader task of national unity, the aesthetics of the IPTA was to construct a singular narrative of the nation, borrowing from the existing multiple units of performance culture, which were often incorporated as the traditions of the 'real people', the 'working class', and the 'peasants' (influenced by the Communist Party's logic) of the Nation. When in 1946, a certain section of the Communist Party felt that the IPTA Central Squad was a 'white elephant' on which the Communist Party had to spend a lot, the Squad was disbanded. What happened as a result of this was that many of the members joined the *Indian National Theatre* of the Indian National Congress and later in Independent India these people became forebears of Indian culture. This chapter's aim would be to focus on these several tensions that became apparent in the performances of the 'people' and to evaluate terms like 'people's theatre' and 'national theatre' in the light of that which was the aim of all these groups—*freedom*.

V. Conclusion to the Introduction

Before I conclude, I would like to clarify that I am not considering the nation as the 'group' but rather the idea of 'group' is used in the Sartrean sense. Within this context, my interest does not lie in locating good nationalisms and bad nationalisms but rather this study explores the several relationships of power and structural configurations that pervade the discursive matrix of a national 'Indian' being and the 'Indian Theatre'. There has been a conscious effort to keep the commercial theatre scenario out of the purview of this study especially of the late nineteenth/early twentieth century although that was also a playground of such equations. Rather the preference has been based on mainly the political agenda of a national subject-creation especially in Chapters 3 and 4. These help us evaluate the efficacy of the theatre as a transformative form as well which might be conscious of its politics but that does not lead anyone to a determinate solution. Especially in the last chapter, this uncertain sphere that theatre leaves its spectators as well as its agents to, is explored. Theatre in this research is hence studied as holding political energies, which is an intrinsic element of the form. Finally, the study is an exploration of my own 'being' as an Indian national through an evaluation of conjunctures in history, theatre, performance, and life—a *theatrum mundi*.

REFERENCES

1. Jean Paul Sartre, *Critique of Dialectical Reason: Theory of Practical Ensembles*, Vol. 1, Trans. Alan Sheridan-Smith (Verso, London, New York, 2004).
2. The group unlike the series, is the instrumentation of a common aim, comparable to one's body (Sartre denies any organic idealism)—it is the end as well as the means. The group project is 'tearing away man from the status of alterity which makes of him a product of his product, to transform him...into a product of the group, that is to say—so long as the group is freedom—into his own product'.
3. A negation of praxis, which exercises its own counterfinality without an author and produces its own idea or rationality by virtue of having been worked by man, who then is alienated within it, theoretically free and sovereign but in reality 'powerless'- a victim of inertia.
4. http://www.thehindu.com/opinion/editorial/preserve-the-idea-of-india/article6017266.ece.
5. Sudipta Kaviraj, 'The Imaginary Institution of India' In *Subaltern Studies VII: Writings on South Asian History and Society*, Eds. Partha

Chatterjee and Gyanendra Pandey (Oxford University Press, Oxford and New York, 1992), 7.

6. Ibid., 8.
7. However this remains contested. 8. Ibid., 35.
9. Peter Brooke, *The Empty Space* (Touchstone Book, New York, 1968).
10. For Walter Benjamin, each moment mankind has lived becomes a citation–*Theses on the Philosophy of History* (Illuminations, Pimlico, London, 1999).
11. Introduction, Shireen Moosvi, *Facets of the Great Revolt 1857*, Ed. S. Moosvi (Tulika Books, New Delhi, 2008), xi.
12. http://www.pap.gov.pk/uploads/acts/6.html.
13. It has been tried to emphasize on the distinction between the two theatres by the use of quotation marks for one and not for the other. It becomes more self-evident as we elaborate more in the chapters.
14. Refer to Erika Fischer–Lichte, *History of European Drama and Theatre*, Trans. Jo Riley (Routledge, London and New York, 2002).
15. In Richard Schechner, 'Drama, Script, Theatre, and Performance' (*The Drama Review: TDR*, Vol. 17, No. 3, Theatre and the Social Sciences, September, 1973), 5-36.

    Schechner tries to give precise definitions to the terms drama, script, theatre and performance in this essay. He calls drama 'the smallest, most intense (heated-up) circle. A written text, score, scenario, instruction, plan, or map', script 'the basic code of the event' of theatre, theatre 'the event enacted by a specific group of performers' and performance 'the whole constellation of events, most of them passing unnoticed, that takes place in both performers and audience...'.
16. Mulk Raj Anand, *On the Progressive Writer's Movement;* In *Marxist Cultural Movement in India: Chronicles and Documents (1936-1947)*, Ed. Sudhi Pradhan (National Book Agency Pvt. Ltd., Kolkata, 1979).
17. Political Scientist, Partha Chatterjee, one of the most influential critics of the nationalist project in colonial Bengal in his most significant contribution to reading of nationalism in India, *Nation and Its Fragments*, outlines his methodological premise through a critique of Benedict Anderson according to whom—'the historical experience of nationalism in Western Europe, in the Americas, and in Russia had supplied for all subsequent nationalisms a set of modular forms from which nationalist elites in Asia and Africa had chosen the ones they liked.' Chatterjee in

his enlightened post-colonial force writes back—'History, it would seem, has decreed that we in the post-colonial world shall only be perpetual consumers of modernity. Europe and the Americas, the only true subjects of history, have thought out on our behalf not only the script of colonial enlightenment and exploitation, but also that of our anticolonial resistance and post-colonial misery... The most powerful as well as the most creative results of the nationalist imagination in Asia and Africa are posited not on an identity but rather on *difference* with the 'modular' forms of the national society propagated by the modern West.' (Chatterjee, 5) He further argues that—'By my reading, anticolonial nationalism creates its own domain of sovereignty within the colonial society well before it begins its political battle with the imperial power. It does this by dividing the world of social institutions and practices into two domains—the material and the spiritual. The material is the domain of the 'outside', of the economy and of statecraft, of science and technology, a domain where the West had proved its superiority and the East had succumbed... The spiritual, on the other hand, is an 'inner' domain bearing the 'essential' marks of cultural identity.' (Chatterjee, 6) Firstly, the *difference* that is realised in a colonised society comes through the formation of the *identity*. The identification of the *difference*, I would argue is not a conscious process that is postulated as contradistinctive to the colonial sovereign state but this happens through a process of political *representation* in the colonised dominion. Here by representation, borrowing from Carl Schmitt, I mean something that assumes that although every state form presupposes a structural *identity* between rulers and ruled, such *identity* can never be fully realized in practice and *identity* on the other hand presupposes the 'unmediated' unity of the people. I would argue here that it was the non-realization of *identity* that led to the realization of *difference* within the colonized natives—the difference which later was stimulated by socio-economic circumstances and events leading to *aporia* that an 'unmediated' unity of the people could be attained. Secondly, political sovereignty cannot exist at two levels within the same dominion as has been suggested by Chatterjee—a dominion he calls the 'inner domain of sovereignty'. Schmitt argues that the interdependence of modern state and liberalism born out of Reformation and disputes over religious toleration corresponds with the rise of something approaching the theory of 'possessive individualism'. Drawing from Abbé Sieyes that the nation's constitution was not a constituted or collective power but rather a constituent or individual power, he argues that liberalism's foundation was in the private sphere where each one of the member of the people had to be a constituent of the power i.e. the Nation. (Carl Schmitt as referred to, by Duncan Kelly, 119) As Sumit Sarkar has pointed out in *Modern India 1885-1947* that the British Government in India was an autocracy of hierarchically organized officials, headed by the Viceroy and the State of Secretary, but gradually there was an attempt to liberalize the system, through induction of native representatives which was later often demanded by the 'initiated' and 'qualified' natives. Thirdly, the nationalist project cannot be reduced to binaries of the material outer domain where the West was sovereign and the spiritual inner domain where the East was trying to mark out its cultural identity, thereby East and West seen as two distinctive homogenous categories. But rather the formation of a cultural identity was a part of the non-realization of identification with the Colonizer, in this case the British sovereign state. The problem is augmented, when the question is that of the formation of a new community which is a *people comprising all communities* with different religious beliefs and also often no religious belief at all. Here, by a people comprising all communities, I am referring to the idea of the Indian state that started shaping up in the early twentieth century. 'An independence pledge was taken at innumerable meetings throughout the country on 26th January (1930), denouncing the British for having 'ruined India economically, politically, culturally and spiritually', asserting that it was 'a crime against man and God' to submit any longer to such a rule, and calling for preparations for 'civil disobedience, including non-payment of taxes' (Sarkar, 284). An 'unmediated unity' was felt by the demand of *Purna Swaraj* or total independence, which took birth from the realization of *difference* and the consolidation of an *identity* of being an Indian, thus, making the rule of the British sovereign state not only unacceptable but completely illegitimate.

18. Rabindranath Tagore, *English Writings of Rabindranath Tagore: Miscellaneous Writings,* Introduction by Mohit K. Ray (Atlantic Publishers and Distributers, New Delhi, 2007), 1117.
19. Urmila Sharma and S.K. Sharma, *Bhawani Mandir in Indian Political Thought* (Atlantic Publishers and Distributors, New Delhi, 1996) 253.

20. See Dipesh Chakrabarty, *Provincializing Europe: Post-colonial Thought and Historical Difference* (Princeton University Press, Princeton and Oxford, 2000).
21. See Marvin Carlson , 'Introduction: perspectives on performance: Germany and America, In *The Transformative Power of Performance: A New Aesthetics*, Erika Fischer-Lichte and Saskya Iris Jain (Trans.) (Routledge, Taylor and Francis Group, London and New York, 2008).

PART I

Thinking Indian Theatre

1

Critical Meanderings: 'Theatre' in Colonial India

1.1 The Beginnings of a Discourse on 'Theatre'

An interesting observation has been made in the book *'Bilati Jatra Theke Swadeshi Thiyetar'*. The title of the book written in Bengali, edited and sub-edited by Subir Raychoudhury and Swapan Mazumdar respectively can be translated as *Foreign Jatra to Swadeshi*[1] *theatre*. What is interesting is the idea of *'bilati jatra'* or foreign *'jatra'*. *'Jatra'* is a performative tradition mainly from Bengal and Orissa. The book begins with the mention of the fact that during the colonial period, theatre was often mentioned as *'bilati jatra'*. This observation opens up in front of us the question, where does the word 'theatre' stand semantically and can we call 'theatre', *'bilati jatra'*? Now *'jatra'* the word in Bengali means journey. As a noun, a *'jatra'* is the journey of devotees who are believers of a certain cult. The devotees make a journey from one place to another in a processional march and then return to the place of origin following the idol or the deity. These processional marches are said to have had their origins in the Vedic society.[2] During that period, after a *yajna* or ritual sacrifice, the festivities of the ritual bath took place, which often involved processions that included dancing, singing, chanting and other performative acts. *Jatra* eventually got associated with fairs and festivities apart from the religious links that it already had. These performer-devotees initiated acting in *jatra* or *jatrabhinoy* or *jatra*-acting. *Jatrabhinoy* involved mainly singing, with a few dialogues here and there in praise of the worshipped deity. *Jatrabhinoy* was also known as *Gitinat* or *Natgiti*, which literally would mean 'singing-acting' or 'acting-singing'.[3] This could also involve dancing at times. It has often been argued that theatre in Bengal evolved from *Jatrabhinoy*. On the other hand, it has been argued that theatre influenced *jatra*, as a result of which the amount of dialogue involved in a *jatra* performance increased. However the analogy between theatre and *jatra* draws attention to the etymology of the word 'theatre' which came to be used in Bengali and other Indian languages from its usage in English. The word 'theatre' in English is derived from the Greek word 'theatron' which basically signifies a space for the spectators or an auditorium. In the late eighteenth century and early nineteenth century, when interest in the drama and theatre of India was at a high, after the discovery of *Shakuntala* by the orientalists, there was much discussion about the existence of auditoriums in India, like those, the Greeks had founded. The claim of the existence of theatre in India was also reinforced by archeological discoveries of the late nineteenth century and early twentieth century. *The Archeological Survey of India Report of 1903-1904* by a certain Dr Bloch claimed the discovery of a small amphitheatre at Ramgarh Hill in the area of Laxmanpur on the Bengal Nagpur Railway line. Dr Bloch writes:

> ...the small amphitheatre in front of the cave with its hemispherical rows of rock-cut seats rising in terraces above each other and with the pathways between them arranged somewhat like concentric circles and radiants, bearing a somewhat similar resemblance to the plan of a Greek theatre cannot, I think be overlooked. And it will likewise be admitted that the shape of a Greek theatre in an Indian building that served similar purposes has a strong bearing upon the question of the Greek influence on the Indian drama.[4]

That the very existence of theatre in India might have been influenced by Greek theatre became one of the speculative factors. However, the performance of *jatra* does not involve a *theatron* or the physical space of the theatre, as one would understand in the Greek sense. It rather could be performed on makeshift ramps usually open on all sides. So the *jatra*/theatre analogy here seems a little misfitting given that if quintessentially theatre is to involve the physical space of an auditorium, *jatra* and theatre have different formats. However, the *Natyasastra* does mention the playhouses. The playhouse of the mortals were said to be only thirty-two yards long and sixteen yards broad, much smaller in scale than the Greek theatre. There have been speculations about the use of the temple courtyard or the temple space, which was called the *Natmandir* (*natya-mandira*) for performances during this period.[5] M. Christopher Byrski mentions that the theatre-hall of the classical Sanskrit theatre of Kerala, which is also called *Kuttampalam* has many affinities to a temple.[6] Performances in the temple space, in the eighteenth and nineteenth centuries, around the time when the colonial settlers were building theatre auditoriums, were very common. One of the earliest theatres that came into existence in India under the patronage of the British was the 'Calcutta Theatre' that was built in the 1750s. It was located in the Lal Bazar region of the present day Kolkata.[7] The Chowringhee Theatre in Calcutta soon followed. A theatre house was built in Bombay in 1776 for the English population and subsequently several others came up. That the theatre in these newly developing urban spaces was 'foreign' given that the very nature of theatre performances involving an auditorium, was distinct from already existing performances like that of the *jatra* was hence evident.

The 'foreignness' of the theatre was also highlighted by the discourse on drama that followed during this period. The formation of such a discourse was initiated by the translation of Sanskrit dramatic texts to other European languages. *Sacontala Or The Fatal Ring: An Indian Drama* was the first such dramatic text to be translated to English by the Anglo-Welsh philologist William Jones, the founder of The Asiatic Society, in 1789 in Calcutta. The translation of *Shakuntala*, the play originally written in Sanskrit by *Kalidasa* engendered such an enthusiasm about dramatic-literature and theatre-arts of the Indian sub-continent, that soon it was translated into German by Georg Forster in 1791, into Danish by Hans West in 1792, into French by A. Bruguiere in 1803, and into Italian by Luigi Doria in 1815.[8] The play in the literal sense became a discovery of an eastern cultural tradition and hence followed a discursive thread around the origins of this tradition or the origins of the theatre in India. Ursula Struc-Oppenberg in the study *Friedrich Schlegel and the History of Sanskrit Philology and Comparative Studies* notes that in the late eighteenth century German literature, India along with the orient in general were 'magic words evoking a magnificent legendary image of a former unity of religion, morality, mythology, and philosophy, contained in literary works which presented the complex simplicity of ancient oriental life'.[9] Sue-Ellen Case in the essay *Eurocolonial Reception of Sanskrit Poetics* argues that the German preoccupation with both Sanskrit drama and the language itself had to do with 'intimations of a glory long past—an aesthetic plenitude now spent'.

Goethe in 1791 wrote:

> *'Will ich die Blumen des frühen, die Früchte des späteren Jahres,*
> *Will ich, was reizt und entzückt, will ich, was sättigt und nährt,*
> *Will ich den Himmel, die Erde, mit einem Namen begreifen,*
> *Nenn' ich Sakontala, dich, und so ist alles gesagt.'*[10]

Horace Hayman Wilson in 1827 translated more such dramatic texts in three volumes that he called *Select Specimens of the Theatre of the Hindus*. These volumes are primarily the translations of certain Sanskrit plays. In the first volume Wilson introduces the theatrical form of these plays. What becomes apparent from his narrative is that the text was essentially written for a reader outside of the people, it concerned. The 'Preface' to the first volume and the first chapter *On the Dramatic System of the Hindus* asks a qualifying question of civility and by the end, like William Jones the translator of Shakuntala declares— '...the Hindus had a national drama'! But this affirmation of the Hindus possessing a 'national drama' comes with questions of its purity of origin and judgment of its adeptness. Wilson like many other orientalists of the time tries to analyze the possibility of any connection that the Hindu civilization might have had with the Greeks. He writes that although the science of the Hindus and may be even the legends are borrowed, but not so the dramatic compositions as they have their distinctive character. He highlights the lack of unity of time, place and action that on the one hand lack the extravagance of the Chinese dramas and on the other lack the severe simplicity of the Grecian tragedies that make them stand for themselves. In fact, following up on the argument of August Wilhelm Schlegel, he writes that in the few dramatic pieces that the Hindu civilization had ever produced which ranges to only sixty, there were no tragedies and no comedies like in Ancient Greek literature. He elucidates on the theory of dramatic forms based on his analysis of the Hindu dramatic-literature:

> The Hindus in fact have no Tragedy, a defect that subverts the theory that Tragedy necessarily preceded comedy, because in the infancy of society, the stronger passions predominated, and it was not till social intercourse was complicated and refined, that the follies and frivolities of mankind afforded material for satire.[11]

He arrives from the theory of drama to an anthropological revelation about the Hindus:

> In truth, however, the individual and social organization of the native of India, is unfavorable to the development of towering passion, and whatever poets or philosophers may have insinuated to the contrary, there is no doubt, that the regions of physical equability, have ever been, and still are, those of moral excesses.[12]

Within the parameters of a rigorous inspection of the dramatic-literature of the Hindus that he attempts in this short essay, in which he also questions the poetic and philosophical capabilities of Hindus, he constantly moves from dramatic analysis to anthropological comment on character. However, the analysis is never based on 'the thing itself' but a comparative study that was in fact intended for the non-native readers' comprehensibility of the theatrical language.[13] It presupposes *knowability* and judgment based on the familiar Greek dramatic and theatrical forms. The Hindu theatre becomes knowable, and fully graspable through the existing forms of cognition for the writer as well as the reader it intends to address. The cognizance and its veracity become so much dependent on establishing similitude and difference, that Schlegel commenting on *Shakuntala* wrote:

> ....the Drama of Sakontala presents through its oriental brilliancy of colouring, so striking a resemblance upon the whole to our Romantic Drama, that it might be suspected the love of Shakespeare had influenced the Translator, if other Orientals had

> not borne testimony to the fidelity of his Translation.[14]

In the very *sayability* of the Hindu theatre, by not one orientalist scholar but by a group addressing a certain specific reader group, the Hindu dramatic-literature and theatre-art appear, not by its own, but by a form that it receives, through the creation of the other or that which is different from one's own. This presupposing structure as Giorgio Agamben highlights in the essay *The Thing Itself*[15], 'is the structure of tradition'. Hindu civilization hence was knowable from the Hindu dramatic-literature and theatre-art and in appearing as the other, acquired a structure in being uttered, and thus became in itself the bane of Hindu tradition. Even in post-independence Indian-theatre-histories, one keeps coming back to this origin. The origin however once established couldn't defy itself. Commenting on the portrayal of women in 'Malati and Madhava' (whose translation he provides in the first volume) and 'Ratnabali', Wilson declares that the purity of Hindu-ness was adulterated by the coming of the Muslims in the region. 'It may be suspected, however, that the former piece presents a purer specimen of Hindu manners from the latter. It seems probable, that the princes of India learnt the practice of the rigid exclusion of women in their harems from the Mohammedans', he writes. The appreciation of the Hindu theatre was furthered by sociologists like Max Weber, and linguists like Ernst Windisch who saw no difference or the 'other' in the form, but rather a similitude with Greek theatre that suggested the same origin or rather a forgotten history of acquisition which had now started emerging by their efforts. Weber suggests 'a certain influence on the evolution of the Indian drama'.[16] Ernst Windisch's study *Der Griechische Einfluss im Indischen Drama* published in 1882 presented to the Congress of Orientalists held in Berlin is more exhaustive. It looks at the form of Sanskrit drama and Greek drama and proposes:

> It is difficult to imagine that the Indians knew and analyzed the written texts of Greek plays. But it was sufficient for them to attend a Greek performance or to learn by heresay the subjects of some plays for imitation to follow...[17]

This debate on the similarity and difference continued in works of Richard Pischel's *Die Rencension des Sakuntala*, his doctoral thesis, where he vehemently positions himself in support of the distinctiveness of Sanskrit theatre in the first extensive study of sorts of Indian theatre by Sylvain Levi published in 1890, which also resulted from his doctoral work. In *Le Théâtre Indien* written in two volumes, Levi argues for the singular existence of the ancient dramatic-literature and theatre-art of India, though it would appear that apart from Sanskrit dramatic and theatrical forms which are inherently linked to the upper caste in India, there existed no other forms. He even laments the fact and writes,

> The theatre as a means to defend and propagate the ancient traditions must give up its aristocratic isolation and accommodate itself to the taste of an illiterate audience. The mentality of aristocratic Brahmanism which, in former days, dictated the terms of dramatic aesthetics, loses its position and another spirit prevails. The classical drama had been primarily a literary work which, while propounding an ideal view of life, did not claim to be an instrument of propaganda, but a highly pleasurable entertainment. The modern drama, on the contrary, while aiming at pleasing, has the positive and practical purpose to teach... In Greece, the New Comedy flourished on the ruins of the ancient tragedy. In France, the tragedies of Corneille and Racine died with the regime which had nurtured them. A political, social and religious revolution gave birth to the Romantic drama, which, in its turn, made room for the Comedy of Manners. A common law seems to preside over the evolution of the dramatic art in all countries. The future of the Indian theatre is thus bound up with the future of world theatre.[18]

Levi understands theatre as an entirely upper-caste pursuit totally ignoring the other forms of performances that were existent whether upper-caste or not. What tangentially his argument here tries to state is that without dramatic-literature, theatre is not possible. The lack of drama hence signifies a lack of theatre in India. The other question that Levi raises here, which is integrally related to the enlightenment logic of nineteenth-century Europe[19], is that of a rational consciousness which lay in case of India, according to him, in its future. In fact, he begins his second volume of the study with what would have perhaps seemed like sarcasm, if it were not written and was rather a part of a conversation in reality. Talking about the origin of theatre as is propounded in Bharata's *Natyasastra* he writes,

> In their taste for the marvellous the Indians like to colour *history* with legends and fairy tales.

Adorno and Horkheimer in their work *Dialectic of Enlightenment*, elaborate the study of the impact of enlightenment work on Western history. Its overpowering emphasis on reason and rationality is exposed in the study of anti-Semitism. They write, 'Enlightenment is Totalitarian', where 'It wanted to dispel myths, to overthrow fantasy with knowledge'. Hence, although some writers like Levi believed in the existence of an Indian civilization and in its own power of creativity and art from the beginning, yet that power remained in darkness, away from any rationality and 'the day when reason will rule the world'[20] was soon to come. But this hope was at the same time, what in post-colonial studies has been a recurring phrase, 'the white man's burden'. And this burden of empowering the 'other' with knowledge is what becomes the tool for its own power. Through its enterprising effort in 'conquering superstition', it created its own myth or rather the 'superstition' of the belief that it can enable the other, to speak like itself, and to mimic it, in which it obtains its own pleasure of being the source, the origin, the pure—the human!

A. Berriedale Keith's *The Sanskrit Drama: in its Origin, Development, Theory and Practice* was written thirty-two years after Levi's *Le Théâtre Indien*. Like Levi's thesis, Keith's work becomes something like waiting for Godot, as he tries to trace drama in the Vedic literatures of India. Like most Orientalists suggested, the Vedic Age came to be known as the golden age of the dramatic-arts in India. However talking about the elements of drama found in the Rig Veda, one of the oldest Sanskrit scriptures available from the Vedic period, Keith argues that:

> Unless the hymns of the Rig-Veda present us with real drama, which is most implausible, we have not the slightest evidence that the essential synthesis of elements and development which constitute a true drama, were made in Vedic age.[21]

Drama, which was a sustained lack in India according to these literatures, compels one to ask—but what is *drama*? According to Oxford English Dictionary, *drama* is *a play for theatre, radio, or television.* It came into use in Greek from late latin. In Greek, *drâma* is action (of a play), equivalent to *drâ* (*n*) to do + -*ma* noun suffix. Aristotle in the treatise on dramatic art *Poetics* explains that in drama the imitation is primarily that of action of good agents or bad agents. The effect that is achieved in the course of the actions through *protasis, epitasis* and *catastrophe* (the beginning, middle and the end), *hamartia* or error of judgment by the protagonist or tragic hero who is noble but not entirely virtuous and a *dènouement* or resolution leads to *catharsis*, a kind of emotional purging. Hence drama has an essential link even etymologically to action, which is what is primarily imitated in order for drama to happen. In *Natyasastra*, Bharata explains that which is imitated in a performance, quite differently. He elucidates that the object of imitation is *bhava* or roughly translated as mood or emotion or feeling in its variations and phases as a result of which a certain effect is created on the spectators, which he calls *rasa*.[22] It is rather an experience that does not necessarily qualify actions although the imitation of *bhava*s relate to human actions (*narânâm karmasamúrayam*), to human conditions and reactions of all kinds.[23] For Levi, the Sanskrit equivalent of the word drama is *nataka*. Bharata describes *nataka* as,

> That which has as its theme a well-known story, a well-known hero of exalted nature, which concerns the story of a royal sage and his family, in which there are superhuman (*divya*) elements, which speaks of the various aspects of glory, grandeur and success of love-affairs and which has acts and prologues is a Nataka. In a Nataka there is the story of kings, various *rasa*-s and emotions and sorrows and pleasures.[24]

However, this is not the only kind of dramatic-art possible. There are ten forms of plays that include *Prakarana, Samavakara, Ihamrga, Dima, Vyayoga, Anka, Prahasana, Bhana, Vithi*, apart from *nataka*, which Bharata talks about. All these forms have their own formal structures, which often intermingle with each other. At the same time for Aristotle, drama can have its impact as much as in reading or as in watching a performance of it, whereas for Bharata, *natya* or articulate expressions of connected meanings communicating *rasa, nrtya* or interpretative dance relating to a *bhava* which communicate *rasa* and *nrtta* or purely dance movements that do not necessarily relate to any *bhava* are essential for a performance. *Gita* or music is also an essential part of it. Thus a written text like a drama cannot really create a total experience in this case. Hence, that Levi finds in *nataka* the equivalence of drama as a written text becomes in the first place a bit disconcerting. It is interesting to note how the word travelled to such a variegated signification, as it is understood in English as a written text. In *jatra* whose origin is traced back to the fifteenth century in Bengal, the word *pala* would roughly mean the subject of performance rather than essentially a written text for performance. The other word that was known both to Pali and Sanskrit was *ranga,* which fundamentally means a theatre, stage, scene or arena.[25] In J.L. Austin's study of the speech act[26], performative utterance is rendered hollow or void if said by an actor on stage. Where, theatrical performance is understood in literary terms as a mode of speaking scripted words, according to Austin, this process of citation leaves theatre hollow. Performance thus reconstitutes the text and survives of a parasite, while the text itself assumes authority of being the origin of utterance. Although Austin's thesis of the hollowness of theatre in this regard is a contestable argument, given the *event-al* character that every performance in the here and now assumes, however, the fact that the text, at least in the West, had enjoyed a position of enlightened authority, cannot be debated. Such textual hegemony of colonial power had often been a trope to dominate and exploit the 'other'. This happened in the case of many of these theatre-histories, first by establishing the lack of the text, or by establishing the lack within the text. Hence the 'other' is not only a binary opposition of the 'self' but also a perpetual 'lack' in comparison to the 'self' that establishes itself through writing, knowing and letting know of the 'other'. The confusion created by Levi's text about *nataka* is somewhat resolved in Keith's study, which does not assume, drama to be *nataka*. His study unfolds the work of Asvaghosa[27], whose manuscripts of three plays unleashed the possibility of an earlier beginning of the writing tradition for theatre. Keith highlights the fact that writing a play script was probably never high priority and even if it were written, it was mainly a craft of the upper caste Brahmins.

The search for defining that which appeared similar, but at the same time dissimilar when parameters of technical considerations were applied, made 'theatre' a considerably mutative category, which in itself became prominent. Within a colonial context, theatre became apparent as what Gerard Genette calls an *archigenre*. Genette defines *archi*—as that which overarches and includes 'ranked by degree of importance, a certain number of empirical genres that—whatever their amplitude, longevity, or potential for recurrence—are apparently phenomena of culture and history; but still (or already)—*genres*[28], because... their defining criteria always involve a thematic element that eludes purely formal or linguistic description.'[29] Genette sees genres attributed depending on 'mode of enunciation' in Plato and Aristotle. So the question of who is speaking became fundamental[30]; however each genre was defined by specification of its content that was in no way prescribed by definition of its mode. Hence there was a possibility of dissimilar generic and modal criteria. In the romantic and post-romantic division, he argues depending on thematic elements (however vague), 'real genres' started to get defined that no longer had anything to do with modes of enunciation. He attributes this confusion to 'deep-seated respect for orthodoxy' at the end of Classicism and in the twentieth century to 'retrospective illusion'[31]. He writes 'the vulgate is so well established that imagining a time when it did not exist is very difficult'.[32] Gerard Genette critiques this erroneous creation of 'real genres' and argues that 'there is no generic level that can be decreed more 'theoretical', or that can be attained by a more 'deductive' method than the others'. He sees them as empirical classes that cannot escape historicity. The colonial attribution of hierarchical status depending on technical considerations like the use of written text or drama, existence of auditorium etc. while studying taxonomic definitions only open up the confusion around the word 'theatre' to ideological leanings of the period. It cannot be seen outside any historical reality as essential problems of the term 'theatre' itself. In fact, such colonial and other cultural interactions of the late nineteenth– early twentieth century did have real consequences to the understanding of 'theatre' itself even in the geographical location from where the word travelled to India. The word itself even today has several variations in terms of what it expresses depending on its historical-cultural background. These variations and their study require a separate research platform. Right now, the concern is to see how taxonomic confusions within a colonial situation of present day India were directly associated with colonial ideologies and what consequences that had on its socio-political system. When the question became to have or not to have theatre, several technical considerations of the colonizer were directly borrowed and several others manipulated... some even invented. In the process, the form 'theatre' itself was not collapsed but only revisited making evolution of identities possible through its intrinsic property of coalescing, coagulating, and bringing together of individuals to form a community.

1.2 Discovery of an Identity

In the previous section, we discussed how the question of the 'theatre' was related to drama, which was seen as its intrinsic property, and from that were drawn anthropological evaluations of a 'group of people' that were the other. This group was mostly identified with a certain religious-cultural group, which in turn aided in narrativizing the emerging 'other-ed' identity. HH Wilson's thesis onwards, the 'Hindu' theatre in theatre-histories travelled across the nineteenth century to the twentieth, and theatre of the Hindus that had been categorized as national drama of the Hindus, became more and more synonymous with national–Indian identity. EP Horrwitz's witty fairy-tale like version of the Indian-theatre called *The Indian Theatre: A Brief Survey of the Sanskrit Drama*, constantly evokes this national identity that followed from the Sanskrit and Prakrit dramas; however he ends his work with a disclaimer:

> When the Mohammedans became rulers of India, they followed in the Prophet's footsteps, and abolished every music hall and playhouse. But coercion is bound to evoke reaction; that is a

> universal law which holds good at home and in school, in politics and religion, in society and on the stage. In spite of the Moslem precepts, dramatic activity was once more in full swing towards the end of the fourteenth century.[33]

He also highlights the willingness of the Hindus to blend with all other religions, be it the Muslims, even the Christians and now with the world. Although the book's aim is to trace the origin of Indian theatre, it is largely a commentary on Sanskrit and Prakrit texts. In 1858, British occupied India was already declared a nation-state vested in the Queen by liquidation of the British East India Company. India's location as a nation, by such a declaration of the Government of India Act 1858, henceforth, got written. It could be argued that before 1858, therefore whatever little was written and translations that started circulating outside in Europe, were largely identified with the language they were written in. Hindu civilization got associated with this discursive framework and soon it became synonymous with Indian civilization. As a result, the linear narrative vision of theatre-histories of India faces a vacuum post 1000AD—a vacuum that has been explained by various historians in multiple ways. This period has also often been called the age of traditional performances or folk performances. Hemendranath Dasgupta wrote that even though the 'golden age' of theatre had faded, still only Bengal could be 'credited with worthily maintaining its reputation of having, drama, art, and stage. In *The Indian Stage,* he does an extensive study of *Jatra* in Bengal. He also mentions other forms from Bengal such as *Kavigan, Half-akhrai, Panchali, Kirtan* and Bengali drama in Nepal, Assam and Manipur. RK Yajnik's analysis of the medieval forms covers a wider scope compared to that of Dasgupta. Although in the sub-title of his book he mentions that his focus is mostly on western India, he tries to incorporate forms from the east, west, north and south in talking about Indian traditional theatre. He negates the argument of European orientalists like R.W. Frazer that there is no relation between ancient Sanskrit drama and medieval traditional and folk performances and continues:

> ...it is obvious that with the ruin of the classical drama proper, after the rise of the Mohammedan power, the lower species came

> more into prominence and then contributed largely to the village drama. Of course, artistic subtlety disappeared. The old rules of decorum were violated in order to satisfy the desire of the masses... Despite all this certain elements of the old school lingered in the medieval dramatic performances.[34]

So, although some of the historians did not completely disown medieval theatrical forms, to them, those forms remained 'degraded forms', unlike the Sanskrit theatre since they lacked drama. In all the history writing, one factor remained common, that is the coming of the Muslim invaders and the subsequent deterioration of representative art practices. Hemendranath Dasgupta in *The Indian Stage*, published in four volumes between 1944 and 1946 writes:

> Sanskrit dramas for the first time began to decline with the advent of the Mohomedans rule in India. It was the dark age for the Hindus and a good many Hindu institutions began to decline and some disappeared from the land for good... The Mohomedans were without any national theatre and it received no tangible support from them. Political subjection, on the other hand brought about a radical change in Indian life and the Hindus lost much of their early freedom, simplicity and ease, their life and property were insecure and their well-being depended upon the sweet will of their rulers... A good deal of artificial restraints were introduced into society. It pushed back Indian women, excluded them entirely from society and introduced the 'pardah' as a protection against all profane gaze. The Hindus in course of time grew stoic and joyless and became almost a lifeless people. They began to deprecate many innocent public festivities and the drama and art began to decline from that time.[35]

This view about the theatre, being lost by the invasion of the Mohomedans initially found voice in the theatre-histories of the western orientalists like Arthur Berriedale Keith's *The Sanskrit Drama in its Origin, Development, Theory and Practice*. He writes:

> The invasion of the Mahomedans into northern India, which began in earnest with the opening of the eleventh century, was a slow process, and it could not immediately affect the progress of the dramatic art. But gradually, by substituting Mahomedan rulers— men who disliked and feared the influence of the national religion,

> which was closely bound up with the drama—for Hindu princes, the generous and accomplished patrons of the dramatists, it must have exercised a depressing effect on the cultivation of this literary form. The drama doubtless took refuge in those parts of India where Moslem power was slowest to extend, but even there Mahomedan potentates gained authority, and drama can have been seldom worth performing or composing, until the Hindu revival asserted the Indian national spirit, and gave an encouragement to the renewal of an ancient national glory.[36]

Hence, the discourse around the theatre carried two main arguments. Firstly, that the Indian theatre existed, but it ceased to exist because of Muslim invasion and rule; and the second one being, the possible association of Indian theatre with the Greek theatre which was being argued by several European orientalists. HH Wilson's *Select Specimen of the Theatre of the Hindus*, refers to the Greek theatre on several occasions and tries to understand Hindu theatre in the light of Greek theatre. The lack of unity of place and time as against Greek plays, the division of acts in Hindu theatre as against prologue, episode and exode in Greek theatre, sensuality of love being less in Hindu theatre and the lack of chorus singing all became elements that helped find the right place for an Indian rather Hindu theatre. While in Keith's history, the possibility of influence is not entirely negated and he writes that 'the Indian genius has known how to recast so cleverly and to adapt what it borrowed so effectively that the traces which would definitely establish indebtness cannot be found'[37], Hemendranath's *The Indian Stage*, categorically denies such association. Hemendranath Dasgupta writes that, 'there is not the least vestige of doubt that Indian drama was purely of indigenous origin and growth'[38] Keith and others also held Sanskrit theatre to be congruent with mystery or miracle plays as in medieval Europe given their religious nature. However, later scholars especially Indian scholars completely disagreed on limiting Sanskrit theatre to religious foundations alone. Both Hemendranath Dasgupta and R.K. Yajnik point to the concern for the 'social' in the Sanskrit plays. Yet what remained constant in all the historical narratives is a lamentation, of a loss that had occurred due to largely unknown reasons, while very few were known, like that of the invasion by the Muslims and later rule and subjugation. So most historians would argue that with an English theatre built at Lal Bazar in 1755-56, a new age of the theatre began not only in Bengal but in the whole of India. It was a revival of the Hindu/Indian theatre, a getting back of what the Indians or Hindus already had in the past as it were. The coming of the theatre happened, and of course it happened with the English theatre! Theatre-historians rejoiced this 'coming' in their narratives often linking it to the fact that the theatre is an ancient institution in India and it could not have attained so much perfection and popularity unless there were efficient actors or persons skilled in histrionic arts from the very beginning.'[39] P. Guha-Thakurta in *The Bengali Drama: Its Origin and Development* first published in 1930 wrote:

> When European theatres first appeared in Bengal, they immediately captured the people's imagination and appealed to their mind as a very interesting and suitable instrument of both pleasure and education. They had, of course, their Yatras and performances of similar nature, but with the coming of new ideas they were beginning to be dissatisfied with them. In the English play-houses they discovered for the first time an entirely novel and, indeed, more profitable source of entertainment and conceived a desire to make full use of it and to adapt it...[40]

Hence, it can be said that the discourse around theatre in India during the nineteenth century and early twentieth century has been one that highlighted a 'lack'. It not only repeats the doctrine of the lack but also the incapacity or incapability of the colonial subject. For the native writers it has been the narrative of a 'split' which according to Homi Bhaba,

> ....constitutes an intricate strategy of defense and differentiation in the colonial discourse. Two contradictory and independent attitudes inhabit the same place, one takes account of reality, the other is under the influence of instincts which detach the ego from reality. This results in the production of multiple and contradictory belief. The enunciatory moment of multiple belief is both a defense against the anxiety of difference, and itself productive of differentiations. Splitting is then a form of enunciatory, intellectual uncertainty and anxiety that stems from the fact that disavowal is not merely a principle of negation or elision; it is a strategy for

articulating contradictory and coeval statements of belief.[41]

On the one hand, there is agreement on the fact that the nation's narrative is one that had points of victory like in the Sanskrit theatre but at the same time a disavowing of any complete vacuum of non-existence. Within the discourse of the Indian-theatre history, it is the non-existence of the Hindu, who remained subjugated by the Muslim rulers and hence they did not seem to appear—either in revolt or in performance as *One*. The attempt by Hemendranath Dasgupta, and R.K. Yajnik has been to feebly, if not unnoticeably highlight the nation's singularity and existence as the land of the Hindus through the later medieval 'traditional' performances. Yajnik even goes to the extent of calling them the performances of the 'people', within an ambivalent discursive matrix of a missing community of Hindus within the medieval times, —attempting a revival of a lost community as it were, in getting them together—in coagulating them within the grand narrative of a world of theatre, where the Muslims were outside the circular ladder of the *homo hierarchicus*.

Now let us deliberate on the term traditional as performances since 1000 AD till the present day are known. The term traditional is understood as against the term modern. It is a term in opposition to modern, and here arises another colonial dilemma because within the discourse of theatre-history of India, the traditional does not stand in opposition to the modern but it co-exists with it till the present. To understand the concept of the modern, Paul de Man borrows from Nietzsche and argues that modernity, 'invests its trust in the power of the present moment as an origin, but discovers that, in severing itself from the past, it has at the same time severed itself from the present'; whereas 'modernism' becomes conscious of its own strategies 'in the name of a concern for the future—it discovers itself to be a generative power that not only engenders history, but is part of a generative scheme that extends far back into the past.'[42] Within the temporal reality of the colonial subject, within a modernity that emerged out of interactions with the British, the colonial subject discovered itself anew—not sure of its own positioning within any linear narrative but at the same time disinclined to see itself in disappearance. Theatre that supposedly started in the mid-nineteenth century had yet to find its counterpart in the native languages and by initiatives of the natives. Hence it remained foreign or '*bilati*' but at the same time the medium of the theatre was understood as something familiar, something almost as familiar as the *jatra* of the natives. In 1831, when *Uttara Rama Charita* of Bhavabhuti, a Sanskrit play, was performed under the guidance of its translator HH Wilson, who taught the native actors acting technique and stagecraft, many native young men who had watched the performance had called it *Ramlila*.[43] That any analogy could be drawn between theatre-arts as Wilson might have taught the English educated theatre enthusiasts and the local form of *Ramlila* that does not consist of many of the fundamental necessities of the theatre like the auditorium or the dramatic text (the Ramlila has often improvised texts by the actors) is interesting in itself. Theatre was brought down to a kind of bareness of itself as it were—which is that of *theatricality*. Theatricality, as Marvin Carlson would define is 'an essential element in the continued vitality and enjoyment of both theatre and performance and beyond that, as a positive, indeed celebrative expression of human potential'[44] and this very potential created a dialogue between the forms that were foreign to each other but not quite, creating a rupture in any discourse of divide that existed. Theatre's scripting in colonial India thus happened within the purview of such a dialogue that evolved and further got transfigured in its own potentiality. This potentiality did not get manifested in the happening of the theatre alone but also in creating sites of interaction. Not only amongst that which happened within the *intra-scenic axis* of theatre i.e. what happens between the immediate elements of the theatre but also in its interaction with what Hans-Thies Lehmann has called *theatron axis*[45] i.e. the elements present within the reach of the theatre space itself that includes the audience. Colonial interactions made the colonized subject conscious of what elements interacted within the *intra-scenic axis;* however this consciousness also made him aware of a new identity that was collective, given theatre interacted at a second level which is within the *theatron axis* that housed the potentiality of a becoming.

1.3 Discovering Indian Theatre

The qualifying adjective 'Indian' came to be associated with drama with the translation of Shakuntala by William Jones in 1789. However the term remained interchangeable with the word 'Hindu' as in most cases the study of drama and theatre was shown to have origins in the Sanskrit tradition, and the coming of Islam in India—the reason for its disappearance. We already discussed this earlier. The English theatres that were started by the English population in the urban centres inspired the English educated native elite who were often invited for these performances. A certain section of the elite felt the need to build their own theatre where they would entertain themselves like the British. Prasanna Kumar Tagore were one such native elite who had had his education in the Hindu College and was a practising lawyer. Hindu College was one of those educational institutions founded by the British in the early nineteenth century that aimed at converting the native individual to a proper British colonial subject.[46] Prasanna Kumar Tagore along with other associates founded the 'Hindu Theatrical Association' in 1831 in order to provide guidance to the theatre group he founded which was called the 'Hindu Theatre'.[47] However that some natives were to create their own theatre was not received very well by all. One Englishman proposed that instead of doing theatre, the native population should focus on the education of their fellow countrymen and only when they were able to appreciate theatre should they think of building native theatre.[48] Nevertheless the first production of the Hindu Theatre was decided upon, and the drama to be staged was Bhavabhuti's 'Uttara Rama Charita'. That the Hindu Theatrical Association had found glory in its Hindu past when they had 'national drama', as was declared by some orientalists, was not surprising. However it was decided that the play would be performed in English and H.H. Wilson the author of *Select Specimens of the Theatre of the Hindus* was asked to translate the play from Sanskrit. He also happened to direct it. The invited audience for the play were mostly the English or the English educated native elite. English continued to remain the language of theatre for the Bengali elite population for some time. In fact, in the same year, a play was written by Reverend Krishnamohan Bandhopadhyay called 'The Prosecuted'.[49] This too was in English. In the course of the nineteenth century, several theatre-houses that were founded in Calcutta mostly had English names like 'National', 'Great National', 'Bengal', 'Emerald', 'City', 'Kohinoor', 'Classic', 'Minerva', 'Star' etc.[50] In Bombay, the Grant Road Theatre founded by the English was sold to the Parsi businessman Jamshed Jejeebhoy in 1835 due to lack of funds. Later Jejeebhoy along with Jagannath Shankarseth and Framji Cowasji founded a new theatre there. All performances held there till 1853 were in English, which were performed by both amateurs and British actors. Often touring artistes from England, Europe and America were invited. In March 1853, for the first time, a Marathi play was staged based on the Ramayana. Vishnudas Bhave who is often claimed to be the first playwright of the Marathi language directed the play. However some others argue, that his plays were actually improvised lines by the actors who played them based on a broad idea of the characters in the play and hence Bhave cannot be called the first playwright. Bhave who had already directed some plays for the court at Sangli near Bombay had watched English performances at the Grant Road Theatre. The neatness of the place, seating arrangements, curtains and scenes had highly impressed him. His play that was later staged at this theatre was influenced by the stagecraft of the English theatre. A review of his play published in the Bombay Times notes that the gods and goddesses in the play based on the Ramayana sat on chairs and couches and 'the combat between Luxuman and Indrajit was carried on (the weapons being bows and the combatants dancing fiercely round each other) in an English looking parlour'.[51] During this period, certain theatre groups were also founded by the students and ex-students of the Elphinstone College of Bombay which performed in English. The plays were structured in European conventions of division into acts and scenes. That mid-nineteenth century onwards, the conventions of performance followed a dictum of the existing English theatres in colonial India cannot alone be explained by the colonized's desire to mimic the colonizer. Gauri Vishwanathan makes an interesting observation in this regard. She argues borrowing from Gramsci in the essay *Currying Favour*: The Politics of British *Educational and Cultural Policy in India 1813-1854,* that cultural domination by consent often precedes domination by force. So, the inclination of the colonized subject towards the culture of the colonizer is understandable but at the same time the proliferation and propagation of the study of English literature was a strategic device employed by the British to establish their stronghold over the colony. That good governance over the colony was possible only by understanding each other's culture was realized by the late eighteenth century. Orientalism hence worked for the English administrators tacitly as a policy to rule and assimilate with the culture of the natives and at the same time institute a paternalistic government. By the Charter Act of 1813[52] the government had already decided on taking on the responsibility of promoting education amongst the natives and had also opened up India for missionary activities about which until then it was hesitant. An increasing involvement in education initiated the study of English as a subject in the educational institutes. However it had to be taught with the same dignity as the classical languages like Latin and Greek enjoyed in England. Cultural supremacy of the British increasingly manifested itself in the way curricula were decided for the educational institutions founded in India. Hence English dramatic literature came to gain ascendancy in the colonial world of theatre. It is interesting to note that the first theatre of the natives came into existence in 1831 and in 1835 the English Education Act was passed which made it obligatory for the colonized population to submit to the study of English literature. However the growing theatre-performances in the urban centres by the English-educated elite population slowly started to question this process of acculturation. At the same time, that the language was a foreign one on stage was a practical problem since a huge segment of the population still did not know it. At least for commercial benefits, the language had to be one known by the locals although as Kathryn Hansen notes, in the case of theatre in Bombay 'architectural setting, stage construction, management and publicity, the naming of companies after royalty, and countless other public signs'[53] were such as to allure the English metropolitan culture. In Calcutta, a certain wealthy section of the native society invested a lot of money in theatre performances they organized in their own houses. The stagecraft in these performances with an invited audience would be in imitation of the English theatres. This was followed by the coming of the amateur clubs. In 1867 was founded 'The Bagbazar Amateur Theatre' by Girish Chandra Ghosh, Nagendranath Bandhopadhyay, Dharmadas Sur, and Radhamadhav Kar. Initially the performances happened with donations. The first play it performed was Michael Madhusudan Dutt's Sermistha that was followed by a social play called *Shodhobar Ekadoshi* by Dinabandhu Mitra. By 1872, the club changed its name from 'The Bagbazar Amateur Theatre' to 'The Calcutta National Theatre' followed by only 'The National Theatre'. During this period Nabagopal Mitra was associated with the club. He was the editor of the newspaper 'National' along with Rajnarayan Basu and also the founder of the 'Hindu Mela', an organization that was founded in 1867 in order to promote nationalist feeling amongst the educated youth. He was also known as 'National Nabagopal' because of the frequent use of the word 'national' he made to everything he was associated with. Around this time, the need for ticketing of performances was felt by the members of this club in order to generate funds for the plays. Girish Chandra Ghosh was against such a proposal. He argued that ticketing a performance would mean that rich and the poor alike could come to watch these plays. But when they would see the glamour of the set design they would feel repulsed. Hence he thought they had no right to call this kind of theatre 'national'.[54] A consciousness about the nature of performances on stage was already developing by the end of the nineteenth century. Newspapers often termed performances by theatre clubs like those of the Sangli Hindu Dramatic Corps or Amerchand Wadi Hindu Dramatic Corps and many others as versions of 'national theatre'. That the national theatre had to be dealing with native subjects, relating to their social concerns, from popular mythological tales or by native playwrights was felt. The very nature of theatrical performances also received a hybrid character in the search of the 'national', which was perceived as that which included the audience of the traditional performances. According to Girish Chandra Ghosh, he started playwriting out of 'sheer necessity' to attract more audience to the theatres. He comments—'Plays had to be written keeping in mind the audience of jatra, kathakatha and half-akhrai. Is there any other way but to take refuge in the mythological to entertain such an audience? If one writes the history of Bengali theatre one has to specifically keep this in mind. Let alone the subject of the stage.'[55] It was within this larger paradigm of a search for a form that was right for the colonial native masses, a new nationality, that was recognizably the other but at the same time coagulated, and transformed into *one* with the multitude, maintaining its difference with the colonizer, what Homi Bhaba describes as 'a subject of a difference that is almost the same, but not quite' that a new discourse of modern Indian theatre developed in the late nineteenth century/early twentieth century. It was a Swadeshi[56] theatre by which indigenous or traditional forms were not necessarily meant but a new form that was manufactured à la deshi or national character whether invented by the revisionists or the vanguards of modern theatre in India, both of which also dealt with subjects that the masses related to, which means that they were conscious of their own aesthetics and content. On a larger view, by the 1880s the educated elite inspired by western culture and ideals of patriotism had slowly started being repulsed by foreign rule. Lord Lytton, the Viceroy of India between 1876 and 1880 complained—'Babus, ...we have educated to write semi-seditious articles in the Native Press'. The growing consciousness of aesthetics and content led to the theorization of theatre which more importantly was driven by the consciousness of an identity that was mainly national in character. Tagore's essay 'Rangamancha' written in Bengali in the month of Poush of 1309 according to the Bengali calendar, which would be roughly December-January 1902 in the Gregorian calendar, has to be understood within such a discursive matrix. The essay was published in English translated by Surendranath Tagore eleven years later as 'The Stage' in

December 1913, the year Rabindranath Tagore received the Nobel prize. Tagore's critique in the essay is against the imitation of western theatrical tradition, which sought the portrayal of reality as it was. He argues like Girish Chandra Ghosh that, 'theatres that we have set up in imitation of the West are too elaborate to be brought to the door of all and sundry.'[57] The main thread of his argument remains that the theatre does not require the help of the other arts as such to evolve. Acting according to him, to some extent requires drama, but apart from that, it is not enslaved by any other form, not even realism as one sees on the western stage. He rather would like the theatre-art to flourish by itself with the help of the creative capacities of imagination of the members of audience. Tagore's essay takes note of the fact that what theatre creates is a space of togetherness that according to him is also a space for mutual creativity. In the 1913 published English essay he interestingly refers to Richard Wagner's idea of the 'combined arts' as against which he proposes the solo of the theatre. However the 1902 Bengali essay does not have any such comparison. Possibly the English translation was published seeking an international readership in the post-Nobel era[58] of Tagore's life. Hence a comparison is deliberately made to a text that functions as a guideline for modern theoretical engagement with the theatre as against which a claim to an essentially different understanding of the theatre is posed. However Tagore does not alienate the theatre arts itself from its historical development in India. It is not a borrowed form for him. In fact he dissolves any possibility of estrangement by beginning the essay with the example of the Natyasastra. He writes the Natyasastra does not talk about sceneries or divisions into scenes of a play. For him, it did not even cease to exist as he relates it to the Jatra and explains how it is a performative means that unfolds through the interaction between the performers and the audience members. According to him, drama could evolve, as a separate form of art and it does not necessarily need the stage for representation. At the same time what evolves out of a dramatic text does not necessarily need a literal translation on stage as the stage could play around with its own elements. He gives the example of Kalidasa's Shakuntala, where the poet takes his liberty to imagine a chariot pursuing a flying deer. However according to Tagore that would be possible on stage with a different theatrically creative engagement. Tagore's Bengali essay is more of a call to his fellow countrymen to discard the 'foreign childishness' (*bilati chhelemanushi*) of showing off wealth. Interestingly, the English essay omits what Tagore writes next. He writes in the Bengali essay—'*Baganke je obikol bagan ankhiyai khara koritey hoibey ebong streechoritra okrittrim streelokkey diyai obhinoy koraitey hoibey, ei roop ottonto sthul bilati borborota porihaar koribar shomoy ashiyachhe*' which could be translated as 'That the garden has to be painted exactly as the garden and that women characters have to be performed by real women, it's time to discard this kind of extreme uncouth foreign barbarity.' Women started performing on stage since the early days of 'theatre' performances in the houses of the nobility. However that they would perform on a professional stage was not acceptable by the educated bhadralok[59] section. To the extent that having women members in the audience was also not acceptable. When the National Theatre invited women for one of their performances, the 'National Paper' (18.12.1872) wrote that during these times of change until the unrestrained whimsical elements are removed from stage, women cannot be asked to come to the theatre. Nevertheless women were introduced on the stage in the professional theatres in August 1873 at the Bengal Theatre with Michael Madhusudan Dutt's play Sermistha. However Tagore's consideration in this regard after more than three decades of women having performed on stage probably has to be seen in a different light than to link it to any kind of prejudice he might have had about women performing on stage. In fact, Tagore had introduced women in his own performances. In 1887 he performed along with Dwijendranath Tagore and female members of the Tagore family Saratkumari and Barnakumari in the play 'Emon kormo aar korbo na' written by Jyotirindranath Tagore. In 1889 he performed the play 'Raja o Rani' with the actresses Gyanodanandini and Mrinalini at Saint Paul's Cathedral in Calcutta. In fact, women were active participants in the performances of Shantiniketan where Tagore founded the Vishwa-Bharati University.[60] Possibly he is pointing to the lack of creative engagement in performances that tend to portray everything as is real. Female-impersonation had been a trend in not only 'theatre' performances but also in many existing performance forms in India. For Tagore, 'theatre' needed to develop independently using its own elements and he calls for a theatre that moves beyond any kind of colonial mindless imitation. Removing the paragraph from the English version however makes one suspicious about the intentions of Tagore in having written what he wrote in the Bengali essay. Was it a puritan position in disfavour of women performing on commercial stage, which often employed prostitutes as actresses that he later reconsidered? We do not know. For Tagore not the existing theatres of Calcutta, but the folk performances were exemplary for the stage. The near minimalist approach of these performances, according to him is ideal for the socio-economic situation of a 'famine-stricken' country. As Christopher Balme notes the essay draws a 'connection between the capitalist-driven politics of colonialism and the artistic products accompanying and established by it.'[61] Such critical evaluation of western obsession with realism and looking back at traditional forms of performances became a modernist method to build a new theatre and performance tradition for India that began in the late nineteenth century and continued till the 1940s when the Central Squad of the Indian People's Theatre Association attempted to incorporate folk performances in order to propagate a sensibility of a one national people. By the early twentieth century, the sensibility of Swadeshi[62] had been popularized by Gandhi who called out to the nation to look back at the villages. His sensibility of going back to the village handicrafts was based more on his understanding of indigenous livelihood and exploitation caused by industrialization and urbanization. For Gandhi it was about being committed to one's own nation's natural resources and systems that lay in the villages. He had his differences with Tagore as he found the poet romanticizing life as he portrayed beautiful pictures of birds singing hymns of praise while he had 'had the pain of watching birds who for want of strength could not be coaxed even into a flutter of their wings.'[63] Tagore's essay that tries to theorize theatre in colonial India however only shows that Gandhi had had his own misconceptions about Tagore's work. A certain Mrs Fould or Tandra Devi as she was known published the pamphlet *Village Theatres: The Foundation of Indian National Theatres* in 1938 in the same light that in an impoverished country, art is but a luxury. She is uncompromising about art's effect on life and believed that it, in her context the theatre, played a significant role in creating a community bond. According to her, the western urban slum dwellers who lived in psychologically arid conditions were in worse conditions than the Indian villagers. Theatre, she argues expresses the architecture of the soul and that art loses its power once it is personalized. According to her, the cult of the star had degraded modern drama. Earlier however she writes that the actor wore the mask in order to escape this weakness and the mask would externalize the poet's vision. In villages due to lack of available amenities, puppets were created which also ensured the 're-creative education of the peasants'.[64] Borrowing from an Indian critic and patron of art he calls puppetry of India the *harijan* in the theatre-arts due to its declining status. *Harijan* was a term used by Gandhi for the *dalits* or lower caste people. It also means children of God. According to her, puppetry is the 'only real and creatively blessed theatre they (people of India) can ever have.'[65] In order to make it a national theatre she calls upon the poets and thinkers to join her cause, as she believes theatre is a combination of various art forms. Revival of different theatrical forms of India was already becoming one of the foremost agendas from the 1920s onward when the nationalist consciousness amongst the educated youth had become more self-determined. Rukmini Devi Arundale's encounter with *sadir*, a form mainly performed by Isai Vellalar or the Devadasi[66] community, which she reconstructed as Bharata Natyam can be seen in this light. Rukmini Devi was a nationalist and a theosophist. She was inspired by Anna Pavlova, the ballet dancer, who had apparently asked her to revive the art of her own country. She took up the form of *sadir* and associated it to its ancient past at the same time detached it from its immediate context of performance by the Devadasi community. She made the performance suitable for the Victorian morality instilled educated middle class and upper class natives.[67] During this phase of revivalism of the arts, Uday Shankar, a painter/dancer had an encounter with Anna Pavlova in London who like Rukmini Devi inspired Shankar to look back at the forms existing in his own country. Uday Shankar who was not trained in any dance form as such recreated them through observations from paintings. He created ballets, a form Anna Pavlova inspired him to do. Rukmini Devi also had ballet as part of the curriculum of Bharata Natyam dance training. Hence intercultural weavings became an integral element in the modernist phase of national performance creation. Uday Shankar's aim gets highlighted in the brochure of the Uday Shankar India Culture Centre that he founded in 1938—

> ...it is intended that the traditional and folk forms of Indian dancing and music should be studied at the Centre in order to establish definite standards of production. By this means, the harmony underlying the seemingly confused state of India's dance art may be re-discovered or recreated. Through a technique of dancing, drama and music, designed to reveal the inner significance behind the outer forms of expression, the Centre hopes to give a new interpretation to these arts.[68]

While the dramatic performances in the nineteenth century that got inspired by western 'theatre' continued to be often called Sangeetnatak, Natgiti, which were a conglomeration of forms, that presupposed a kind of hybridity of the art forms, by the twentieth century, the need to define form compartmentalized them to some extent. Nevertheless, the forms in character were to be identified with a national people. Let us have a look at the brochure of Uday Shankar's India Culture Centre which elaborates training thus:

TRAINING COURSES

THE courses offered in dancing at the Centre are intended to give the student not only training in the particular style of dancing in which he wishes to specialise, but also to widen his artistic horizon and help him in his artistic achievements by providing facilities for the study of all connected arts.

COMPULSORY COURSES :

Each student will be required to take the following courses :

I. DANCING

Technique of Dancing

This will include training in the methods obtaining in various schools of dancing. The course is calculated to give to the student the suppleness of body and facility of movement required to execute any style of dancing with confidence and

Students at work in the open-air classes

ease. The student will be required to learn foot-work as well as the symbolic gestures of the hands, facial expressions and body movements essential for the different sentiments and types of dancing.

Folk Dances

Probably no country can equal India in the wealth and variety of folk dances characteristic of different groups of the population or of different parts of the country. A special effort will be made to teach folk dances, and to revive this art in India.

Improvisation

Students will be encouraged from the very beginning to create new dance movements, thus providing an opportunity to develop their own creative abilities. The themes, simple in the beginning, will become more complicated and complete each year, till in the final year students should be able to compose a whole dance by themselves. These dance movements and dances will be criticised in the class, and by this means the student will be helped to a more critical standard of his or her own work.

Students at work

Composition and Rhythm

Composition here indicates the effective sequence in which movements are to be arranged, with a gradual rise to a climax of dramatic effect. Such movements are governed by a strict law of time and rhythm. These will constantly be stressed in both music and dancing during the whole course of study.

Production

Students will be taught the technique of arranging dances for presentation. Details of movements will be taken into consideration from the stand-point of the audience and the particular sentiments to be evoked.

Lighting

Stage lighting is a most important factor in professional performances. Students will be shown how to produce the lighting effects suitable to the different moods of the dances.

Stage and Costume Design

Costumes for dances will be carefully studied in accordance with stage requirements. Costumes may be historically correct, accurate from the point of view of local usage, or specially designed to meet the imaginative needs of a composition.

Make-up

Students will be made conversant with the most up-to-date methods of make-up, and will be taught how to make up so that they can heighten the character and the effects of their dances.

The work outlined in the preceding paragraphs will be distributed over five years as follows :

First Year

Elementary physical exercises
Expressive movements
Development of the sensitiveness of the body
Improvisation - concentration - imagination
Group feeling
Observation

Second and Third Years

Development of the foregoing in a constructive form, plus:
Knowledge of spade and the psychology of movements
Sense of colour and line
Relation of dance to drama

Fourth Year

Development of creative power
Characterisation and elementary make-up
Refining of technique

Fifth Year

Composition
Dance direction
Costumes, ornaments, make-up
Stage lighting

II. MUSIC

Every dance student must also study music. This study will be continued over five years. At the end of the course a student will have a fundamental knowledge of the Ragas, capacity to recognise and reproduce notes, take down melodies in notation, recognise and be able to sing the important Ragas and produce on the drum the important *Talas* with variations. Special stress will be laid on voice production, and also in arranging music to suit different dances.

III. THEORETICAL TRAINING

Students of each year will have a certain portion of theoretical study combined with practical training. This will include lectures on the history of the arts and the developments and theory of dancing, acting and music, as embodied in the *Natya Shastra* and other treatises. Students will further be required to familiarize themselves with mythology and the philosophical and psychological background of dance, music and drama in India.

OPTIONAL COURSES

In addition to the regular course students may take up either *Kathakali* or *Bharata Natyam*.

KATHAKALI:

First Year

Kathakali exercises
Fundamental steps with simple *Talas*

Second Year

Thottayam
Kalasams

Third Year

Purappara

Mudras

Eyes and Expressions

Fourth Year

Acting of small pieces with *mudra* and *abhinaya*

Fifth Year

Full stories in complete Kathakali technique

BHARATA NATYAM:

First Year

Fundamental foot movements *(Arava)* to main rhythms

Second Year

Hand movements added to the above

Third Year

Dance movements with different rhythms, without music and songs.

Fourth Year

Dance movements with songs and drumming

Fifth Year

Abhinaya and polishing up the complete technique

[69]

A training methodology for the performer as is evident from the Almora Centre's brochure was a conglomeration of methodologies that aimed at reinventing a new language for the performing body. It borrowed from the vocabulary of dance as a category of performance as in the West yet incorporated from Natyasastra's 'abhinaya' for 'polishing up the complete technique' as it were. Its focus on 'folk dances' resonates earlier concerns over indigenous forms of performance. This concoction of forms borrowed from different spatio-temporal realities fully aware of the available technologies worldwide was also focused on formation of the new. Hence it is not surprising that improvisation received utmost importance in the training process along with awareness of 'group feeling'. Insofar as Uday Shankar Culture Centre at Almora insisted on invention of a new language of performance, it was modernist in approach with the loci based on an Indian national past, the folk traditions of India and western performance techniques. Possibly this insistence on inventing led to several of its performers becoming later-leaders of performing arts movements and institutions in India. The Indian People's Theatre Association's Central Squad which has been discussed in a later chapter happens to be one such site of coming into being spearheaded by Almora Centre's performers.

Baldoon Dhingra's 1944 essay *A National Theatre for India* begins identification through establishing fundamental differences with the West. He argues that Indian acting is a poetic interpretation of life and western acting mere imitation. In the West, only in dance forms does such poetic expression exist although historically it began in Greek theatre. Theatre in ancient India in Baldoon's essay is almost idyllic. As much as it is perfect poetic expression, it is also democratic where the four pillars of the stage signify the four different castes and women traditionally performed the roles of women.[70] It is characterized by spectacle, and lyrical in action and music. In the modern times however, according to him, drama of Bengal under writers like Tagore and Dwijendralal Ray has been able to maintain such a poetic vision unlike in other parts of India where it was just imitation of the West. In a detailed manifesto for a national theatre, he demands a non-commercial theatre unlike the ones in Bombay, Calcutta, Lahore or the other urban centres. The national theatre was rather to be a theatre owned by the community with distinctive regional features. The project of a national theatre was not to be funded by the government but by 'private liberality' with no profit involved. His frequent point of reference in the manifesto is post-revolution Russia. In fact, he goes to the extent of saying 'We require in India exactly what the Russians have in their country: social spirit and principle'.[71] The actor was to be the People's artist. This reference of 'People's theatre stars the people' is found in the slogans of the Indian People's Theatre Association (IPTA) that was active during this period. Dhingra makes no reference to the organization whatsoever although by 1943-44, IPTA's work had become significantly popular especially after the Bengal famine of 1943. Dhingra's vision of a theatre was not the theatre for the impoverished population of India as is in the IPTA performances. Nor was the aesthetics of this theatre determined by the taste of the populace as in case of Girish Chandra Ghosh or Rabindranath Tagore. The national theatre was to have the best and the most modern of equipment. National theatre as much as it would be multi-lingual, targeting the diverse population of the country, it would also be in English for the bi-lingual and tri-lingual communities. He calls India a 'theatre-less' country at present and demands that a national theatre is required for a national soul. In 1945 was published Kamaladevi Chattopadhyay's essay *Towards a National Theatre*. Kamaladevi was associated with the nationalist movement and later in independent India she became the founder of the National School of Drama at New Delhi. She opens up her study on a reverential note on the theatre-arts of ancient India. Commercial theatre and cinema are the reasons for its decline in modern India according to her. She claims that theatre can best flourish when it is a community affair rather than an individualistic one. Her vision for a national theatre is the one in which the national community by its own choice engages in the art form like the amateur theatre groups for whom any professional theatre seems to be a threat. Every community, be it in the cities or villages, of different class backgrounds, should have its own theatre. She writes that theatre is a conglomeration of all the other forms of art, and realism was mere imitation, which did not leave space for creative potentiality of the art form. In fact, what she further writes in this context is worth noting:

> One of the features of the present-day Indian stage may be said to be the preponderance of song. Distinctions like musical plays, operas, ballets are not made to distinguish them from plain prose plays. Every play in fact, is a song play, with one song to every few sentences or so... What is most disconcerting is that the actors burst into song on every single occasion, whether they are in terror or in grief, whether running for their lives or in hot chase, or on a sick bed breathing their last. Once a foreigner after watching such a performance saw an animal come on stage, and turned to his Indian neighbour quite seriously and asked: 'And now I suppose the animal is going to sing'.[72]

Like many others who had complained of the 'hapazardness' of theatre in modern India, Kamaladevi sees such non-categorization as a problem for the theatre arts although theatre itself, she claims is a conglomeration of all the other art forms. Although she is not seeking realism here but something more dignified, presentable to the foreigner in front of whom the national theatre should not seem to be an embarrassment. The discourse of the theatre-arts in India, like in several other fields constantly struggled with notions around shame and pride. The issue of national honour had been a significant element in the formulation of any kind of project. A national project's vulnerability within such a discourse is guided by the very principle of nationalism. Nationalism that primarily functions through the representation of a body politic also seeks personal dignity and authority in the representation. India although within colonial rule, never ceased to be of immense interest for countries outside, especially for Europe but at the same time, its being exposed to foreign rule, made it conscious of its own being. Theatre's development into 'national theatre' is grounded on this principle of dignity of the body politic. Rukmini Devi's national theatre project like the other visions of national theatre hence aims at creating a platform which is fundamentally a community affair but not conscious of distinctive class structures but rather that has universal elements with national character. The transformative aim of the national theatre was based on its ability to generate 'constructive value' by people 'who have the urge to raise the roof and the walls of the new social structure'[73], it could not hence be an embarrassment.

By the mid-twentieth century, theatre's potentiality had already been tested during the anti-colonial upsurge. We will discuss this in the following chapters. As it got linked to culture and tradition that added to the project of identifying a 'homo nationalis', it became an asset for the nation. At the same time there was a need felt to assimilate it, organize it and bring it under controllable visibility whereby on the one hand it became unprofanable and at the same time segregated into categories i.e. genres tagged like in a museum, as happened in the case of Bharata Natyam. However it was also to become propaganda for the nation (like Baldoon Dhingra clearly notes in his essay). For the national theatre's aim was only to create the 'homo nationalis' as it were, a national being who was to be represented through theatre but in a way such that he or she becomes archetypical of collective dignity.

REFERENCES

1. 'swa' in Sanskrit means self and 'deshi' is of the country; during the Indian Independence struggle the term was frequently used to mean self-made or that which is made by the people of the country for themselves.
2. Vedic period is roughly c. 1500 to c. 500 B.C.E.
3. passim, Jatra, Ajit Kumar Ghosh, *Bangiya Lokosanskriti Kosh* (Encyclopedia of Bengali Folklore), (ed. Barunkumar Chakraborty, Aparna Book Distributors, Kolkata; 2007).
4. Dr Bloch as quoted by P. Guha-Thakurta, *The Bengali Drama: Its Origin and Development*, (Greenwood Press, Connecticut, 1974 reprint), 34. Originally published in 1930 by Kegan Paul, Trench, Trubner and Co., London.
5. *The Natyasastra: A Treatise on Hindu Dramaturgy and Histrionics ascribed to Bharata Muni*, Vol. I (Chapters I-XXVII) (Trans. Manmohan Ghosh, The Royal Asiatic Society, Kolkata, 1950), LVII.
6. M. Christopher Byrski, *Concept of Ancient Indian Theatre*, (Munshiram Manoharlal Publishers Pvt. Ltd., New Delhi, 1974), x.
7. P. Guha-Thakurta, 40-43.
8. Rakesh H. Solomon, *Modern Indian Theatre: A Reader*, (ed. Nandi Bhatia, Oxford University Press, New Delhi, 2009), 9.
9. *Canadian Review of Comparative Literature*, Autumn 1980.
10. Wouldst thou the young year's blossoms and the fruits of its decline/And all by which the soul is charmed, enraptured, feasted, fed,/Wouldst thou the Earth and Heaven itself in one sole name combine,/I name thee, O Sakontala, and all at once is said. (Trans. E.B. Eastwick)
11. *Select Specimens of the Theatre of the Hindus* (trans. H.H. Wilson, Vol. 1, second edition, London, Parbury Allen and Co., 1835), xxvi.
12. Ibid.
13. Wilson in one of the introductory pages of the book after dedicating it to George IV whom he calls 'The patron of oriental literature', writes 'to familiarize his British subjects with the manners and feelings of their fellow subjects in the East'.
14. As quoted in the *Preface*, ibid., xii.
15. Giorgio Agamben, *The Thing Itself* (Trans. Juliana Schiesari, *Substance*, Vol. 16, No. 2, Issue 53, Contemporary Italian thought 1987). In this essay, Agamben discusses Plato's seventh letter.

Here through Plato he tries to understand the 'thing of thinking'. He writes that for every entity, knowledge comes through three things- name, discourse and image. Any entity or the thing itself has its place in language 'even if language is undoubtedly not perfectly suited to it' (21). Plato calls this a 'weakness'. He elaborates that like in the Stoic logic the entity depends on the *onama* or the signifier, *logos* or the signified or virtual referent and the *image* or denotative or the actual referent. He thus writes that 'the thing itself is no longer simply an entity in its obscurity, an object presupposed by language and by the cognitive process, but instead..., that through which it is knowable, its own knowability and truth...' (22-23) The 'weakness' of *logos* consists in its inability to bring to expression this knowability and this sameness; the language pushes back like a presupposition, the very knowability of the entity which is revealed in it. Language is therefore, always pre-supposing and objectifying. Hence, sayability remains unsaid and knowability lost in what one knows about what there is to be known. So the thing itself is not the thing but the *sayability*, where we presuppose and betray the thing itself, hence sinking it. On this 'foundation' Agamben writes 'upon which—and only upon which-something like a tradition can constitute itself'. Tradition he writes is the 'presupposing structure of language'.

16. As quoted by Sylvain Levi, *The Theatre of India*, (Vol. 2, Trans. Narayan Mukherji, Writer's Workshop, Calcutta, 1978), 54.
17. As quoted by Levi, ibid., 59.
18. Ibid., 132.
19. Refer to Adorno and Horkheimer, *Dialectic of Enlightenment*, (Trans. Edmund Jephcott, Gunzelin Schmid Noerr, Stanford University Press, Stanford California, 2002).
20. Ibid., 133.
21. A. Berriedale Keith, *The Sanskrit Drama: In Its Origin, Development, Theory and Practice* (First Indian edition, Motilal Banarasidass Publishers Private Limited, Delhi, 1992).
22. An interesting analogy could be drawn here to Charles Batteux's definition of lyric poetry that imitates feelings, ,portrays nothing except the unique state of the soul' as it were. (See Gerard Genette, *The Achitext: An Introduction*, Quantum Books, 1992, 32).
23. Anupa Pande, 'Concept of Drama: Bharata and Aristotle' in *The Natyasastra Tradition and Ancient Indian Society*, (Kusumanjali Prakashan; Jodhpur, 1993), 13.
24. *The Natyasastra*, (Trans. Adya Rangacharya, Munshiram

Manoharlal Publishers Pvt. Ltd., New Delhi, 2003), 148.

25. Referred to *Samsad Bangla Obhidan* and Digital dictionaries of South Asia of the University of Chicago. (In a modern Bengali dictionary like the *Samsad Bangla* the meaning of *natak*, is similar to drama. Here, it means a written text used for a play-production.)
26. J.L. Austin, *How to Do Things with Words* (Oxford University Press, Oxford and New York, 1976).
27. Ashvaghosha is considered to have been a Sanskrit dramatist prior to Kalidasa between 80 to 150 AD.
28. Genette's enquiry although limited to literary classifications but he emphasizes that the fact of genre is common to all arts.
29. Gerard Genette, *The Architext: An Introduction*, 64.
30. ...where the enunciative mode could be pure narration, mixed narration and dramatic imitation. However genres could cut across modes. (For more details see Gerard Genette)
31. The term 'genre' doesnot even appear in the *Poetics.*
32. Ibid., 61.
33. E.P. Horrwitz, *The Indian Theatre: A Brief Survey of the Sanskrit Drama,* (Blackie and Son limited, London, 1912), 176.
34. R.K. Yajnik, *The Indian Theatre: Its Origins and Its Later Developments Under European Influence with Special Reference to Western India,* (George Allen and Unwin Ltd., London, 1933), 53.
35. Hemendranath Dasgupta, *The Indian Stage*, (Vol. 1, Metropolitan printing and publishing House, Calcutta, 1934), 87.
36. Berriedale Keith, 242. 37. Ibid., 356.
38. Dasgupta, 82.
39. Ibid., 4.
40. P. Guha-Thakurta, *The Bengali Drama: Its Origin and Development* (Greenwood Press Publishers, 1974), 40.
41. Homi Bhaba, *The Location of Culture* (Routledge Classics, London and New York, 2007), 132.
42. Paul de Man, 'Literary History and Literary Modernity', (*Daedalus*, Vol. 99, No. 2, Theory in Humanistic Studies, Spring, 1970), 384-404.
43. Vishnu Bose, *Babu Thiyetar*, (Srishti Prakashan, Kolkata, 2001), 12.
44. Marvin Carlson, 'The Resistance to Theatricality' (*SubStance*, Vol. 31, No. 2/3, Issue 98/99, Special Issue: Theatricality (2002), University of Wisconsin Press), 249.
45. *Postdramatic Theatre,* (Trans. by Karen Jürs-Munby, Routledge,

Oxon, 2006), 127.

46. An interesting insight in this respect is provided by Gauri Vishwanathan in the essay 'Currying Favour: The Politics of British Educational and Cultural Policy in India 1813-1854' in *Dangerous Liaisons: Gender, Nations, and Postcolonial Perspectives* (Ed. by Anne MacClintock, Aamir R. Mufti, Ella Shohat, University of Minnesota Press, 1997). It has been discussed later in this section.
47. Vishnu Basu, 11.
48. Ibid., 11.
49. This play has been further discussed in Chapter III.
50. *Bilati Jatra Theke Swadeshi Thiyetar* (Ed. Subir Raychoudhury and Swapan Mazumdar, Dey's Publishing, Kolkata, 1999),.69.
51. Shanta Gokhale, 'Introduction 1843-1943' (In *Playwright at the Centre: Marathi Drama from 1843 to the present*, Seagull Books, Kolkata, 2000), 8.
52. With the Charter Act of 1813, the Parliament of United Kingdom renewed the charter issued to the British East India Company and the Company's rule continued. However its monopoly in India was ended except in Tea trade.
53. 'Languages on Stage: Linguistic Pluralism and Community Formation in Nineteenth Century Parsi Theatre', (In *Modern Asian Studies*, Vol. 37, No. 2, May 2003), 388.
54. Raychoudhury and Mazumdar, 37.
55. Ibid., 39.
56. Here the term is not used in the sense of the political movement discussed later in Chapter III.
57. In *Modern Indian Theatre*, (Ed. Nandi Bhatia, Oxford University Press, New Delhi, 2009), 434.
58. Tagore received the Nobel Prize for Literature in early 1913.
59. People belonging to families of well-repute.
60. Darshan Choudhury, *Unish Shotoker Natyabishoy* (Pragya Bikash, Kolkata, October 2007), 77.
61. Christopher Balme, *Decolonizing the Stage: Theatrical Syncretism and Post-colonial Drama*, (Oxford University Press, New York, 1999), 30.
62. Not to be confused with the Swadeshi movement discussed in Chapter III.
63. 'A house on fire; The village reconstruction', (Ed. Anand T. Hingorani; Bhavan's Book University; 1998), 11.
64. Tandra Devi, *Village theatres: the foundations of Indian National Theatres;* (Foreward by Nandalal Bose, Tandra Devi Publications,

Tandrashram, Kashmir, 1938), 6.

65. Ibid., 7.
66. The Sanskrit term 'devadasi' could be roughly translated as the 'slave of god'. The Tamil word for 'devadasi' is *tevaradiyal* which literally means 'at the feet of god'. They are women who through the ceremonies of marriage dedicate themselves to god or any ritual object. When in the late nineteenth century anti-nautch campaigns were at a high, especially championed by Christian missionaries and other social reformers, the devadasi system got associated directly with prostution. (For a more detailed study refer to Amrit Srinivasan, *Reform and Revival: The Devadasi and Her Dance*; Economic and Political Weekly, 1985)
67. Janet O'Shea, 'Rukmini Devi: Rethinking the Classical' (In *Rukmini Devi Arundale (1904-1986): A Visionary Architect of Indian Culture and the Performing Arts,* Ed. Avanthi Meduri, Motilal Banarsidass, New Delhi, 2005).
68. MSS EUR F191/159, The Uday Shankar Culture Centre, Almora, India, The British Library, London.
69. Ibid., 7-11.
70. Baldoon Dhingra, *A National Theatre for India,* (Padma Publications Limited, Bombay, December 1944), 10.
71. Ibid., 41.
72. Kamaladevi Chattopadhyay, *Towards a National Theatre;* (Published for the All-India Women's Conference by Aundh Pub. Trust, 1945), 29.
73. Ibid., 34.

Part II

Performing Indian Theatre

2

A New Sociability: The Colonial *Urbes Prima*[1] Goes to the Theatre

2.1 Towards a Study of Colonial Sociability

> The European élite undertook to manufacture a native élite. They picked out promising adolescents; they branded them, as with a red-hot iron, with the principles of western culture, they stuffed their mouths full with high-sounding phrases, grand glutinous words that stuck to the teeth. After a short stay in the mother country they were sent home, whitewashed. These walking lies had nothing left to say to their brothers; they only echoed. From Paris, from London, from Amsterdam we would utter the words 'Parthenon! Brotherhood!' and somewhere in Africa or Asia lips would open ... thenon! ... therhood!' It was the golden age.
>
> – Jean Paul Sartre in the *Preface* to 'Wretched of the Earth' by Franz Fanon

A dictionary would tell us about the English word 'sociability' that it is the quality of being sociable or being in interaction with people. The theatre is, as we discussed in the previous chapters, such a space of sociability. Within the colonial situation, this space of interaction is marked by a very unique dynamic. The colonial space is often seen as a space of *encounter* between two different sociables that are always in a play of power; however it is arguable and we have discussed that earlier in the Introduction. Essentially these are two incommensurable sociables, that have gotten together in space and time for reasons beneficial and often detrimental. We have called this *interaction*. The reason for such an unequal interaction, or its incommensurability is somewhat inherent to the very logic of their coming together, which was not aleatory and hence we have not called it an encounter. Nevertheless, they remain affected by each other. The question of reform, central to how the colonized sociable identified itself as a subject was also key to how the identity of the colonizer was created where each one identified the other as distinct. However there is no reason to believe that the colonial psyche was built overnight. The curiosity of the other's existence had been an integral part even before. Only that within this new space of interaction, initially, there had been far more willingness to adapt than to identify a knowledge system about an 'other' that needed to be worked upon. To validate my argument, an interesting case study would be the interactions of the *theatrical* that happened between India and Europe in the sixteenth century. It is often understood to be 'the first strong Western cultural infiltration' at least in the south of India.[2] The coming of the Portuguese in the area and subsequent missionary activities by them initiated a process of acculturation. *Chavittunatakam* evolved out of this interaction although some scholars believe that it had already started evolving from the times of the Syrian Christians[3] in Kerala. *Chavittunatakam,* which literally means stamping-theatre, has often been compared to miracle plays of the West. It has been argued that the Syrian Christians imitated the use of drama in pagan religions and therefore in India they continued with the tradition. With the Portuguese came the Roman Catholic Church, which considered drama as the 'citadel of adverse moral influences', but nevertheless was unable to stop such performances and hence biblical themes came to be their subject, in order to avoid conflict with the Church. Performances like *Genova Natakam* exalting the deeds of a Roman Emperor, *Kaaralman Charitam* based on the life of Rollang, a military chief of Emperor Charlemagne who attained martyrdom and many other such performances that used realistic action, detailed characterization, curtains on stage etc., highlighted influences both of western theatre and *Kathakali* the most popular theatre form during that period in this area. The form was patronized by the Portuguese missionaries. The *Chavittunatakam* of Kerala also influenced religious performances in Tamil Nadu and

Ceylon, which were popularized by the missionaries especially in Tamil speaking areas. In Tamil Nadu, the form is also known as *Terukkuttu*. In some Catholic villages of Ceylon a form called *Nadagama* is performed which shows major influences of the *Chavittunatakam*. However, the evolution of these performances which were integrally related to Christianity never really moved any further from the south. Although it is believed that *Chavittunatakam* replaced pre-Portuguese Hindu art forms like *Kuuttu* and *Kuutiyattam* but the form itself almost ceased to exist later. So the interaction between the English East India Company and subsequent British rule in India was not the first of the occurrences of cultural hybridization in the subcontinent. There has been a historical evolution of performance forms through cultural interaction even before. However, the reason for an unequal interaction could be traced in the unwillingness of the British colonizer to adapt to cultural elements within its own vocabulary as it realized itself as the ruling/colonizing power in the sub-continent. The events that led to the Mutiny of 1857 'uprising' played a significant role in chalking out boundaries. Although there were several aspects for the rise of discontent amongst the Hindus and the Muslims who formed the majority population of colonial India, leading to the events of 1857, one of the significant triggers was religious intrusion by Christian English colonizers. The East India Company's patronage of Church activities and at the same time the suspicion of the colonized population regarding reforms that threatened religious traditions played an important role in the rising discontent. The uprising of 1857 was brutally suppressed. By 'The Government of India Act of 1858', the Company's territories in India were vested in the Queen and a conscious attempt was made from England to stay away from religious activities of the natives. At the same time, the colonial nature of government created a public sphere fundamentally different from that in England and France.[4] Like Sandria Freitag has argued in *Collective Action and Community: Public Arenas and the Emergence of Communalism in North India*, what emerged in India was not a public sphere that would participate in collective rituals identifying itself with, as also moulding an ideological framework, coming to equate the community to the nation.

Rather what transpired were public arenas based on distinctive community rituals rooted in dominant religious practices. Its distinctiveness was maintained by the colonial government's apparent no-interference policy. While communities, religiously sanctioned, got a chance to thrive within such a context, the English population in India as a result got as much chance to stay aloof from collective activities of the natives. 'Theatre's' so-called emergence in such a context cannot be seen as aleatory but it needs to be seen in a different light that is rather historical. The late eighteenth century interaction between the English and the colonized population's elite found 'theatre' as just another tool of sociability that at the same time negotiated power relations. This chapter tries to locate the emergence of 'theatre' within such a historical conjuncture.

2.2 Sociability in the Premier Cities—The Case of Bombay and Calcutta

In the early years of colonial rule, the English preoccupation with trade left little interest for activities, which were not so profitable. Culture was not something that needed to be cultivated as such in this new space, although the English found ways of entertaining themselves in the distant land. Possibly that is why we see disinterest amongst the settlers to invest too much in the newly developing urban habitats which they created for themselves and this gets reflected in their architecture. The Calcutta Theatre or the New Playhouse supposedly had 'no architectural beauty'.[5] For the early settlers of the East India Company entertainment meant dance halls, amateur theatrical activities, dinners and the *nautch* or dance performances for which they were often invited by the native *zamindars* or feudal lords. Hence it is not surprising that a permanent playhouse breathed its first almost a hundred years after the British started settling in India which was in the middle of the eighteenth century when it felt it had more grip on the land. In the plan of Fort William, which the British built in Calcutta, the city that was founded in the late seventeenth century by Job Charnock, a theatre with a dance hall is seen to have existed in 1753.[6] This theatre is also often referred to as the

Old Playhouse. The English during this period had only trading rights, which were granted to them by a Mughal *firman*. They were merely rent collectors and had no sovereign rights. In 1756, Nawab Siraj-ud-Daulah, the Mughal successor in Bengal got suspicious about the activities of the British when they started shoring up Fort William. Curious, Siraj-ud-Daulah on June 19, 1756 started for Fort William and on reaching Dum Dum a nearby area saw that the British had set some native markets ablaze. This infuriated the Nawab and hence his army attacked the Fort and captured the inhabitants there.[7] Hemendranath Dasgupta in his extensive historiography of Indian theatre points out that because of the strategic location of the Theatre-cum-dancehall right opposite the fort, it was used by the army of Siraj-ud-Daulah to seize the fort. The theatre got destroyed in the process. The British inhabitants were incarcerated in a famous event, which is often known as the Black Hole of Calcutta in which several captives were pushed into a small cell where they suffocated to death. Robert Clive who had come to India as the Company's writer was sent as the Commander with a troop to Bengal. When they reached Fulta (Falta) about forty miles downstream from Calcutta, Naba Krishna Deb, a Hindu landlord provided for their food as the troop stayed on, in the anchored ships. In December, one night, Clive and his troops with support from Siraj ud-Daulah's uncle Mir Jafar recaptured Calcutta, marking the beginning of British rule in India. Once Calcutta was recaptured, the need to build a church was felt at the site of the Old Playhouse. However the church never materialized. Dasgupta mentions a second playhouse that came to be known as the New Playhouse or 'Calcutta Theatre' built in 1775 or in the early part of 1776. However these dates are subject to dispute. Geoffrey Moorhouse in his book *Calcutta* writes that the earliest theatre in Calcutta was established in 1745 and was demolished when Calcutta was sacked by Siraj-ud-Daulah in 1756. However a replacement was built in 1772 and the New Playhouse followed three years later.

Around the same time, in Bombay, was built the first playhouse in 1770, which is also known as the Bombay Theatre. The British Crown acquired Bombay in 1661 from the

Portuguese as dowry for Charles II when he married Catherine of Braganza. Eight years later it was transferred to the East India Company. This sparsely populated swamp ridden cluster of seven islands came into prominence in the late eighteenth century when the export trade of cotton and opium from this region was at its peak. The growing trade scenario and the strategic location of this port city with the vast hinterland that the East India Company had by now acquired, turned the city into a vibrant commercial centre.[8] It was during this time that the Bombay Theatre was built on subscriptions in this certain area called the Bombay Green. *The Gazetteer of Bombay City* writes:

> The ground upon which it stood was granted by Government unconditionally and the building was vested in trustees. Unfortunately the proceeds of the performances did not suffice to keep the building in proper repair, and in 1818 it had become so dilapidated that Government were obliged to make a fresh grant for its renovation, on condition that it was used *solely* for public theatrical entertainments. The renovated building was finally opened in 1819 with a debt of Rs. 17,000, which gradually increased to Rs. 23,000 in about 1836. The chief creditors were Messrs. Forbes and Company. Government thereupon discharged the debt, took possession of the theatre and sold it for Rs. 14,870, the remainder of the debt being defrayed from the proceeds of the sale of the site which realized Rs. 27,000. This left a balance in the hands of Government, which it was decided, at a public meeting in the Town Hall in 1836, should be devoted to building a market and subsidising a central library and dispensary.[9]

The newly developing urban centres expanded around the immediate needs of the white settlers rather than any schematic plan that guided the city's construction. As the main motive of these settlers was trade, they encouraged people from other ethnicities to come and settle in these areas. Catholic Portuguese, Armenians, Jews and Tamils from Madras, Parsis and Gujaratis from Bombay and Bengalis from Calcutta all settled in and around these urban centres. In fact, in Bombay, the Parsis who were closer to the English than the others had defended the city from Mughal invasion during the early phase of the city's history.[10] However within these new sociables, the white area and the black area were clearly demarcated. Especially in Calcutta the white part of the town was largely distinctive. The construction in the non-white part was more haphazard where big houses were built right next to houses of servants who built their houses themselves.[11] On the other hand, the white towns or the English settlements were replicas or nostalgic articulations of spaces back home in England. In their attempts to create an atmosphere of a performance culture, as it existed back in England, they took help from professionals in England, as was the case in building one of the first theatres in India. Four gentlemen in the East India Company's service in Calcutta gave a commission for the purchase of theatrical scenery and scripts to the captain of one of the Company's vessels about to depart for home. David Garrick, the famous British actor had apparently helped in sending the material and later he received an acknowledgement letter, which was dated as April 21, 1772[12] and two madeira pipes. David Garrick's association with the theatre in India was not limited to facilitating the purchase of and sending resources from Drury Lane. On being contacted by the founders of the New Playhouse, he responded by sending out an actor named Bernard Messink. Messink was largely responsible for setting up the New Playhouse or the Calcutta Theatre as it was often known. His contributions were greatly praised by Gilbert Ironside, a Colonel in the East India Company's forces. Ironside wrote to Garrick from Patna:

> I have some thoughts of setting at work his happy invention for Machinery, and the skill he has in the artificial slights or deceptions of the Stage, in manufacturing a Pantomime by way of Vehicle for the introduction of the fashions, habits, dances and music of this Country.[13]

The attempts of Messink in setting up a theatre and his contribution in these 'distant quarters' were not always appreciated. Messink who was also connected to the India Gazette was often ridiculed as 'Barnaby Grizzle'[14] by the founder/editor Augustus Hicky of the Bengal Gazette, which was a rival newspaper of the India Gazette. Hicky wrote about Messink's venture into the print media:

> Ye Gods what Havock does ambition make. The Ambition of a

> certain Theatric Manager, who after playing a variety of parts, with universal applause, has been seized with the strange infatuation of making his appearance in the character of a Printer's Devil. This is likely to prove the destruction of Dramatic amusements in Calcutta.[15]

Messink from establishing himself as an actor/administrator moved on to become the theatric manager and then the co-proprietor of the Calcutta Theatre. In 1780, within a couple of years of becoming the co-proprietor of the India Gazette, he ceased to manage the theatre. Having lived in India for about a decade and earned a fortune, he headed back to England. He died on the way. Messink was succeeded by Francis Rundell, a Company surgeon and aspiring actor. William Hickey (not related to Augustus) who was much in favour of Rundell wrote in his memoirs about Rundell's enterprising ability of collecting funds for the theatre which apparently helped in the improvement of facilities and the performance standards. His resourcefulness also included 'getting three very tolerable female performers from London and some male understrappers.'[16] About his performance skills, Hicky mentions one Mr William Burke who had praised Rundell's act in Hamlet as 'quite equal to Garrick'. However Rundell started giving in to heavy drinking, which reduced his stage activity and he started keeping unwell. Finally for a change of air on the way to Bombay he died at sea on September 2, 1791. The matters of the theatre continued to remain sponsored by subscription principally because of the enthusiasm of the amateurs. Often the fate of the theatre was solely dependent on the interests of amateurs like Messink and Rundell who were either government officials or their family members or in some other form of service. The theatre, which required an audience for its survival also became a space where a congregation happened, that of the British expats coming together. But their willingness was not in culturing through a new form of existence or any Aristotelian aim of citizen formation because ultimately most of them planned to be back 'home' in the long run only to which they felt they belonged. Their coming together was mostly to merrily perform matters of daily life, fashions and classics from England within the limits of a form that was a memory of the patria—the theatre followed by a ball and supper/dinner afterwards. Amal Mitra notes in the essay *The English Stage in Calcutta, circa 1750*, that although in the earlier performances of the Calcutta Theatre, some enthusiasm was seen in putting up texts like Macbeth, The Merchant of Venice, Richard the Third, Venice Preserv'd, The Revenge etc. but soon it was taken over by light comedies and farces. It was also felt that the mediocrity of these plays was what led the Calcutta Theatre run into debt. In the Bombay Theatre were showcased similar performances that included musical comedies, farces, and pantomimes with a few productions of Shakespeare, all performed by amateurs. When a certain Lady Nightingall, the wife of Sir Miles Nightingall, the Commander-in-Chief was scheduled to leave for England on January 1, 1819, Holcroft's 'The Road to Ruin' was staged at the renovated Bombay Theatre in her honour and also marking the first anniversary of the battle of Koregaon. The Bombay Gazette on January 6 wrote that 'the whole of our society that were not prevented from attending by ill-health or very urgent business' were present to watch the performance.[17] Joachim Hayward Stocqueler who came to India as a cadet of the Company in 1819 writes in his memoirs about his experience at another theatre which was an improvised artillery theatre at Matoonga near Bombay and I quote it at length here:

> There were no soldiers' libraries fifty years ago. The men were left entirely to their own devices for recreation. The most popular form of entertainment was the theatre. A pretty little edifice had been raised by the officers out of the slender material available in the village of Matoonga. Bamboo walls, columns of the cocoa-nut palm, a thatched roof composed of the leaves of that useful tree, the whole of the edifice excepting the outer roof being either whitewashed or its simple substances connected by pink and white calico tastefully disposed, presented a beautiful interior. The building was oblong, and divided into boxes—in reality stalls—and rows of seats behind them without backs or cushions; there was an orchestra, a classical proscenium, and a stage 15 feet broad by 20 feet deep. We acted farces. The quarter-master-sergeant, one Dixie, was the manager. He had been a member of Richardson's company at Bartholomew and other fairs, and was the comic man of that particular body of Thespians. He was rather illiterate—in fact he could not read at all, but he had a half-caste

wife who read his parts to him, and thus he mastered them. One instance of his deficiency of education will suffice. He had to say as Lazarillo in Two Strings to your Bow—"By the church clock it is eleven, but by the mechanism of my bowels it is dinner-time." He pronounced 'mechanism' mechanichism; and when he had to speak of the University of Salamanca, he called it the University of st. Helena. My dramatic aspirations reviving with the completion of the theatre, I joyfully accepted the duty imposed upon me of reciting the opening address. It was written by a gunner, and the first few lines recur to me at the present moment. They ran thus:

> *Forced forward in an humble cause to plead,*
> *A timid advocate—confused, dismayed—*
> *At this tribunal with submission stands,*
> *To deprecate your frowns, engage your hands.*
> *A tender scion of dramatic sort*
> *Requires this night your fostering support—*
> *Cherished, it blooms—its sweets and flowers arise;*
> *Blasted by apathy, it falls and dies.*
> *Could memory floating o'er the tranquil mind,*
> *Retrace those scenes reluctantly resigned,*
> *Recall the splendid pile, the concave wide,*
> *Raised by a state in architecture's pride,*
> *Our plain ungilded stage you'd scorn, we fear,*
> *And for its homeliness condemn the cheer.*
> *Say, shall the unassuming straight bamboo*
> *Obtain the praise to polished pillars due?*
> *Or can the useful cocoa branch procure*
> *The plaudits gaudy roofs alone ensure?*
> *Futile our labours, our expected joys;*
> *The glaring contrast every life destroys.*
> *&c.&c.&c.*

Then followed a propitiation of the performers. They were not used to the gentler offices of life; their business had been to 'scare the Mahrattas;' even the representatives of the female characters could handle the sponge staff and rammer.

> ...our dames are cannoneers!
> Let not the formidable sound amaze you—
> Equipped in stays, they strive to-night to please you;
> And, leaving keener weapons, hope in form
> With peaceful petticoats your hearts to storm.

> The performances on the whole were not bad, and were loudly applauded by the audience, which consisted of the *élite* of Bombay society—the staff and civilians—who readily accepted invitations to the theatre, because the entertainment was invariably supplemented by a ball and supper in the mess-room of the officers. The band was a very good one, and the caterer for the mess understood his *métier*. There was a good deal of competition among the gunners for engagements in the dramatic recreations, because the officers desiring to retain them at Matoonga, placed them in the headquarters offices as clerks, and, they were not rendered liable, therefore, to be sent up the country. Two sources of advancement were open to steady soldiers—his to be a Scotchman or an actor ensured a man promotion.'[18]

On 20 March, 1819 a journal, Bombay Courier, wrote that the Matoonga theatre had been enlarged and made more commodious and some new scenery had also been added that reflected credit of the amateurs. It was thought that the theatre at Matoonga would soon become the formidable rival to the Dum Dum artillery theatre.[19] About the Matoonga theatre, Sir D.E. Wacha in his memoirs wrote that in 1820, the Bombay Society including the Governor, 'flocked there to witness a performance called *Miss in her Teens and the Padlock*'. The performance was followed by supper and a ball that were organized in a large house in the vicinity of the theatre.[20]

In the initial years of the 'theatre's' coming in the British Raj i.e. the late eighteenth century/early nineteenth century as Kumudini Arvind Mehta puts it, in case of the Bombay Amateur Theatre—'It was the settlement with its civilians, its heads of commercial houses and officers of the Company's regiments which formed the backbone...'[21] Therefore the colonial establishment as a whole was never interested in promoting theatre as such and the need to have professional actors on stage was not at all encouraged. The whole thing majorly depended on the whim and fancy of the Governor General. Amal Mitra writes:

> In Hastings' time and thereafter too Government officials would frequently appear on the stage. But for some reason or other Cornwallis was opposed to this practice. A situation in consequence wherein theatres were virtually obliged to remain closed for lack of actors.[22]

In case there were actors, their indulgence would many a time be as T. Williamson in *The East India Vade Mecum* writes:

> Gentlemen of property, fashion and Consequence, were not easily controlled, they would have new dresses, for every character, and were to be kept in humour, by good suppers after each rehearsal, some tickets for their friends etc. etc. so that, when all was reckoned up, the receipts were invariably less than the disbursements.[23]

Nevertheless this colonial sociable made sociability possible not only through playfully running its theatres but also sometimes by generating funds for charity in the theatres. R.K. Yajnik quotes from an original advertisement for production at the Bombay Theatre, which had mentioned that a seat in the pit was as expensive as Rs.8 for the show and nobody was to be allowed behind the scenes:

> On Tuesday evening, the 12th instant, will be performed the Favourite Farce of the *Apprentice*, after which the Interlude of the *Manager's Ante-Room* to conclude with the *Village Lawyer*. A moiety of the net receipts to go to charity.[24]

An interesting case of a fund-raising performance is noted in the letters of Emily Eden written to her sister. She writes in a letter dated June 9, 1838:

> We went to the play last night. There is a little sort of theatre at Simla[25], small and hot and something dirty, but it does very well. Captain N. got up a prospectus of six plays for the benefit of the starving people at Agra, and there was a long list of subscribers, but then the actors fell out. One man took a fit of low spirits, and another who acted women's parts well would not cut off his mustachios, and another went off to shoot bears near the snowy range. That man has been punished for his shilly-shallying; the snow blinded him, and he was brought back rolled up in a blanket, and carried by six men also nearly blind—he was entirely so, for three days, but has recovered now. Altogether the scheme fell to the ground, which was a pity, as the subscriptions alone would have ensured 30*l*. every night of acting to those poor people. So when the gentlemen gave it up, the 'uncovenanted service' said they wished to try. The 'uncovenanted service' is just one of our choicest Indianisms, accompanied with our very worst Indian feelings. We say the words just as you talk of the 'poor chimney-sweepers,' or 'those wretched scavengers'—the uncovenanted being, in fact, clerks in the public offices.'[26]

2.3 'Handsome Actresses', Colonial English Sociability and Prodigal Energies

The 'Indianisms' of the amateur performers also got reflected in the 'uncovenanted service' of the theatre often as hyperbolical sexual insinuations. During the early days of the East India Company, often the English women would not accompany their husbands and lovers. Stocqueler remembers about his journey as in the 'dark recesses of the deck, the filth, the nausea, the corroding indolence, the vile salt junk, the watered scum, the coarse ribaldry of the sailors, the apprehensions founded on ignorance when squalls caused lurches, the screams of the poor women, the evidences of scurvy...'[27]. Even if they came, they remained in the cities while their husbands were posted in far-flung areas. Apparently there were in eighteenth century Calcutta about two hundred fifty European women as compared to four thousand of the menfolk.[28] Therefore, these men were often not only in practice of keeping native mistresses or *bibis* but at the same time the occasion of socializing that is the 'theatre-ball-dinner' scheme common to the settlements, was that of vying for a partner. As has been already mentioned earlier, professional actors were not allowed in the early years, but given such a situation, actresses were also not allowed on stage. And the reason being,

> The Court of Directors... feared that handsome actresses in India might arouse a spirit of intrigue among the junior servants of the Company; and, doubtless in those days when English women were so scarce, the advent of actresses would have created a great stir and possibly have led to scandal.[29]

From a letter of Emily Eden written from Meerut dated February 11, 1838, we know that till as late as this date, 'except in Calcutta, such a thing as an actress does not exist...'[30] So for the female parts often what one saw was, 'very tall lancer with an immense flaxen wig, long ringlets hanging in an infantine manner over his shoulders, short sleeves, and, as Meerut does not furnish gloves, large white arms with very red hands'[31] or 'buttocky clerks playing Victorian ladies without bustles (how scandalous), and heavily-mustached NCOs playing ladies complete with the whiskers they refused to forego'.[32] Given that the stage was a restricted area for the female performer, what the theatre worked as within the 'theatre-ball-dinner' scheme, was an usher for the later events of suitor seeking. Dewar reminisces that at the public ball, the custom was to lead the ladies out to the minuets according to the rank of their husbands. In case their husbands were not in the service of the company they were led out according to the order they came into the room. This was also the case for unmarried women. Country-dances were generally more in favour and one notice of such a ball said 'the lively country dance runners were bounding and a bounding'. In fact there was a teacher to teach 'the Scotch step in its application to country dancing' and other such steps in addition to 'the athletic and agile' to both men and women for hundred rupees. Apparently one Mr Mackrabie had said about such dancing in India,

> By dint of motion these children of the sun in a very few minutes get as hot as their father, and then it is not safe to approach them. In this agitation they continue, literally swimming through the dance, until he comes himself and reminds them of the hour.[33]

In fact, most of these programmes would be late night affairs in the colony, transforming the craving of the colonials to go back home into prodigal energies of ritualistic performances before the following hot sultry day was faced. What was staged throughout the early years of British theatre in India was this home-bounded desire, which did not cease to be reflected even in the later years. But at the same time the colonial experience of the eighteenth century-early nineteenth century was one that of conflict between the growing middle class sense of propriety as was developing in England which necessitated the ban on women performing on stage but distinctively so. There in England although the social acceptance of the actress was increasing, still there had been ambiguity[34] about her private life while in India, 'a spirit of intrigue' about the actress figure caused her to be banned. When Isabella Birchell, later Mrs Vincent and an erstwhile actress, married to the Black Hole (1756) survivor James Mills came to India, this intrigue as Busteed in his memoirs writes was reflected as she was

A Ball at Governor House, Calcutta.
Notice that the military officers are in full-dress uniform. The illustration is taken from *Tom Raw—The Griffen,* by Sir Charles D'Oyly, Bart (Douglas Dewar, 174-175)

introduced as a 'bewitching widow' and 'a celebrity on the English stage, much admired both as Miss Birchell and as Mrs Vincent for her melodious voice and amiable, simple disposition'. Apparently she had acted as Polly Peachum of Drury Lane's Beggar's Opera in 1760 and featured in Churchill's Rosciad (1765). However they returned before the end of the century and nothing is known about her ventures in Calcutta.[35] Hence, that women started performing on stage in colonial British India within domestic parameters of a private theatre is not surprising. Amelia Wrangham[36] or Emma Wrangham, the daughter of a former Governor of St Helena (Hutchinson) married to John Bristowe, an officiating captain was to start such a private theatre at her Chowringee residence in Calcutta. For what reason Emma was in India is not quite known, nevertheless her physical beauty and ball appearances would be a part of Hicky's Gazette regularly between 1781-1782 making her a much sought after lady till she got married at the age of nineteen. But the fascination around her, took a different turn when encouraged by her husband she opened a theatre at her residence. On May 7, 1789, the Calcutta Gazette published that Mrs Bistrowe's theatre was 'a perfect theatre differing only from a public one in its dimension and agreeing within the essential point of being appropriated to amusements without which we might fear that we had tasted joy only to lament the loss of it.'[37] The lack of the white female performer that was felt in the public theatre was in a way fulfilled by the ones of the private theatres where the audience would be an invited one repeating itself especially from the ranks of the influential ones, within the limited numbers that the colonial sociability allowed during the times of Lord Cornwallis. Mrs Bristowe became popular especially for her comedies and humorous singing. The character of Polly Honeycombe of the play by the same name was apparently her favourite role. It is interesting to note that this theatre-loving damsel found her favourite in George Colman's satire about the novel-loving woman. Orientalism played its own nostalgic role even in the private theatre. Orientalism in this case was not any perception based on contact with the culture of the East, it was rather a reliving of fantasies sexual and otherwise played out on stage as was being done back home. Bristowe's recreating of the harem scenario as the English slave in the Ottoman Seraglio, the art-décor, and the charms of Mrs Bristowe all apparently justified the 'extravagances of the amorous Sultan' in the play.[38] In the process, such oriental excesses justified the amorous or sexual desires of the male spectator/voyeur who pitched his gaze on the English woman performing the 'slave' to their desires. Mrs Bristowe was back to England in 1790 and whether she returned to continue with her pursuits is not quite known. However she initiated the trend of amateur women performers who often also played male characters. The overtly sexual bearings continued with the female actresses that followed her. A Calcutta newspaper in 1790 apparently published on a certain actress appearing as Lucius in Shakespeare's tragedy Julius Ceasar at the Calcutta Theatre—

> When with new powers to charm our partial eyes,
> Thy beauteous form appears in virile guise,
> Such tempting graces wanton o'er thy air,
> By gentle Love's enchanting wiles I swear
> Each throbbing youth would...

H.E. Busteed who quotes this passage from the paper in his memoir notes that the poet gets so carried away with his theme that he cannot be quoted any further.[39] The theatrical activities around Chowringhee soon procured for itself the title of 'Calcutta's Drury' after Drury Lane of London. And shortly followed the star of 'Calcutta's Drury', the 'Mrs Siddons of Bengal'—Esther Leach's tryst with the stage.[40] She was a 'country-born' as against others who had come to India to exploit their fortune. Born to a soldier stationed in Meerut in India in 1810, she was orphaned by the age of seven. She grew up around military surroundings and studied at an English military school. Her theatrical debut began as a child artist in the army plays.[41] At the age of twelve she got married to John Leach who at that time was stationed at the Dum Dum barrack. She was invited to perform at the Dum Dum artillery theatre for a monthly salary of sixty rupees and was soon noticed by the wealthy Calcutta officials who often would come to Dum Dum—their escape from the city.[42] John Leach was transferred from Dum Dum to Calcutta where he moved with his wife. His wife was invited to perform at the Chowringhee Theatre, which had opened in 1813. Stocqueler in his memoir writes that John Leach was not the first man 'who owed his advancement to his wife.'[43] About Esther Leach, Stocqueler remembers—

> Extremely pretty, very intelligent, modest, and amiable, possessing a musical voice and good taste, she adapted herself to all the requirements of the drama. The ingénue and the soubrette, the leading parts in such plays as Othello, the Wife, the Hunchback, and the Lady of Lyons, the highest flights in comedy, the pantomimic action of La Muette, and some minor parts in Italian opera when a small buffo company took Calcutta en route from Bologna to Macao via Lima, thence to the East Indies, were all alike to this clever child of nature.[44]

Esther Leach having made repute for herself as the Sarah Siddons of colonial India, after working at the Chowringhee Theatre for twelve years sailed back to England. A grand farewell was organized for her departure. However she returned soon with her two daughters Alice and Julia leaving her son back home to continue with his studies there. When she returned, the Chowringhee Theatre had already burnt down. She initiated the process of building a theatre in another part of the town. As contributions started pouring in liberally for constructing the new theatre, the venue of 'a long room beneath a bookseller's store was engaged and converted into a temporary home for the drama under the title of the Sans Souci.'[45] The subscription money being not enough, the property had to be mortgaged in order to raise funds. By March 1841, the San Souci theatre building with an enormous portico supported by six doric columns was completed. Stocqueler apparently had asked for two actresses to be sent to India and by his wish was sent 'two actresses, marked, S, Mr Stocqueler'. The Englishman of May 9, 1840 notes that they had been brought in with a salary that would be considered handsome in England.[46] One of the actresses Mrs Deacle from the Adolphe Theatre in London who had became popular by playing the role of Cleopatra played roles of Portia, Juliet and Lady Macbeth in India. After the tragic death of Esther Leach who met with an accident during a performance, as her dress caught fire from the candles placed as footlights, Mrs Deacle took up her role as the next actress-manager. What was interesting about these women was their total control over the space of the theatre. Bishnupriya Dutt in the essay 'Historicizing Actress Stories: English Actresses in India (1789-1842)', borrowing from Tracy Davis, argues that like in the case of the British actress Genevieve Ward to whom Esther Leach was often compared, the age of 'actressocracy' began in India at this point. However even during the times of Mrs Bristowe, her prowess was seen in her ability to attract people to her theatre. The politician and pamphleteer Philip Francis wrote in a letter in 1796 to the 'most dear and worthy Ceilings' in Calcutta—

> For three or four years past Mrs Bristow has sworn to me by all her gods that she would take you and your affairs under her immediate patronage and protection. I saw her last night at the opera, and I think her perjuries seem to agree with her mightily: every vow she breaks creates a new charm, and there! Am I such a fool as to tell her so? Encouraged by my success in my care of the East, I have lately turned my thoughts to the West, from Hindoos to Negroes. And Mrs Bristow says, 'What signify negroes? Aren't they black? And don't I make a slave of every man I meet?[47]

But Leach's abilities in gathering resources for the public theatre and keeping in control every situation within such a public space is probably what made the Calcutta Literary Gazette write in 1839 that 'she has no equal, male or female on the Indian scene'.[48] Even the entry of James Vining who was announced to be the first professional leading man and stage manager from a well-known theatrical family who had established himself as a major actor in England could not overshadow Leach's aura. But this success story was accompanied by stories of actresses like Madame Dhermainville or Madame D. as Stocqueler calls her. Madame Dhermainville, an English actress married to a Frenchman, 'master of a trading vessel' came to India from Sydney in search of better opportunities. It was soon found that the ship in which he was travelling was a stolen one and thus anticipating the legal consequences, he committed suicide. The shocked Madame Dhermainville after a while of grief obtained protection of an officer of the Bengal army. Stocqueler writes—

> At the expiration of a few weeks, the captain manifested a feverish anxiety for her appearance on the stage, that she might assert her independence and earn an honest livelihood. I readily gave her the opportunity. She made her debut as Madame Monnette in the poor farce Mischief-making.

The officer, her 'protector' who had occupied a private box in the theatre for her performance, after the show shot himself. In a suicide note written to friend Stocqueler he revealed that his wife was about to return from England, and knowing not how to face the situation, he decided to end his life. Madame Dhermainville apparently unable to deal with her misfortune and unwell of cholera died within ten days of the incident.

2.4 English 'Publicity' and Colonial English Sociability

From all these narratives what is evident is that the theatre remained fraught with scandals and talk of the town. It was a space of common being of the English population in India. It was also a space of dissemination of information in its entire nostalgic garb, a space of congregation that in coming together performed the function of a reunion. But the reunion every time aimed for a union with the institutionalized congregation of the distant homeland that was made possible using the theatrical medium; nevertheless it was also a space of escaping the institution. It was becoming English and unbecoming the same that made colonial English theatre of the early years distinct from that in the homeland. How the East India Company officials led their lives in the colony soon became a matter of concern for England. The debauchery, the loot of people and most importantly the total lack of representation of the nation-state is what made the Parliament in England more and more suspicious of the Company's activities. England's own taking shape as a modern democracy from the existent form of monarchical and aristocratic rule paved ways about thinking of the 'people'.[49] In fact in 1786 Edmund Burke, the anti-revolutionary thinker who also chaired the Commons' Select Committee on East India Affairs since 1781, moved in the House of Commons to impeach Warren Hastings, the Company's former Governor General (1773-85), for the crimes the Company administration had committed in India which Burke claimed to be the violation of property, the destruction of native customs and institutions and the dishonouring of native women. This impeachment move, which was one of a kind in England's history, was open to ticketed viewing by public. Burke argued that the crimes that the nabobs or English merchant-administrators had committed in India were evidence to the way merchant imperialism had corrupted the nation-state and above all the Parliament. His main concern remained however that imperialism threatened the British civil society, which under such a situation will always be in a 'concealed state of war', and 'the civilized self and civility a mask constructed out of the conventions of print culture and performed in the public sphere.'[50] In India after Warren Hastings, and especially during the time of Lord Cornwallis who was appointed in the same year as the move for impeachment of Hastings, that there was much care taken in the behaviour of the *nabob* in public is predictable. Possibly this is why Cornwallis was not in favour of the officials performing on stage and did not encourage theatrical activity as such. The question of public visibility and 'publicity' as Burke demanded for the sake of the British civil society also has to be kept in mind in this regard. Burke repeatedly highlighted the necessity to respect organic traditional developments of societies. The conspicuous wealth of the *nabobs* when they returned to England, the state's tottering credit at this point when the biggest revenue for England came from the Company which had frequently been unable to make its annual payments to the state or to the shareholders had also made the Parliament suspicious of its activities. Such growing distrust by the late eighteenth century/early nineteenth century culminated in the Charter Act of 1813 that dissolved the trade monopoly of the Company in India also bringing in several reforms through parliamentary intervention in England.

2.5 Colonial Knowledge Formation and 'Discovery' of the 'Other'

Questions of visibility and publicity of the English outside of national boundaries made the colonizer aware of its role as a governing body. David Ludden in the essay *Orientalist Empiricism: Transformations of Colonial Knowledge* argues that around this time a new sort of attention was paid to Indian intermediaries between the Court of Directors of the Company and the Indian subjects. In order to subordinate the intermediaries, the need to appropriate knowledge about India that was 'locked away in the minds of Indian commercial, judicial, military, and revenue specialists' was felt. It was by appropriating this knowledge that the European colonizers discovered India for themselves, in their own terms by converting knowledge from native sources into English language through a so-called process of 'systematic, scientific, and accessible to means of truth-testing' which also became pride of European culture.[51] It was this authoritative gathering of facts at the wake of the distrust that the administrators had around the native specialists, that drama became the signifier of a 'written truth' about the Indian civilization. Of course, behind this 'will' was also the will to establish the justification of the material well-being of the colonized that the Empire was carrying forward in the colony by leading ahead a civilization that had halted in time. William Jones the philologist who 'discovered' Shakuntala in 1789 had originally come to India when appointed as the puisne judge of the Supreme Court of Bengal in 1783. In fact, in a letter written in 1788 by William Jones to Cornwallis, he proposed a grant to be commissioned to compile a 'Digest of Hindu and Mohammadan laws' in order to write civil law in accordance with native customs (something Burke had also argued for). He had already shown concern during Warren Hastings' times in 1784 in this regard. He writes, 'I can no longer bear to be at the mercy of our Pundits, who deal out Hindu law as they please...' and to Cornwallis he wrote, 'Every native of Hindustan, I verily believe, is corrupt':[52] It was while undergoing this process of compilation that he came across Shakuntala. Regarding the so called 'discovery', Jones in the preface to the published play writes, 'In the north of India there are many books, called Nátac, which, as Bráhmens assert, contain a large portion of ancient history without any mixture of fable'. Clearly Jones did not want fable in the story of India and that is why possibly the Brahman replied this way. Jones continues about his own 'discovery-story' that he had a different experience once he learnt the language of the Brahmans who could now no more fool him. They said, 'the Nátacs were not histories, and abounded with fables; that they were extremely popular works', and Jones' own knowledge of the oriental languages helped verify this. If they were 'popular works' as the Brahman said, so then, they were a 'discovery' for whom? – Of course for the 'discoverer', the European colonial administrator who was ignorant of the culture it was in and needed to create a knowledge bank to 'rightfully' for the sake of its 'civil society' back home, rule the colony that was the main source of its regular income. Jones continues:

> At length a very sensible Bráhmen, named Radhácánt, who had long been attentive to English manners, removed all my doubts, and gave me no less delight than surprise, by telling me that our nation had compositions of the same sort, which were publickly represented at Calcutta in the cold season, and bore the name, as he had been informed, of plays. Resolving at my leisure to read the best of them, I asked which of their Nátacs was most universally esteemed; and he answered without hesitation, Sacontalá... I soon procured a correct copy of it; and, assisted by my teacher Rámalochan, began with translating it verbally into

> Latin, which bears so great a resemblance to Sanscrit, that it is more convenient than any modern language for a scrupulous interlineary version: I then turned it word for word into English, and afterwards, without adding or suppressing any material sentence, disengaged from the stiffness of a foreign idiom, and prepared the faithful translation of the Indian drama, which I now present to the publick as a most pleasing and authentick picture of old Hindu manners, and one of the greatest curiosities that the literature of Asia has yet brought to light.[53]

The impact of the 'discovery' of Shakuntala has been discussed in the previous chapter. Drama remained a thing of curiosity for not only theatre enthusiasts but also the colonial administrator as how it portrayed life, its imitative potential, seemed 'authentick' to the colonial administrator in its project of creating an administrative system in par with the 'authentick' situation of the colonial subject. This drive of authenticity kept drama at the centre of political discourse as pre-colonial texts figured as 'sources'[54] to be evaluated by modern scientific model of the West. As late as 1874 J. Talboys Wheeler, who had been the Assistant Secretary to the government of India in the foreign department and the Chief Commissioner of British Burma in his History of India published in five volumes wrote:

> The theatre of the Hindus opens up a new insight into the civilization of ancient India. It forms valuable supplement to the information furnished by Greek writers and Chinese pilgrims. Moreover the dramas are more reliable than the sacred books of either Buddhists or Brahmans. They do not appear to have been compiled by pious sages, or to have been interpolated and garbled to any appreciable extent by an interested priesthood.[55]

In the series of volumes, which are supposed to be, the history of India is 'objectively' gathered through the study of not only historical events but also myths and epics especially in the first two volumes that he calls 'prolegomena to history'. The quest in the third volume that carries a chapter on 'The Hindu Drama' is supposed to be 'the first volume of the history of India properly so called.'[56] What the dramas seem to do according to him is to open up 'inner life of ancient times', which the Greeks or the Chinese ambassadors were unable to capture. What the chapter really does is to describe the plots of a few plays like the 'Toy-cart' that shows glimpses of the social life of middle and upper classes, the 'Signet of the Minister' which he calls the next 'historical drama' in terms of importance to the 'Toy-cart' and criticizes it for having 'an artificial air of unreality' about it. Then he moves on to describe 'Sakúntalá, or the Lost Ring' which he thinks mostly gives an idyllic picture about ancient India and then he follows up on the play 'Málatí and Mádhava' which he finds interesting because it portrays the conflict between Brahmanical idea of marriage and the Buddhist idea which seemed to him to be the ideal play for the Hindu-*zenana* or the women's space within a house. Finally after brief descriptions of social lives from these ancient plays of the Hindus or Indians which he finds are interchangeable given the lineage of the colonial society where the 'Mussulman' are characterized as just the invaders who in fact are studied in an entirely separate volume (while the Portuguese are placed in this third or rather the first 'proper' history of India), he declares:

> But social development amongst the Hindus is of slow growth; and even in the progress of centuries the outer life of the people undergoes but few important changes. The Sanskrit Theatre furnishes valuable illustrations of that resignation and habitual self-control, which specially mark the Hindu people.[57]

The canonization of these dramatic texts work at two levels here that is required to be connected to the political discourse around which they were 'discovered'. As has been discussed earlier, they worked as 'sources' for a lost past by which the true colonial subject could be identified. These narratives are characterized by their Hindu-ness. Further validation happens in the case of dramatic literature by the very missing/vanishing of the 'sources' during the medieval times. The discourse of Indian theatre hence, from the very beginning was coloured by communal categorizations where not theatricality as such but the 'text' decided the course of any narrative on the theatre. It was a narrative of identity—a lost one that needed to be reclaimed precisely because at a collective communal level it held the potential of mirroring the 'real' people of India. This 'real' people was Burke's 'natives' who needed to be justly ruled and rescued from the Indian intermediaries as also the *nabobs* given to debauchery. This is why it could be argued that by the early nineteenth century the English actress in India from the mere 'entertainer-woman' had now become the woman representative of Victorian English morality and virtuosity in colonial India. A Sarah Siddons, the epitome of 'serious, virtuous and maternal (devotion)'[58] was made possible on the colonial British stage in the form of Esther Leach in the courtroom and parliament of England. But this also called in the slow death of dramatic activities by the colonial English population, which was more interested in entertaining itself than to create a genuine sense of engagement with the arts as an English community. 'Publicity' of the officials made their public endeavours in terms of theatrical activities in the colony feeble. Like the older theatres Calcutta Theatre which was sold to Gopey Mohun Tagore in 1808 who turned it to a market and the Bombay Theatre, which closed down in 1835 after running in debt most of the time, Sans Souci theatre also was closed for longer and longer durations due to lack of resources 'until one day came an announcement that next season the building would be used to accommodate a circus!.'[59] The feeble dramatic activities of the English community continued through the nineteenth century into the twentieth. A book published in 1927, which is mainly a guide to Indian life for the Europeans elaborate on the aspect of public life of the British in India:

> The fact may be lamented, but it must nevertheless be accepted, that Europeans in the East refuse to take the theatre seriously, nor are many of them very keen on the drama. Rather do they wish for a light and cheery entertainment, something in the nature of a musical liqueur to round off a good dinner. They are apt to be captious and intolerant of any play that requires a certain amount of serious attention, and prefer the soft strumming of the Hawaiian steel guitar to the wit and sarcasm of Bernard Shaw or the subtle humour of A.A. Milne. Needless to say, the play or entertainment which savours of what is popularly known as "highbrow" ingredients is doomed from the word go, and the "tag" will be spoken to many vacant stalls, while the chinking of glasses in the theatre bar merrily tolls its requiem.[60]

The author A. Claude Brown, a former editor of the newspaper *The Empress* writes that in the theatres that would begin late in the night, the audience usually would be late to enter often interrupting the performance. However he quotes an incident whereby the intervention of one actress Miss Marie Tempest, the number of latecomers decreased. The author argues that post the war (he probably means the First World War) due to the rise in transportation charges, it had become difficult for touring companies to come to India. Moreover taxes like the entertainment tax imposed by the colonial government had made it difficult for theatrical activities to bloom apart from other infrastructural problems that the travelling troupes faced. The author poses the nightlife of the European residents in Calcutta as against the nightlife of the natives who according to him have 'humble' ways of amusing themselves. Of the Indian theatre, he writes that while the European ones began after nine-thirty and are over by mid-night, the Indian ones go on long into the early hours of the following morning. He writes:

> Long speeches and a certain amount of knockabout fun are indulged in by the players, while the audience, not to be outdone, bandy shrill cries with friends or acquaintances in distant parts of the theatre, and at other times hold animated conversations with their near-by neighbours...One visit to an Indian theatre will probably suffice to satisfy the curiosity of the average European, for the plays being entirely in the vernacular will mean nothing intelligible to the Westerner; moreover the atmosphere will quite likely be considered distinctly oppressive, and somewhat ultra odoriferous. Should you sample the Indian theatre you will get lots for your money, as the "show" will continue until two o'clock, or even later still into the hours of the morning, and you will come away dry inside but thoroughly wet as far as your outer man is concerned.[61]

Here possibly the author means the *jatra* performances of Bengal, but nevertheless while the European theatres were struggling with the sad state of affairs in terms of theatrical activities amongst the European community what flourished meanwhile was the native theatre—a theatre which has often been seen to have had an 'intercultural'[62] beginning.

2.6 'Parthenon! Brotherhood!'–the Other Discovers Itself

> I am aware, my dear fellow, that there will be in all likelihood, be something of a foreign air about my drama; but if the language be

> not ungrammatical, if the thoughts be just and glowing, the plot interesting, the characters well maintained, what care you if there be a foreign air about the thing? Do you dislike Moore's poetry because it is full of Orientalism? Byron's poetry for its Asiatic air, Carlyle's prose for its Germanism? Besides that I am writing for that portion of my countrymen who think as I think, whose minds have been more or less imbued with Western ideas and *modes of thinking*; and that it is my intention to throw off the fetters forged for us by a servile admiration for everything Sanskrit.[63]

The case of 'Indian' theatre remained within a dichotomous relationship of the foreign with the Sanskrit, since its inception. When Michael Madhusudan Dutt published the play *Sermista* in 1859, taking on the responsibility of moving on from the existent Sanskrit plays that were being repeatedly played and overplayed in the *babu* sociable, he was criticized for the language of this Bengali play which was seen to be too 'high' for those who patronized this kind of theatre. It was in this context the poet-playwright wrote the above lines. The beginning of 'theatre' as is highlighted here as well, was possible due to the patronage of the gentry in the newly developing urban centres like Calcutta and Bombay. In fact, the tastes of this section of the society had a huge role to play in the development of drama and 'theatre' in India. The landholding class in and around Calcutta and the businessmen of Bombay and also Calcutta who had been settling in these areas since the coming of these establishments in the late seventeenth century were in direct contact with the British. In Calcutta, this class who came to be known as the *babu*-s and in Bombay mainly the Parsis[64] apart from the Gujaratis comprised this section. Interaction with the British had begun in the early years of the development of English settlements in these regions. By the late eighteenth century—early nineteenth century there was supposedly a cordial relationship between the upper class native and the British colonials. In Calcutta, the British seem to have frequented the house of the affluent Bengalis during festive occasions. *Nautch* or native dance performances were organized with lavish food and drinks with the aim to attract the European guests' attention. Although there is evidence of the Englishman often visiting such *nautch* performances, nevertheless these performances were often seen as obscene. A certain Bishop Heber's wife refers to one such *nautch* performance she saw at a *zamindar* (landholding gentry), Ruplal Mullick's house that she found disgusting. Another Miss Fanny Parks in her memoirs *Wanderings of a Pilgrim in Search of the Picturesque* writes of having witnessed a *nautch* in 1826 at the home of an opulent Hindu gentleman. Maria Nugent who visited Calcutta in 1812 writes about the lavish entertainment provided to European guests by Raja Ramchunder Roy of Calcutta on the occasion of his son's wedding ceremony.[65] Similarly, this section of the native society both in Calcutta and Bombay was often invited to entertainment events organized by the British that included 'theatre'. Like Kathryn Hansen argues 'sociability and mutual hospitality reinforced economic collaboration' in this way.[66] These everyday matters of ceremony, celebrations and entertainment evenings led to a certain desire in the native to imitate the customs of European guests. Fanny Parks mentions that she had attended a ball thrown in English style by a rich native gentleman called Rustomjee Cowasjee that was attended by several English guests like Misses Eden, sisters of Lord Auckland who later became the Governor General. Raja Nabakrishna Deb of Calcutta organized a birthday party for Emma Wrangham, the actress, with a costume ball.[67] The invitees of these events at the native houses were strictly limited to certain elite groups of both the native houses and the English. In fact, doors would remain closed for anybody other than the invited. Reverend Ward notes of a *nautch* performance he was invited to by the Raja Rajkrishna of Sovabazar (Calcutta) in 1806.

Soon after the invited guests left from the venue at midnight, 'a vast crowd of natives rushed in almost treading upon one another'. These natives were waiting for the next performance, which was that of *kabigaan*, not meant for the viewing of the English but that of the 'uncultivated' and 'uncouth' natives.[68] In colonial India, the question of public morality was put centre-stage by the influence of Judeo-Christian values. Sumanta Banerjee in his seminal work *Unish Shotoker Kolkata o Saraswatir Itor Santan* notes that within Calcutta popular forms like *kabigaan, jatra, panchali, tarja, kathakatha, khemta* etc. which were forms performed by the lower section of the society and often

A nautch girl dancing before three Europeans.
This picture is taken from *The European in India*, illustrated by Sir Charles D'Oyly, Bart (Douglas Dewar, 28-29)

patronized by the elite got obliterated as concepts like 'oshleel' which means obscene or indecent, 'oshobhya' or uncivilized entered the daily discourse of public life in Calcutta. He traces the beginning of such a discourse to the late eighteenth century-early nineteenth century when the British in India often criticized behavioural patterns, and ways of dressing of natives. Discussing a comment made by Bishop Heber in 1823 where he says that the natives cannot be judged according to the standards of vulgarity of the white people because their colour is different, Banerjee argues that although many idealistic Englishmen considered the native population to be uncivilized and to civilize them to be their mission, they thought of these people like primitive children, without any sense of the good or the bad or without the sense of sin like Rousseau's noble savage. For Heber therefore it was his duty to convert these people to Christianity and in turn civilize them.[69] With this main imperative, the ecclesiastical institutes in India opened up schools for primary education. It has already been argued earlier how with the Charter Act of 1813, the colonial model of education was institutionally imposed and the spread of English education was a huge part of it. Within a certain colonial discourse of public morality and decency and the orientalist view about existing performance cultures, few forms continued to be patronized by the elite while others were discarded. Meanwhile, that vacant space was taken over by this new form '*natok*' or that which was the 'theatre', a genre that came to be defined by its use of dramatic writing.

2.7 A Detour—Gerasim Stepanovich Lebedev and his Bengali Language 'Theatre'

Before we move on to studying 'theatre' as it supposedly emerged and became popular amongst the people of the colonial cities of Bombay and Calcutta, an interesting observation needs to be made. It is a story about the 'theatre' that has already been mentioned in several theatre history books and is often considered an example of the first theatre production in any native language in India. The story is that of Gerasim Stepanovich Lebedev from Yaroslavl in Russia. Lebedev who landed in Madras in 1785 began his career in India as a musician. He was influenced by the rising interest around ancient Indian language and culture and learnt Tamil. But he still wanted to learn Sanskrit. As it was difficult to learn the language from the local experts who wouldn't teach the language to lower castes or foreigners, he moved to Calcutta.[70] In Calcutta in exchange for music lessons he learnt Sanskrit from a Brahmin called Goloknath Das. Although he couldn't really master the language he eventually ended up learning Bengali. This was around the time when William Jones had first translated *Shakuntala* and Charles Wilkins had translated Bhagavad–Gita. Given that the literary vocabulary of superior Bengali at that point was so much similar to Sanskrit that when he spoke what he had learnt he could not communicate with the local people. Goloknath hence suggested to him that instead of translating the vocabulary he should try writing dialogues. He started with this exercise and decided to translate a couple of plays. The next step to this exercise naturally became staging these plays and Golaknath apparently promised to provide him with native actors and actresses. He applied to rent the New Playhouse and was rejected. So he decided to construct one himself and interestingly got permission from the then Governor General Sir John Shore. Lebedev chose to perform an almost unknown play *The Disguise* of Richard Jodrell and Moliere's farce *Love is the Doctor*. About his choice, Lebedev argued that 'Indians prefer mimicry and drollery to plain grave solid sense, however purely expressed'.[71] As the preparations of Lebedev's endeavour progressed, the English in Calcutta mocked it as a 'Don Quixotic plan'. He invested his own savings to construct a theatre and to stage the plays. *The Disguise* was adapted to the context of Calcutta. The playbill announced 'decorated in the Bengalee style' the play would be performed 'by both sexes' and would begin 'with Vocal and Instrumental Music, called The Indian Serenade'.[72] He also made it clear in the second run of the show that the play was 'for the Asiatic Inhabitants... at and in the Vicinity of Calcutta, to attend'. The play was apparently very successful. Given the success, he applied for the license 'for full permission to perform both English and Bengalie plays'. Meanwhile in a feud with the scene designer and later his partner Joseph Battle he got entangled in a legal battle and the English community in Calcutta refused any help. Several other cases of debt were thrown on to him leading to the end of his theatre career. It has been argued by Hayat Mamud that the English were suspicious of his endeavours in Calcutta and as they were trying to settle themselves at that point, they did not want any foreign intervention of any kind on the matter. Lebedev's theatre in the Bengali language could not initiate native theatre in Bengal but nevertheless it is said to have influenced the *jatra* of the time. In fact, the newsmagazine *Samachar Darpan* had apparently called Lebedev's theatre 'notun jatra' or new *jatra* and 'opurva jatra' or wonderful *jatra*. His play was also introduced as 'natok' in the newspaper *Calcutta Review*.[73]

2.8 Colonial Sociability, 'Theatre' and Native Elite Brotherhood in Calcutta

In Calcutta, the early theatre performances often known as '*babu* theatre' or 'theatre' of the gentry began with Prasanna Kumar Tagore's 'Hindu Theatre' in 1831. Prasanna Kumar Tagore a rich landowner was a student of the Hindu College, one of the first educational institutes to be founded in 1817 to introduce English education in Bengal. Prasanna *Babu*, a lawyer who was later to become the clerk assistant of the Legislative Council of the Governer-General[74] initiated the performance of the English translation of the Sanskrit play *Uttara Rama Charita* and soon after Shakespeare's 'Julius Caesar'. Clearly such a choice reflects the larger discourse around the mid-nineteenth century that was about the orientalist idea of the original Indian culture, which was basically Sanskrit textual supremacy, which was supposedly at par with English high culture and Shakespeare was symbolic of that. The invitees in the performances included people like the judge, Edward Rayan, Colonel Young and Radhakanta Dev one of the founding members of the Hindu College. However these plays performed in English met with a lot of criticism. The 'East Indian' wrote:

> We hear that the performances are to be in the English language. Who advised this strange proceeding we know not, but it is surely worth re-consideration—what can be worse than to have the best dramatic compositions in English language murdered outright, night after night, foreign manners misrepresented and instead of holding the mirror upto nature caricaturing everything human? We recommend our Hindu patriots and philanthropists to instruct their countrymen by means of schools and when they are fitted to appreciate the dramatic compositions of refined nations, it will be quite time enough to erect theatre... A theatre among the Hindus with the degree of knowledge they at present possess will be like building a palace in the waste.[75]

Clearly 'theatre' was regarded as the high art which was no easy job for even the native elites to practice. It should be noted here that the editor of the newspaper *East Indian*, Henry Louis Vivian Derozio was a teacher of the Hindu College and had influenced a huge section of the student community who later came to be known as the Derozians or the Young Bengal. In the same year as the performances of these two plays, the first play in English by a native was written. Krishna Mohan Banerjee, a disciple of Derozio wrote 'The Persecuted'. The play which possibly is based on his own life story is about a Hindu boy Banylal who was given to beef eating and was asked by his father for formal penance. But Banylal refuses to give away his 'inner truth' and hence has to leave home. The play tries to bring out the hypocrisies of the society that enjoys drinking brandy and sends their children to English schools but nevertheless do not accept their 'inner truth' and publicly pretends to be religious.[76] The play is a reflection of the rebellious student community that was churned out of the Hindu College in the 1830s who were mostly atheists, given to drinking and beef eating, something that was not allowed in popular Hindu belief. But these rebels at the same time had their soft corner for the British colonial ruler, which gets reflected in the above comment in the *East Indian*. Sumit Sarkar notes that this new community who later on became influential as it generated public opinion and created forums of discussion about religion, women's emancipation etc. in the upcoming societies, *samaj* or *sabha*[77] were critical about the Company's monopoly rights and administrative practices but basically they remained loyal to the British.[78] Prasanna Kumar unlike the other Derozians had not entirely given up on religion, possibly which is why, he was attacked by the *East Indian*. The desire to establish a theatre materialized with Prasanna Kumar's efforts but nevertheless there had been an ongoing cry to start one. According to Brajendra Nath Banerjee, post Lebedev's endeavour a number of *jatra* performances had deviated from their earlier structure. Although Banerjee argues that they cannot really be called 'dramatic performances', the growing desire for the so-called 'dramatic performances' in an atmosphere of co-habitation with the English got voiced in the newspapers of the time. Banerjee cites *Samachar Chandrika* and *Asiatic Journal* of the 1820s to prove his point. He quotes from the *Asiatic Journal* of August 1826:

> In this extensive city public institutions of various kinds and novel descriptions have lately sprung up for the improvement and gratification of its inhabitants; but their amusement has not yet

> been consulted, and they have not, like the English community, any place of public entertainment. In former times, actors and actresses were attached to the courts of the princes of India, who represented plays, and charmed the audience with graceful poetry and music, and impassioned action. We have had of late some Saker-Jatras exhibited, which though not perfect, gave great diversion to the people; they have been, however, unfrequent. It is therefore very desirable, that men of wealth and rank should associate and establish a theatre on the principle of shares, as the English gentlemen have done, and retaining qualified persons on fixed salaries, exhibit a new performance of song and poetry once a month, conformably to the written *nataks* or plays, and under the authority of a manager; such a plan will promote the pleasure of all classes of society.[79]

It needs to be reiterated here that all the English theatres were mainly meant for the entertainment of the English population living in the colonial cities. However they often had native elites as shareholders. Dwarkanath Tagore for example was one of the trustees of the Chowringhee Theatre. When the theatre went into massive debts, he proposed it be sold. He later bought the ailing theatre in August 1835. HH Wilson became one of the trustees.[80] 'Theatre's' origin in India or rather re-inventing is usually traced to such interactions amongst the native elites and the English men of office.

2.9 Colonial Sociability, 'Theatre' and Native Elite Brotherhood in Bombay

In 1843, the King of Sangli, a princely state in the south of Maharashtra commissioned Vishnu Amrit Bhave commonly known as Vishnudas Bhave, the court poet-story teller to create a performance. The King is believed to have seen a Bhagwat Mela[81] performance in 1842 that influenced him to commission Bhave. It was in response that Bhave created *Sita Swayamvar* and staged it before the court on November 5, 1843. This performance is often seen as the first 'theatre' performance in western India in a native language. However there is a glitch. This 'dramatic performance' was not based on a drama, which means it was not based on a written text that in English is known as the drama. Rather Bhave expected his actors to improvise their lines based on certain character types and development of the plot. In this context, Shanta Gokhale makes an interesting observation in the book *Playwright at the Centre: Marathi Drama from 1843 to the Present*. She writes –

> ...his drama came closer to the root meaning of the word 'play' than to the formalized concept into which it evolved in later centuries. The Marathi word for a theatrical show, *khel*, has exactly the same meaning as 'play'.[82]

However, within a discourse of the 'Indian theatre', a *khel* or play was of a different genre and not the 'theatre' itself at the time. Bhave travelled extensively with the performance of *Sita Swayamvar* and even went to Bombay in 1853 with it, where the 'play' was performed in open air, dead-end alleys, inner courtyards of large mansions or in temporary *shamianas*.[83] Around 1853, in Bombay, there existed the Grant Road Theatre, which was built by Jagannath Shankarseth with contributions from Jamshedji Jejeebhoy in possibly 1846. Its initial intended audience was the English for whom the location of the theatre was not very convenient as it was slightly away from the Fort or the Malabar Hills in Bombay that they inhabited. But the theatre was at the border nearing the native town.[84] Some of the most regular performances at the Grant Road Theatre, until other theatre companies like Elphinstone, the Victoria Theatre, the Hindi Natyashala, the Grand Theatre or the Ripon came up, were the English amateur performances and the touring opera companies to which the Parsi businessmen were regular visitors. With the coming of the Grant Road Theatre funded by Shankarseth and Jejeebhoy, the audience composition had largely changed from the 'theatre on the Green' or Bombay Amateur Theatre which were predominantly visited by the English population with the local native businessmen being often invitees. Apparently the newspapers of those times complained of 'antics of drunken Jacks', 'late comers' or 'Parsees' with their 'rotund Pugrees'.[85] Kumudini Arvind Mehta argues that at the Grant Road Theatre, it was rather the presence of the 'wits' that made it different. By the mid-nineteenth century, Bombay saw the coming of the student dramatic clubs that were predominantly the clubs of the Parsi students who were often encouraged by their English teachers to perform one of the English dramas. Shakespeare soon became a popular choice that was performed by them in English. Although newspapers complained of young Parsis spending more time in the activities of these clubs rather than focusing on their studies or the Hindu youth being corrupted by the enticements of the theatre[86], these were the activities that changed the theatre scenario of Bombay largely. English education was slowly changing the cultural scenario of Bombay where unlike the late eighteenth century—early nineteenth century when theatre was merely an entertainment activity of the British with few native audiences, the mid-nineteenth century was turning to be serious engagement with European drama and at the same time Sanskrit texts which by then had become the element of pride for the native population. The Parsis, who had their own tradition of Persian myths, often had them represented on stage. Amateur theatre societies or clubs mainly comprising Parsis indebted to the educational institute from which they came like the Elphinstone College called themselves Parsi Elphinstone Dramatic Society or Elphinstone Stage Players etc. On the one hand, they produced Troughton's *Twelve Months' Honeymoon*, Morton's *Going to the Derby*, Moliere's *Mock Doctor*, Shakespeare's *Othello* or *Merchant of Venice* and on the other hand, new plays were being staged based on Persian myths like *Sulemani Samsher* or *Pakdaman Gulnar*. Growing competition amongst these clubs which often turned from amateur theatre companies to professional ones led to the formation of several other clubs like the 'Victoria Natak Mandali' or 'The Zoroastrian Theatrical Club', or 'Natak Uttejak Company' or 'Empress Victoria Theatrical Company' or 'The Alfred Natak Mandali' etc. As the names suggest these clubs readily named themselves based on their loyalty to the English or even highlighting their own Parsi roots. In fact, theatres were built for such clubs by rich Parsi men. C.S. Nazir for example a Parsi playwright/actor built the New Elphinstone Theatre in 1876 for the Parsi Elphinstone Dramatic Club.[87] While the Parsis created their own niche for theatre performances in Bombay, the Maharashtrian amateurs did the same in their own way. One of the Marathi amateur clubs was the Kalidas Elphinstone Society. The affinity of this club lay more in performing the European classics and the Sanskrit ones. They were predominantly from the Pathare Prabhu community. To attract all kinds of audience they would perform something as serious as Shakuntala intersected by comic sketches or topical songs. This was apparently common amongst English dramatic companies. The English community of Bombay was not very enthusiastic about performances of these sorts although there were some conscientious Englishmen and teachers who helped them prepare for performances. However at an institutional level, dramatics and especially performing Shakespeare was encouraged. In 1864, in Elphinstone College, the Shakespeare Society was formed and the newspaper *Times of India* of 8 April, 1864 notes that the professors of the college had 'sanctioned the formation of a dramatic corps for private theatricals within the walls of the college'.[88]

2.10 Native-English interaction, Cultural Hegemony and Distinctive Features of the Urbes Prima Sociability

The spread of 'theatre' activities amongst the educated section of the Bombay elites marked on the one hand, a total submission to colonial power which had successfully established its cultural hegemony over this growing city which by the late nineteenth century was characterized by the presence of a vast business community. Like it has been argued, these communities were mostly a social public congregation that interacted but at the same time was aloof in matters distinctively religious or racial. It was not Habermas' public sphere that was largely a class-based homogenous group that one encountered in Bombay but rather a conglomeration, which was class-based but yet not uniform. The theatre resided in this space which to use Sandria Freitag's words could be called a 'public arena'. While public interaction within the public arena only intensified with the growing awareness to form as also re-form itself to sustain the definition of a nation set forth by the colonial ideological apparatus, at the same time, such an interaction dulled down amongst the English colonizers with the awareness of its responsibility as a colonial ruler. Talking about the English theatre of the late nineteenth century, Kumudini Arvind Mehta writes:

> The real and serious difficulty facing the English theatre in Bombay during these last two decades of the nineteenth century was the gradual dwindling away of patronage from Indian audiences and the poor support from the European community. The opening night of a new season, a special Benefit Night, or a pantomime programme at Christmas sometimes attracted full houses. But, as a whole, English dramatic performances were no longer much of a draw.[89]

In Calcutta, the eastern counterpart of the city of Bombay, the scenario was not much different. Educational institutions greatly promoted the development of what by now in the mid-nineteenth century had become a cultural skill that was the drama. However, the participation of the natives in especially the English dramas were not always much appreciated by the European community. Their work at least in the initial years was limited to technical help. It was only in 1848 that a Bengali actor Vaishnav Charan Adhya acted in the role of Othello in the Sans Souci theatre although after that he never figured in the Calcutta theatre scenario.[90] Apart from the 'theatre' in the elite landowning and business class households or the '*babu* theatre', simultaneously what developed were dramatic activities in schools and colleges. This phenomenon increased with recitations or performances of scenes from textbooks. On 29 March, 1837, apparently students of Hindu College recited parts of *Merchant of Venice* and other poetic and dramatic pieces at the Government House at a prize distribution ceremony. A similar performance of *Merchant of Venice* by students of David Hare Academy is reported in 1853 in newspaper of Calcutta *Sambad Prabhakar*. It reports that Englishmen and English women and almost six to seven hundred wealthy and highly educated gentlemen were in the audience to witness a performance comparable to the standards of the Sans Souci Theatre. The students were apparently trained by Mr Clinger, the Headmaster of the English Department of the Calcutta Madrasa.[91] Similarly another educational institute, the Oriental Seminary collected money to establish its own school theatre that would stage Shakespeare. Once again, the students were trained by Mr Clinger and an English woman named Miss Clara Ellis. About a performance by the students of the Oriental Seminary the *Hindoo Patriot* on 22 February, 1855 wrote:

> After the lapse of nearly a year, the Oriental Theatre reopened on the 15th instant with the performance of Shakespeare's Henry IV, part first, and a farce entitled the Amateurs, written expressly for the Chowringhee Theatre by Henry Meredith Parker C.S., in those days in which civilians and military men did not deem it vulgar to amuse themselves with the rational pleasures of the stage. The managers of the Oriental Theatre in their endeavours to nationalize a more intellectual species of amusement than their countrymen were hitherto accustomed to throw away their money upon, complain of having had to encounter heavy losses. Their complaint is more mortifying from the fact that those who have the power to aid them successfully, although hugely patronizing the despicable *tamashas*[92] that abound in the country—*bulbul* fights[93] and dancing girls,—would not lay out a farthing for the thousand times more gratifying shows which the Theatre is capable of affording. Perhaps the majority of the rich in Calcutta, are from their ignorance of the English language, insusceptible to the exquisite delight which an English play well acted can impart to the spectator. Yet if even all those whose education has furnished them with a refined taste and enables them to appreciate the Drama of the west, took that interest in the new theatre which they ought to take, its managers could not certainly despair of success. Shakespeare's plays acted by Hindoo youths is a novelty which none assured should miss, and such acting as we observed at the Oriental Theatre on Thursday last may well make us proud of the versatile and extraordinary genius of our countrymen.[94]

Although performances in the English language in the educational institutions had become somewhat popular by the mid-nineteenth century, 'theatre' in Calcutta really took a popular turn as it turned to Bengali as a medium. However, the luminaries of Bengali theatre like Madhusudan Dutt, Keshav Chandra Mukhopadhyay, Priyonath Dutt, Girish Chandra Ghosh and others had initiated the process of learning about the drama and the 'theatre' by observing it in the English language and performances at English Theatres. Especially knowing the works of Shakespeare and ways of performing his texts were considered a sign of intellectual competence.[95]

Yet, to reach out to a larger audience the need to perform in Bengali was felt. In fact the Hindoo Patriot in the same article wrote that in this regard:

> We wish also that the managers of the Oriental Theatre will hereafter think of getting up Bengalee plays after the manner of our very spirited brethren of Bombay who are now starring it at the Grant Road Theatre.

The new sociables in Calcutta saw inspiration in the similarly emerging urban spaces like that of Bombay but however much they were similar, their development was distinctive in nature. The urban development of Calcutta happened as a space that was definitely guided by the commercial need of the British Empire. Throughout nineteenth century, it remained the 'point of largest outflow of exports from India as well as imports into the country'.[96] With the largest number of the British wealthy population living in Calcutta it was also often referred to as the 'City of Palaces'. However the trade situation started changing in the 1850s and 60s with Bombay taking over its position. With the Parsis, who had migrated from Gujarat during the early years of Bombay's development, emerging as successful entrepreneurs, the character of the city started changing. 'Theatre' evolved by their patronage as a multi-lingual medium that included languages like Gujarati, Urdu and the newly developing Hindustani[97] dialect. David Willmer in his doctoral dissertation *Theatricality, Mediation and Public Space: The Legacy of Parsi Theatre in South Asian Cultural history*[98] argues that the Parsi theatre developed as a resistance to hybridity rather than a willingness to co-opt elements of the English theatre. Although it developed within the city-space that had seen the English theatre, it borrowed elements from various performative forms where Shakespeare and the English theatre were just another 'commodity' in its 'cultural economy' of being an 'eclectic' form. The Marathi theatre that developed in Bombay also developed simultaneously as an eclectic form. Both these theatres became commercially viable forms in the later years. In Calcutta, the *babu* theatre did not see such an eclectic development although the interesting case of Nabin Chandra Bose's theatre can be seen as an exception in the early days. Nabin Chandra Bose, a rich native from north Calcutta set up a theatre in 1833 at his home to perform four to five plays every year. One of the most noted performances at his theatre was that of *Vidyasundar* inspired by a popular Bengali tale written by Bharat Chandra. The performance was choreographed in a way such that it occupied different rooms for different scenes in the house, as the audience moved from one room to the other to keep up with the pace of the performance. The invited audience that included 'Hindus, Muhammadans and some Europeans and East Indians' according to the Hindu Pioneer began at midnight and went on till the morning of the next day. This was not common practice amongst the European theatres in Calcutta. At the same time, that the performance refrained from using painted sceneries is another aspect that added to its innovative rendition of being created across different spaces of Bose's house. However the Hindu Pioneer compared it to Shakespeare's *Romeo and Juliet* and it was seen at that time as an example to 'be followed by an opulent community'.[99] The constant comparison to the English theatre and being truthful to the imitative forces in 'holding the mirror upto nature' made the *babu* theatre conscious of its medium. In *Bambai Chitra* (written around 1889) an autobiographical note by Satyendranath Tagore, the first Indian to be selected for Indian Civil Services, brother of Rabindranath Tagore and from the famous Tagore family of Calcutta, wrote on a Parsi performance of Shakuntala that he saw during his stay in Bombay that,

> Times have a strange pace. Tastes are changing. The old is disappearing to make space for the rule of the new. Now no one likes *nautch, jatra, katha* rather it's the age of *natok*. On that one can hear the *Parsi natok Hindu natok* triumph. The other day the manager of a Parsi group thought of me as the respected one—I had to give in to his proposal. Many a printed handbill were sent to me and I was told that whatever I would want would be performed for me. Unfortunately Shakuntala became my favoured one—I was completely outraged by what I saw. Shakuntala appeared as today's Parsi woman—Dushyanta is a nineteenth century novel reading lad. The dramatic characters started singing in Hindustani. Dushyanta's son is also a boy from today's world; on seeing his father he threw a book at him. And such was the state of the ashram, the son of the sage, the *konnomuni*[100]—I cannot

quite tell what Kalidas would have thought if he saw his own play.[101]

Satyendranath Tagore in this context refers to significant commercialization and 'share-mania' amongst the Maharashtrians and the Gujaratis. He notes that the share market, levels down the English to the native businessman where he does not anymore show off his racial supremacy. He gives the example of a Bhavai performance which rightly portrayed this 'mania'. However such levelling does not come across to Tagore as much appreciated. In Calcutta, the *'babu* theatre' slowly disappeared to make space for the 'commercial theatre' as a result of the unviability of such dramatic performances not only commercially but also in terms of popularity. Girish Chandra Ghosh, the actor, playwright, and director identified it as a problem of the masses' incapacity to identify with the form of the 'theatre'. What started with what Madhusudan Dutt described as the 'foreign air' about the drama soon picked up elements of the native theatrical performances. Ghosh writing in the late nineteenth century notes that he started playwriting 'out of sheer necessity' for an audience that was used to watching *'jatra, kathakatha* and *half-akhrai'*.[102] However like Satyendranath Tagore highlights, the regional distinctions between these emerging forms remained.

2.11 'The Becoming of a Congregation—Is Our's or Their's a Relevant Question?

On 22 March, 1881 Kesari, a newspaper founded by Bal Gangadhar Tilak[103], one of the prominent figures of the nationalist movement published an article in Marathi called *'Amcha Deshatil Sabha Woh Mandalya'* which could be roughly translated as 'Associations and Groups in Our Country'.[104] The article followed in four parts in consecutive issues. What emerges interesting in this rather exhaustive analysis of the phenomenon of group and association formation is that it identifies the process as an imitation of the English ways. The author writes—'At least they have realized that they should do more for their country than only earning their bread.' He welcomes the process calling it 'blood circulation' in a country that was 'sad' so far and he credits English education for the coming of such *sarvajanik sabha*-s (General Associations). However he is at the same time skeptical about the nature of these associations and compares them to the ones in England where he thinks these associations are much more vibrant and people understand 'their rights' and 'why they have a Parliament'. In India, he complains, from ancient times one has this conception that the king is divine. He suggests activities for these associations in order for them to become more relevant like dining together, games and lectures together etc. He also sees publishing of books, magazines, papers and such activities to be appropriate for creating general social awareness about the country. He gives examples of Brahma Samaj, Sarvajanik Sabha, Punarvibaha Uttejaksabha, and Kaushalya Sikshak Mandala in this context. By the late nineteenth century, such a general awareness about public being and conduct and what implications it could have on the society and nation at large had become common within the urban Indian discourse. *Samaj, sabha, samiti, mandala*, associations or groups emerged in trying to understand the new habitat. In a study about the *samaj* where *samaj* is defined as a 'social collectivity', Swarupa Gupta in the book 'Notions of Nationhood: Perspectives on Samaj, c.1867–1905', tries to move away from any 'delinked emphasis on nationalism as the political ideology of the sovereign nation state and rethinks the nation by focusing on 'nationhood''.[105] She tries to locate the historical lineages of ideas of nationhood in such collectivities and questions the 'western-derivate' nature of such concepts. Gupta's argument is rather useful insofar as it claims that understanding around communities had local origins but how far those local origins could evolve as more universal or even national ones need to be rather questioned. The report published in the *Kesari* identifies it as a new phenomenon and goes on to almost prove Anderson right in his claim that nationalism was a 'western-derivative discourse'. But as much as the author of *Kesari* believed so, it needs to be highlighted here that within a larger dominant ideological framework and hegemonic influence of the English colonial administration, all of cultural development as also the cultural discovery of the Indian identity, seemed to be wishful gifts of the colonial ruler. But then one needs to ask can one exist without the other? Is sociology of a pre-colonial India impossible? What does it mean to be 'us' before the British arrived? Given that theatre is that form which requires a congregation of at least a 'two' to happen, what are the implications of a claim that suggests that theatre did not exist before the British or existed only in the ancient times? With these questions one comes back to the basic questions of 'humanly being'. The civilizational aim of English colonial rule liked to believe that 'we' were NOT before 'they' were here. As Sumit Sarkar has argued, it just added to the separatist logic of British colonial rule. Such understanding of the logic of a nation and a national history where a clear periodization was made on the basis of how a communal congregation[106] was formed with a final realization of a national identity made nationhood appear as firstly 'derivative' and secondly was connotative of communal bearings of such an idea. At the same time, to understand ideas of congregation solely in the light of nationhood takes away from the heterogeneous nature of such a congregation as Partha Chatterjee rightly points out. In *The Politics of the Governed: Reflections on Popular Politics in Most of the World*, he elaborates on this picking on Benedict Anderson's idea of the nation which Anderson locates in the 'unbound seriality' of 'every-day universals of modern social thought: nations, citizens, revolutionaries, bureaucrats, workers, intellectuals, and so on.' Chatterjee questions the homogenous nature that is highlighted in Anderson's project about nationalism and he calls for the need to look at 'heterogenous time of modernity'. Rather than calling such congregations 'unbound seriality', Jean Paul Sartre's conception of the 'group' is useful here. In Sartre's *'Critique of Dialectical Reason: Theory of Practical Ensembles'*, a congregation i.e. a group takes place self-consciously recognizing togetherness or *being* with each other. Within such a self-conscious project, the question of 'derivativeness' becomes irrelevant insofar as one does not deny the fact that one can only exist in consciousness of the other. Within a colonial society where such formations hardly resulted in being a part of the Polity, 'social collectivities' played a huge role in determining the politics of the colonized, even if they were the emerging ones within an urban social discourse like in Calcutta or Bombay. In this chapter the attempt was to highlight the emergence of the 'urban' spaces that were claimed by the elites of these localities. Theatre's so called emergence within the urban discursive matrix, the new sociables like the 'samaj', 'samiti', 'mandali' at the crossroads of such a paradigm has been studied here at some length. The following chapters delve into the matter of interceptions that turned the route that many of these sociables took.

REFERENCES

1. 'Urbes prima in Indis' was a name given to Bombay as the foremost city in India by the British. Here it is being used in a plural sense of both Calcutta and Bombay.
2. Chummar Choondal, *Christian Theatre in India* (Kerala Folklore Academy, Trichur, Kerala, 1984), 66.
3. The Syrian or the Saint Thomas Christian tradition evolved in India when the apostle Thomas arrived in Kodungallur in Kerala and established the Seven Churches. Their origin is traced back to the 1st century AD.
4. See Jürgen Habermas, *The Structural Transformation of the Public Sphere—An Inquiry Into a Category of Bourgeois Society* (The MIT Press, Cambridge Massachusetts, 1991) for further details.
5. Douglas Dewar, *Bygone Days in India with Eighteen Illustrations,* (The Bodley Head Ltd., London, mcmxxii), 273.
6. Amal Mitra, The English Stage in Calcutta Circa 1750, *Sangeet Natak,* Number 88, April-June (Sangeet Natak Akademi, New Delhi, 1988), 14.
7. Krishna Dutta, *Calcutta: A Cultural and Literary History* (Interlink Books, New York, 2003), 15.
8. Prashant Kidambi, *The Making of an Indian Metropolis* (Ashgate Publishing Ltd., Hampshire, England, 2007).
9. *The Gazetteer: Bombay City and Island,* Vol. III (Times Press, Bombay, 1910).
10. Partha Mitter, The Early British Port Cities of India: Their Planning and Architecture Circa 1640-1757, *Journal of the Society of Architectural Historians,* Vol. 45, No. 2, June, 1986, 102.

11. Krishna Dutta, 24.
12. The letter designated as part of the 'Calcutta account', is kept in the Victoria and Albert Museum's Forster Collection of Garrick papers.
13. As quoted from Philip H. Highfill, Kalman A. Burnim and Edward A. Langhans (eds.), A Biographical Dictionary of Actors, etc., in London 1660-1800, Carbondale Ill, Vol. X, 1984, 205-7. In *Our Theatrical Attempts in This Distant Quarter: The British Stage in Eighteenth Century Calcutta* by Derek Forbes, Theatre Notebook, June 2007.
14. *Echoes From Old Calcutta: Being Chiefly Reminiscences of the Days of Warren Hastings, Francis and Impey* by H.E. Busteed (W.Tracker and Co., London and Thacker, Spink and Co., Calcutta and Shimla, 1908), 189.
15. As quoted from Augustus Hicky (ed.), Bengal Gazette and Calcutta General Advertiser, numbers LIII of 20-27 January 1781 and XLVIII of 16-23 December 1780 in *Our Theatrical Attempts in This Distant Quarter...,* Derek Forbes.
16. As quoted in *Our Theatrical Attempts in this Distant Quarter...,* Derek Forbes.
17. Kumudini Arvind Mehta, *English Drama on the Bombay Stage in the Late Eighteenth Century,* (PhD thesis submitted to Bombay University in March 1960, TH2643 A & B, Bombay University Thesis Section), 32.
18. Joachim Hayward Stocqueler, *The Memoirs of a Journalist* (Times of India, Bombay, 1873), 38-40.
19. *The Gazetteer: Bombay City and Island,* Vol. III (Times Press, Bombay, 1910), 365.
20. Sir D.E. Wacha, *Shells from the Sands of Bombay being My Recollections and Reminiscences–1860-1875* (K.T. Anklesaria, The Indian Newspaper Co. Ltd., Bombay 1920), 347.
21. Mehta, 33.
22. Mitra, 18.
23. As quoted by Amal Mitra, Ibid.
24. As quoted from *Bombay Courier,* September 2, 1820 in *The Indian Theatre...*
25. It was the summer capital of British India.
26. Emily Eden, *'Up the Country'—Letters Written to Her Sister from the Upper Provinces of India,* (Richard Bentley, London, 1867), 139-40.
27. Stocqueler, 34.
28. Vikram Sampat, *My Name is Gauhar Jaan!' The Life and Times of a*

Musician (Rupa Publications, New Delhi, 2011), 8.
29. Douglas Dewar, *In the Days of the Company* (Thacker, Spink and Co., Shimla, London and Calcutta, 1920).
30. Emily Eden, 129.
31. Ibid.
32. Derek Forbes, 11.
33. H.E. Busteed, 144.
34. Laura J. Rosenthal, *Entertaining Women: The Actress in Eighteenth-Century Theatre and Culture* in *The Cambridge Companion to British Theatre, 1730-1830,* Eds. Jane Moody and Daniel O'Quinn (Cambridge University Press, 2007).
35. Derek Forbes, 8.
36. H.E. Busteed, 211.
37. As quoted by Bishnupriya Dutt, *Historicizing Actress Stories*, Lata Singh (ed.) *Play-house of Power* (Oxford University Press, New Delhi, 2010), 321.
38. H.E. Busteed, 214.
39. Ibid.
40. Denis Shaw, Esther Leach, 'The Mrs Siddons of Bengal', *Educational Theatre Journal,* Vol. 10, No. 4 (Dec., 1958), 304-310.
41. Bishnupriya Dutt, 326.
42. Denis Shaw, 305.
43. Stocqueler, 92.
44. Ibid., 91.
45. Ibid., 115.
46. As quoted by Bishnupriya Dutt, 331.
47. H.E. Busteed, 214.
This also makes it unclear as to whether Mrs. Bristowe returned to perform again in Calcutta. Her husband John Bristowe died in Calcutta in 1802.
48. As quoted by Bishnupriya Dutt, 330.
49. Mónica Brito Vieira and David Runciman, *Representation* (Polity Press, Cambridge, 2008), 45.
50. In passim, The Theatre of the Civilized Self: Edmund Burke and the East India trials by Siraj Ahmed, *Representations*, Vol. 78, No. 1 (Spring 2002).
51. In *Orientalism and the Postcolonial Predicament: Perspectives on South Asia,* Eds. Carol A. Breckenridge and Peter van der Veer (University of Pennsylvania Press, Philadelphia, 1993).
52. As quoted by Ludden, 255.
53. As quoted by Nicola Savarese, *Eurasian Theatre: Drama and Performance Between East and West from Classical Antiquity to the*

Present, Trans. Richard Fowler (Icarus Publishing Enterprise, Holstebro, Malta, Wroclaw, 2010), 212-213.

54. For a more detailed study see Sumit Sarkar, *Writing Social History* (Oxford University Press, New Delhi, 1998).
55. J. Talboys Wheeler, *The History of India from the Earliest Ages,* (Vol. III: Hindu Buddhist Brahminical revival, Trübner & Co., 57 & 59, Ludgate Hill, London, 1874), 282.
56. Ibid., viii. 58. Ibid., 325.
57. Laura J. Rosenthal, *Entertaining Women: The Actress in Eighteenth-Century Theatre and Culture,* 164.
58. Denis Shaw, 310.
59. A. Claude Brown, *The Ordinary Man's Guide To India,* (Cecil Palmer, London, 1927), 101.
60. Ibid., 100.
61. See Rakesh H. Solomon, Culture, Imperialism, and Nationalist Resistance: Performance in Colonial India, *Theatre Journal,* Vol. 46, No. 3, Colonial/Postcolonial Theatre, Oct., 1994, 323-347.

    However, Rustom Bharucha sees this as something that did not work on the principles of 'exchange' and was essentially linked to the assertion of 'cultural superiority'. *Theatre and the World: Performance and the Politics of Culture* (Routledge, London, 1993), 1-2.
62. *Madhusudan Rachanabali* (Collected Works of Michael Madhusudan Dutt) (Sahitya Sansad, Kolkata, 2012), 50.
63. Inhabitants of the Iranian province Persis or modern Fars. They apparently migrated to Western India (in and around present day Gujarat) in the 8th century. However this is often doubted. Jesse S. Palsetia, *The Parsis of India: Preservation of Identity in Bombay City* (Brills Indological Library, 2001).
64. Abhijit Dutta, *Glimpses of European Life in Nineteenth Century Bengal* (Minerva Associates Pvt. Ltd., Calcutta, 1995), 140.
65. Kathryn Hansen, *Parsi Theatre and the City: Locations, Patrons, Audiences,* (Sarai Reader, New Delhi, 2002), 46.
66. Bishnupriya Dutt, 319.
67. Sumanta Banerjee, *Unish Shotoker Kolkata o Saraswatir Itor Santan,* (Anustup, Kolkata, 2008), 70.
68. Ibid., 197.
69. Laurence Senelick, Russian Enterprise, Bengali Theatre, and the Machinations of the East India Company, *New Theatre Quarterly,* Vol. 28, Issue 01, February 2012, 21.
70. Ibid., 23.
71. Ibid., 24.

72. Subir Raychoudhury & Swapan Mazumdar (eds.), 23.
73. *Dictionary of Indian Biography* (Haskell House Publishers Ltd., New York, 1906), 413.
74. As quoted by Subir Raychoudhury & Swapan Mazumdar (eds.), 19-20.
75. Discussed in further detail in Chapter III.
76. Discussed later in the chapter.
77. Sumit Sarkar, *A Critique of Colonial India* (Papyrus, Calcutta, 1985), 30.
78. As quoted by Brajendra Nath Banerjee, *Bengali Stage (1795-1873)* (Ranjan Publishing House, Calcutta, 1943), 7.
79. Amal Mitra, *Kolkatay Bideshi Rongaloy* (Prakash Bhavan, Kolkata, 1374 Bengali year).
80. It's a form of dance-drama which is closely related to the rituals of Hindu temple.
81. Shanta Gokhale, 4.
82. A *shamiana* could be roughly called a tent, Ibid., 7.
83. For a detailed study of the city of Bombay and the Parsi theatre see Kathryn Hansen, *Parsi Theatre and the City: Locations, Patrons, Audiences* (Sarai Reader, New Delhi, 2002).
84. Kumudini Arvind Mehta, 196. 88. Ibid., 177.
85. http://dsal.uchicago.edu/books/artsandideas/text.html?objectid=HN681.S597_23-24_091.gif, last accessed on 25th March 2017.
86. As quoted by Kumudini Arvind Mehta, 188. 91. Ibid., 239.
87. Subir Raychoudhury & Swapan Mazumdar (eds.), 26-27.
88. Brajendra Nath Banerjee, 13-14.
89. A performance genre from Western India.
90. Fights of songbirds called *Bulbul*.
91. Ibid., 16.
92. Subir Raychoudhury & Swapan Mazumdar (eds.), 27.
93. Amiya Kumar Bagchi, *Capital and Labour Redefined: India and the Third World* (Anthem Press, London, 2002),188.
94. It is a pluricentric language that developed with the use of Modern Urdu and Hindi.
95. Dissertation submitted to Ashworth Centre for Social Theory, The University of Melbourne, May 1999.
96. Brajendra Nath Banerjee, 12.
97. A sage by that name.
98. Satyendranath Tagore, *'Bambai Chitra'*, (Adi Brahma Samaj Jantra, Kolkata, 1296 Bengali year), 78.
99. Subir Raychoudhury & Swapan Mazumdar (eds.), 39.

100. Bal Gangadhar Tilak (1856-1920) co-founded *Kesari*, along with its English counterpart *Mahratta* in 1881. By 1890 both the newspapers came under Tilak's ediorship, after a fall out with their co-founder Gopal Ganesh Agarkar. His influence on music and theatre of the time was immense. See Janaki Bakhle, *Two Men and Music: Nationalism in the Making of an Indian Classical Tradition* (Orient Longman Pvt. Ltd., New Delh, 2008), 147-148.
101. Translation assistance by Madhura Damle, Assistant Professor, Presidency University, Kolkata.
102. *Notions of Nationhood: Perspectives on Samaj, c.1867-1905* (Brill, Leiden and Boston, 2009).
103. Sumit Sarkar, *Writing Social History*, (Oxford University Press, New Delhi, 1998), 19.

3

Coming Communities and Vacillating Definitions: The Case of Censorship and *Swadeshi Jatra*

3.1 Theatre - The House of Satan

Harnam Singh was not well. 'Evil' had overshadowed his daily existence. But he recovered when he followed the principles of personal conversion, renunciation of sins and cultivation of higher life that Shri Guru Dev Bhagwan, the founder of *Dev Samaj*[1], expounded. *Dev Samaj* founded in 1887 in Lahore by Pandit Shiv Narayan Agnihotri, the *guru* who soon came to be known as Bhagwan Dev Atma or Guru Dev Bhagwan, was one of the several organizations that aimed at social reform in colonial India. Its members were mostly the upper middle class of the society like the 'graduates, magistrates, doctors, pleaders, moneylenders, landholders and government servants'. One could become a member or a sympathizer by annually paying a fee of ten rupees or turn into a *Nava Jiwan Yafta* i.e. one who had found a new life by following moral codes, which laid stress on honesty, cleanliness, vegetarianism and temperance. A third category of the members was of those who had taken strict religious vows in the pursuit of *Dev Dharm*.[2] Shiv Narayan Agnihotri was initially a member of another social reform organization called the *Brahmo Samaj*. He later had differences with the organization and thereafter became part of the offshoot of the organization called the *Shadharan Brahmo Samaj* and subsequently founded the *Punjab Central Brahmo Samaj*. Moving from the *Brahmo Samaj*, he later established the *Dev Samaj* at

Lahore. But what had happened to Harnam Singh? The article 'An Instructive Example of Regeneration and Self-Sacrifice: People Saw This Wonderful Change in His Life' published in April 1921[3] explores this matter:

> 'The people who knew Harnam Singh before noticed a wonderful difference between his previous course of life and the new one that he had taken, under the action of higher-life forces upon him. What did they see? They saw that this young man who was so fond of theatres that no sooner, he read a notice or handbill he was mad after it, and having spent all his monthly allowance, he would pawn his clothes and his watch, to attend the theatre, and who in the event of failing to attend it hovered at night round the place, began carefully to avoid even to pass by that road so that he may in course of time be free from the theatre mania which had ruined his health, money and studies. They saw that this young man who was so gaudy and showy, who was so fond of singing obscene songs himself and before others when evil friends wished it, had closed his tongue tight and was determined not to utter those impure words again for anybody's sake... For when Harnam Singh went home in summer vacations, his behaviour bore such a contrast to his former life in respect of his reverence for and service of elders that his aged mother came to Dev Ashram and having seen Mata Puniaji (our Venerable Perceptor's wife) heartily thanked Shri Dev Guru Bhagwan for reforming her child'

Harnam Singh's ailment that was 'theatre-going' and talking and singing the obscene was not part of a reformed-educated behaviour that the colonial middle class, informed with Victorian moral codes[4], aimed at. In the nineteenth century, the colonial urban Indian population was thoroughly concerned with society insofar as it was transformed into something that was acceptable by the educated section. Being educated could include the knowledge of English/Sanskrit literature, the engagement with which was initiated largely by colonial education. Although theatre in colonial India often staged canonical texts but what went on in the theatre especially in the early years was often seen with suspicion. There would be antagonism toward certain performances as Kathryn Hansen notes in the essay *'Ritual Enactments in a Hindi 'Mythological' Betab's Mahabharat in Parsi Theatre'*. In 1916, for example, there were communal disturbances surrounding the performance of the *Mahabharat* of Pandit Narayan Prasad Betab in Lahore. But what kind of theatre Harnam Singh was addicted to and whether this addiction was solely an affair of 'going to the theatre' is not quite apparent from the published article which clearly seems to be in praise of Agnihotri's or Guru Dev Bhagwan's abilities in the transformation of social evil – which was theatre in general in this case. What we know from the article are the visible symbols of a malady, which involved 'obscene' singing and social immoralities that were caused by 'theatre-going'.

Like Harnam Singh, Gopinath Sil was a theatre-addict. Gopinath Sil, a fictitious character in Rabindranath Tagore's 1917 short story *Maan Bhanjan*, was married to Giribala. But Tagore writes- *'Swami ache, kintu swami tahar ayotter modhey nai'* (She has a husband, but her husband is not within the parameters of her reach.'). Gopinath Sil was given to going to the theatre and had mentioned the actress Labanga to his wife. Labanga's name had already become famous because of the performer that she was. Giribala even sent her maid Sudho to the theatre to find out if Labanga was the reason for her husband's regular visits to the theatre. Finally, when her husband became completely out of her reach, Giribala decided to go to the theatre herself—an act forbidden for women of her status. But what does she come across? Tagore writes—*'Mone korilo, emon ek jaegaey ashiyachhe jekhane bandhanmukto shoundarjyopurna swadhinatar kono badhamatro nai'* (She thought, she had come to a place where there was no barrier to unbounded beautiful freedom). The theatre-malady had infected her. Tagore writes- *'Neshaye tahar shomosto mostishko bhoriya uthilo'* (Her head became full with intoxication). This intoxication that engulfed Tagore's Giribala, put her in the middle of the action as it were, like in Artaud's Manifesto. Talking about the stage in his First Manifesto for *The Theatre of Cruelty*, Antonin Artaud envisions theatre as a space that re-establishes a direct-communication between the spectacle of the theatre and the spectator, actor and the spectator where the spectator is engulfed and physically affected by it.[5] Giribala's state brings her to the realization that although she is a respected woman of a well-to-do family, still she remains inconsequential, unknown and her life meaningless like that of any ordinary woman. In theatre she saw that she could reside at the centre of the universe. She got transformed to a theatre-addict herself. However, the story moves forward and many evenings in the theatre pass by, when one day insulted by her husband's behaviour at home, Giribala decides to join the theatre as an actress. Giribala—the addict for whom there was no return, unlike in the case of Harnam Singh, cure was not possible as she takes the centre-stage. Now she along with the theatre's spectators creates an infected space. Her husband, for whom Giribala was an unacknowledged possession, could not become a part of this space. Theatre had undone all bindings for Giribala and Gopinath Sil could not accept it. Gopinath Sil in Tagore's *Maan bhanjan* is not the feminized Bengali *babu*, as the figure of the *babu* came to be known. He was swayed by power, which came into his possession after his father's death. His domain became the public sphere where increasingly he became popular amongst his peers due to his power. He started going to the theatre. In late nineteenth century/early twentieth century Bengal, although going to the theatre had already become a regular practice for the gentry, it still remained taboo for the women. The Bengali writer Bankim Chandra Chatterjee even mocked this section of the society as he defined the word *babu*. He writes—'He whose deity is the Englishman, preceptor the Brahmo preacher, scriptures the newspapers and pilgrimage the National Theatre is a *babu*'[6]. The actress was however, still a *patita nari* or fallen woman although she might be portraying on stage the character of a so-called respectable woman. In Tagore, Giribala's going to the theatre and later becoming an actress are part of 'maan bhanjan'. 'Maan bhanjan' the phrase in Bengali has connotations of amorous involvement. 'Maan' could be translated as unrevealed anger as a result of jealousy etc. towards the lover, whereas 'bhanjan' is to break. Giribala who was married off to Gopinath Sil in her childhood, had her share of exchanging love letters and had had other romantic interactions with her husband. But since Gopinath tasted power, he started ignoring Giribala. As she felt rejected, Giribala's every day became full of 'maan' or anger for her beloved while she wished that at some point he would be back to her and all would be as before. That never happened. It was only to have the key of the money-locker that one night Gopinath came back to her. When Giribala refused to give that to him, hoping that there would be some kind of interaction between the two and he would stay back with her, Gopinath hit her instead and took the jewellery that she was wearing, jewellery, that she wore every day in hope of her husband's return. Giribala left home. Gopinath did not care. He left with Labanga for some place. Male audience members or actors promising a better life to actresses had become almost a regular affair in late nineteenth century/early twentieth century Calcutta. The stage actress Shreemoti Sukumari even married Babu Haridas Dutta, a fellow actor who later abondoned her. Soon in the theatre some other actress took Labanga's place. Her performance started to be talked about. Gopinath got curious and alas what he saw was not what he had even dreamt of. Giribala had become an actress! The figure of fascination that Giribala wanted to be, in the hope of which she adorned herself everyday, thinking that one day her husband would come for her 'maan bhanjan', to break the anger that she had within her—Giribala had turned into that very figure. But as the fascinating figure that Giribala had now become, she became inaccessible to Gopinath. The whole world had come centre-stage for her 'maan bhanjan' as it were. Tagore's story although does not use any analogy to a malady for theatre, in Tagore, theatre receives a transformative power that hits, that affects, and creates a disorder in structure not only a social structure but also something which is almost bodily like in a disease- an evil power.

Binodini Dasi (1862-1941) the Bengali actress, who was trained by Girish Chandra Ghosh also known as Garrick of Bengal after the famous British actor David Garrick, talks about the malady in her experience of rehearsing and performing the play *Chaitanyaleela* in her autobiography *Amar Katha*. *Chaitanyaleela* was based on the life and times of Chaitanya Mahaprabhu, the Vaishnava saint of the sixteenth century. The play was performed in two parts and she played the role of Shri Chaitanya. She writes:

> *Hari mon mojaye lukaley kothae. Ami bhobey eka dao hey dekha pran shokha rakho paye* (Hari, having affected my heart where have you hidden? I am alone in this world, give me a glimpse of yourself, keep my life-soul in your feet) I cannot describe in writing what emotions my heart went through while singing this song. In reality, I used to feel then that I was alone in this world; none is there who was mine. As if my soul would run to Hari seeking refuge in his feet. In madness I would dance with the *shankirtan*.[7] On some days unable to carry forward the difficult task of acting I would fall unconscious... A lot of people would come to watch *Chaitanyaleela*...not only performing *Chaitanyaleela* but in my life the performance of *Chaitanyaleela* brought pride when the forgiver of sins Paramhansadev Ramkrishna showed pity on me... After my performance when I went to the office to present myself to his feet, in happiness he started dancing and saying: *'Hari Guru, Guru Hari'*, repeat Maa[8] *'Hari Guru, Guru Hari'*, then he put both his hands on my head cleansing my body of sins and said, *'Maa tomar chaitanya houk'* (Maa, may you have consciousness).[9]

Binodini Dasi like the fictive character Labanga created by Tagore had male admirers. But Binodini's vocation made a conjugal relationship impossible. She belonged to the class of fallen women' who although could be admired by the *babu* but could not become socially accepted as wife. Women were strictly forbidden from certain roles and Binodini resided in that zone. For Binodini Dasi therefore, having audience members of social respectability, which in turn assured her of her existence as an actress to be acceptable, was of immense significance. On that, the presence of *Ramkrishna Paramhansa Dev,* the rustic spiritual guru[10], whose catholicity of spiritual teachings had made him immensely popular amongst a huge section of the late nineteenth century Bengali population, played a cathartic role for Binodini. Sumit Sarkar argues in *'Kaliyuga', 'Chakri'* and *"Bhakti': Ramakrishna and His Times'* that in bhakti[11] literature deliverance comes easily by the recitation of the name Hari. He writes—'The paradox extends further, for women and Shudras (the lowest caste), the two major sources of corruption in all pre-modern Kaliyuga texts, 'can attain good simply through performing their duties' to husbands and twice-born men. Subalternity is privileged-provided, of course, it remains properly subaltern.' For Ramakrishna who had evolved his teachings from various sects, taking the name of Hari, as he suggested to Binodini was like purging all evil that lay within her. However Ramakrishna's idea of womanhood did not care much about the good and the bad woman as heterosexual intercourse itself was like defecation to him and he had acute physical revulsion to the idea of sex, whether it was with the wife or the mistress. Therefore purging the *patita-nari* or fallen woman of the theatre was not such a difficult task, as long as she attained higher consciousness beyond worldly material pleasures. For Binodini Dasi, this possibility of escape came through her performance of *Chaitanyaleela* where she not only performed the role of Chaitanya, the Vaishnav saint but also felt an ecstasy in purifying the evil in her own self. And Ramakrishna's acknowledgement only made her more convinced of this process of catharsis. The psychophysical nature of Binodini Dasi's experience cannot probably be explained as mere communication through what she performed. Her performances had physical implications for herself. So did Giribala's experience of watching the theatre or Harnam Singh's malady, which visibly required cure and the people 'saw it' as the article published in the praise of Guru Dev Bhagwan suggests. Insofar as a malady or a disease could be understood as a disorder of the structure of human or animal body, theatre could be understood as that disease, which disorganized structured orientations, bodily as also that of the society—an 'evil' force, not as a medically curable ailment but which had a certain visibility of disruption. It was a disruption that did not necessarily aim to upturn entire power relations but opened up spaces for new forms of interaction. That theatre became the target of censorship in colonial India, where one saw the danger of a new disruptive space emerging within the colonial establishment is not surprising. Partha Chatterjee also points out to this strength but he directs it more to the rhetoric of the drama and in its use of 'common speech' than 'carefully structured directedness of dramatic action and conflict'[12]. However it is necessary to understand the relationship of the colonial population with theatre within a broader spectrum.

The understanding around theatre evolved not only through theatre's so called coming to the colony but several other factors got intertwined in generating the meaning of the theatre. Colonial education played a significant role in this. The Christian missionaries were already active in India from the eighteenth century[13] onwards and they played a significant role in shaping the colonial subject. The initial effort of the schools founded by the missionaries was conversion of the native population into Christianity but also subsequent eradication of all kinds of 'barbarity' associated with pagan religions followed by social reform. That theatre, in reality, holds the possibility of socio-moral 'evil' or disruption, within established structured forms of life is directly addressed by an article that was published in colonial Calcutta around 1842 by the *Calcutta Christian Observer*. The article is called '*What is the Theatre: An Inquiry Suggested by Some Recent Circumstances*'.[14] The article signed by some author who called himself JMD, was re-published by American Mission Press. Calcutta Christian Observer was started in the 1830s in Calcutta and was conducted by 'Ministers and Laymen of various denominations'[15] with evangelical aims 'in this part of the British possession'. Colonial Calcutta saw several English theatres run by the British who had settled here during this period. Like in different other cities such as Simla (now Shimla), Bombay etc., by the late eighteenth century, theatre-houses had already started emerging in Calcutta. English amateur theatre enthusiasts ran most of these theatres often with aid from England.[16] The above-mentioned article begins with a quote by one such theatre enthusiast made in a *Theatrical Dinner Speech* on January 7, 1842. The quote says:

> I am delighted to see such a strong array of intelligence and talent, so many men of eminent position, and of unquestionable moral and social worth as congregated around this board, openly and publicly repudiating (as they virtually do, by their presence) what I and they too, I am confident, cannot but consider as the 'cribb'd, cabined and confined' notions of the opponents of the drama, who are but too often pleased in their courtesy to designate a theatre, by the elegant and classical appellation of 'THE HOUSE OF SATAN'.[17]

The entire article is not in defence of this quote, which clearly is a criticism of the 'opponents' of theatre, but rather it endorses the claim made by the 'opponents' which is that of the theatre being 'The House of Satan'. JMD justifies his position by highlighting sixteen main points apart from some general observations that he makes. Before getting to the general observations, let us have a look at the sixteen main points in defence of his endorsement of the theatre as the 'House of Satan'. He adds before he starts that, 'We are of course now writing for Christians, who hold the Bible to be the word of God, and therefore supreme, in all judgement of human affairs: he that admits not this, is of course an Infidel.' Firstly, he notes that the theatre '*rejects*, or must reject *the word of God as the standard* of character by which to test the drama.' He complains that the 'friends of theatre' do not consider the Bible to be the law of the stage because that might be inimical to their interests. It is a well-understood fact in England or 'home' and now in Calcutta-the colony. Not only does the theatre not accept the law of the Bible as sovereign but also his second point is that it does not recognize the 'presence of God'. Although he acknowledges the fact that there are other spaces, which equally ignore 'their Father's face', that does not diminish the 'huge system of evil' that the stage is. Next, he sees on stage the rejection of religion 'meaning by that personal piety, which consists of a strict compliance with the whole word of God'. Like in some novels, on the stage, religious characters are often ridiculed and presented in caricatured forms and are seen with contempt and one finds in them 'sanctimoniousness'. Hence even the 'religion of nature' becomes food for farce and comedy. Theatre therefore for him is the site for misrepresentation of piety. Having rejected the Book, God and religion, the stage now takes to sin. He writes:

> Lying, swindling, cheating, intriguing, coveting, seducing, those sins which bring down the wrath of God on this world, are made in the actings of a play, subjects of most exquisite amusements; and that which in hell is the cause of eternal agony, is on the boards of a theatre, the occasion of convulsive laughter! There is for instance a play, (and if we mistake not, it has been acted in Calcutta, and that too in *high life*,) in which the interest is kept up by character who incessantly lies; - and this is accompanied by merriment of the spectators. Now, suppose the curtain of eternity was to drop at that moment and the Judgement to be set, and these words (Rev. xxi, 8) to be uttered, 'All liars shall have their

> portion in the lake that burneth with fire and brimstone!'—Yea, and (xxii, 15) 'whosoever loveth a lie.' Suppose this, and then judge of the safety of that stage!—The very sins for which the Son of God shed His blood on the Mount of Calvary are represented with peals of laughter in the theatres of Britain and of India!

Similarly, the representation of crime, and the pleasures that one receives when murders, duels, assassinations, poisonings, massacres 'in semblance as near as possible to the crime' as they are 'artificially represented' on stage, shrink the mind as the representation and personification of sin are inconsistent with the purity of spirit. Apart from the representation of sins, the author highlights the sixth point to be the 'profanation of the name of the Almighty God'. The seventh point is just a natural continuation as it were, where Satan's name becomes a favourite on stage. Not only are names of God and Satan taken on the same space but also binaries of 'distinctions of sex' are dislodged. He writes, 'We have before us female-men, and male-women'. He argues that such dislodging of gender binaries are 'considered as most necessary and most legitimate, in what are called the purest of all theatres, *amateur-houses*, or in private theatricals'. Not only is his concern the break in gender binaries but also the '*degradation of woman*' because in the theatre 'as a general rule, an actress is an outcast from society'. Not only are men and women potential victims of degradation in the theatre but also 'piousness' itself is a total lack on stage. He asks, 'We have heard of a religious lawyer, of a religious physician, of a religious painter, of a religious sculptor, of a religious merchant, of a religious musician, and a religious editor – but who can tell us of a religious tragedian, a religious comedian?' It is interesting to note here that to him a musician, a sculptor, a painter who are related to other forms of art are not partners in crime of creating the 'evil' as much as the tragedian or the comedian. May be he even tries to answer this question! He writes, 'we boldly say, SCRIPTURAL[18] piety cannot breathe in the air of a system so essentially ungodly, and necessarily irreligious; or in a place where God is disowned, and sin is ridiculed, where the moral law is daily broken, and the gospel of grace is unknown as the standard of professional life.' Is it too farfetching to speculate at this point that he tries to highlight the unscripted nature of the performative in theatre, its disregard for power – in this case, is it divine scripted power? He however possibly ignores the performative aspect of other forms of arts, which are more structured and written as it were according to him. Or does he limit his definition to the 'holy' scriptures alone? Without further delving into this unaddressed question we move to the eleventh point wherein he tries to talk about the 'House of Evil'. He talks about the likes of Harnam Singh and Gopinath Sil here who are the addicts—the 'play-goers'. He makes it clear that he does not count those that go to the theatre because of circumstances or who do not esteem it much. Rather his concerns are those who fill the boxes and the pits of the theatre regularly, who are the habitual 'play-goers' and in whom one finds 'vicious poverty', 'vicious mediocracy' and who are most often 'the cream of aristocratic pride, vanity and scandal'. It is 'the swindler', 'the gambler', 'the forger', 'the horse-jockey', 'the scoffer at religion', 'the backslider from the worship of God', 'the man that never prays', 'the apostate', 'fashionable swearers', 'shameless adulterers', 'married courtesans', 'embezzling clerks', and 'those that never enter a church', in short 'all the very worst classes of society, provided they have money' who love the theatre. He explains, 'The fact is undeniable, that the closest attendance in the theatre is from the least moral part of society—and it is equally certain that such persons go there only for *pleasure*.' That *pleasure* is what makes theatre the 'house of evil' is without doubt to him. It is not only the physical space of the theatre that houses evil but also the neighbourhood he notes in the next point. He asks, 'Why is it that the theatre is the centre of attraction, both for perambulation and residence, to such multitudes, awful multitudes of ruined, guilty, women, living by the wages of iniquity? Is it because, as an Indian judge has gravely said, 'The theatre is a guardian of morality?'' To JMD it is rather the opposite that the theatre does and that one can know from the neighbourhoods of the theatre, which were 'sinks of vice'. And obviously the victims of the 'sinks of vice' were the youth who 'take pleasure in the imitative representations of human iniquity'. The youth given to 'play-going' were not the ones readily trusted by the merchant class. That the 'way to the pit' is also the way to destruction is not unknown according to him. He says, 'Go ask the merchants of London about these things—and let their counting-houses and banks be our witnesses; if 'saints and methodists' are not to be believed, go ask the WORLD!' In principle, the theatre houses the evil and thus according to JMD even if there were some good in it that's not something that should be counted but rather it only adds to the perilous nature of the theatre. He draws an analogy to his assumption, 'We admit that there is occasional good mixed up with it; but the good is made to serve the evil, as Christian slaves were made to serve Algerine or Turkish masters.' Wrapping up, although he declares he has much more to say about the evils of the theatre, he says the biggest proofs are the apologetic testimonies of the men of the theatre—the actors themselves whose hearts were drawn to the evil but at times are saved by the grace of Christ. He exclaims, 'an evil heart loved an evil place'. Finally, he calls out to his readers and shares an anecdote. 'This pious Hervey once travelled in a stage-coach with a lady, who was speaking of the pleasures of 'the play'—'Pray, what are those pleasures? said he—'They are three, sir, pleasure before the play in anticipation—pleasure during the play, in its enjoyments—and pleasure after the play in retracing it.' 'You have omitted one more pleasure, yet to be realized, Madam,' Hervey calmly replied—'What is that, sir?' 'The pleasure which the retrospect of time so spent, and the things so seen, will afford you when laid on a death-bed!' Of course, the lady having seen the point of Hervey turns to God. And the anecdote ends with a moral that dogmatizes the situation. One is here not free from judgement even if one lived life *ad libitum*. In fact, such a way of life itself is the route to sin and theatre the root-cause of sin committed. 'Managers, actors, actresses, amateurs, auditors, spectators and writers, of the stage' none would be spared from 'JUDGEMENT'[19] and this is why the opponents of theatre call it the 'House of Evil' or 'House of Satan'. His grave concerns, which he elaborates with various examples from the theatres mostly in England, are addressed towards the colonizing population who seem to undermine the evil nature of the theatre. He writes, 'The colonial population of Calcutta, a comparatively late element in its society, is growing up in irreligion, dissipation, and gross immorality—and soon crime will be superadded. The elite of society is cultivated—the mass is given up to sin. Theatres will soon have evil enough to live upon. Amateurs will cease to be; —and mere actors and actresses, (as is even now begun,) will take their place; —and on them there will be no check but the acceptance of an evil population.' Hence a theological understanding of theatre opens up the debate of whether theatre should or should not continue to exist within the colony. It is here not only individual cases of psychophysical impact but rather socio-religious concerns especially within a colonial atmosphere. JMD rests his case challenging those in favour of the theatre to do away with the sin that resides in it. However, at the very beginning before he assembles the points in favour of his argument, he makes one interesting observation. The enthusiast of theatre whose speech he quotes refers to the theatre being called the 'House of Satan'. JMD clarifies that the saying goes not as the 'House of Satan' but as the '*Synagogue* of Satan'. He writes that the reason behind it is obvious as men met together in a synagogue of old to serve God whereas in the theatre although unconsciously, men met to serve Satan. Hence it is the 'house of assembly' as some understood it to be. JMD preferred the term 'house' to 'synagogue' as it is more 'generic, comprehensive, and descriptive of permanent and domestic character'. Hence he does not only try to suggest the evil nature of the theatre on more secular grounds effacing all reference to any religion making it a universal evil as it were, but at the same time suggests its impact within the domestic interior spaces. Theatre is therefore not a performance space that generates sporadic coercive elements affecting a few but rather as a whole it affects a congregation, a 'house of assembly'. This 'house of assembly' is 'immoral', 'irreligious' and 'dissipated' but most importantly the *Other*—an *Other* which is not homogenous but rather evolves from an unconscious multitude that participate in the process of theatre which is initiated by 'theatre-going'. It is the unconscious nature of its participation in an assembly that fails to recognize any scripture or abide by it that makes it a perilous *one*—a singular strength. Although JMD mentions in the beginning that the ones with money are given to the theatre but his apprehension is not about them as they are also 'cultivated'. It is rather the mass that he contends will give in to the theatre and assemble to form this *other*. JMD's concern was not an erratic one. Even before him in the late eighteenth century when in Calcutta there existed the Old Playhouse, Captain Philip Dormer Stanhope, author of *Genuine Memoirs of Asiaticus* regretted that in Calcutta there was a playhouse but no Church. Probably in the wake of similar such concerns, after the Old Playhouse building in Calcutta got burnt down during the hostilities of the Battle of Plassey[20], there was talk about founding a church or a public place of worship.[21]

3.2 Sin, Salvation, Censorship and Theatre Within a Colonial Space

The colonial government during the eighteenth and nineteenth centuries was always apprehensive about the Church and its activities. That the state need not interfere with the religious activities of its people, in this case, a colonized people, had its genesis in Enlightenment in Europe. Peter van der Veer suggests that this was associated with the immanent logic of the superior race as one finds in John Stuart Mill's 1859 essay *On Liberty* where he explicitly states that the doctrine of liberty 'is meant to apply only to human beings in the maturity of their faculties'. At the same time, Mill's critique was directed towards toleration of diverse religious opinions. Der Veer notes—'...in a long footnote on the British response to the Mutiny later in the essay he (Mill) accuses both evangelicals and the state of persecuting Muslims and Hindus. His position allows for the toleration of diverse religious opinions, but only if they already belong to modern civilization and thus contribute to the moral principle of progress.'[22] On the other hand, the blood shed in the 'mutiny' of 1857 as Mill also suggests became a crucial indicator of the colonial government's strategy in India which was to henceforth keep matters of the state separate from the matters of religion. However, inherent in this logic was the principle of custodianship. For the subject within the colonial set-up was not one that was 'free' in the sense of John Stuart Mill and had not reached 'maturity' and hence required a despotic government which could rightfully govern it. In post-1857 colonial India, it became an absolute necessity for the British government to establish its sovereignty over this vast colonial land, but so, only rightfully. After the 'mutiny' of 1857 and the subsequent transfer of power to Britain in 1858, the East India Company lost power over the colony. The righteousness of the British Government's rule, started to get highlighted in the role that it played in social reform. However social reform had its lineage in the evangelical missions that were being carried out in different parts of the world. After accession of throne of the United Kingdom in 1837, Queen Victoria became the Patron of the Royal Asiatic Society, which took great interest in oriental studies. She also became involved in various Indian bishoprics. She later married Prince Albert in 1840 who took deep interest in philanthropy and favoured evangelical missions and became a vocal supporter of the Society for the Propagation of the Gospel in Foreign Parts.[23] At the same time, he was not in support of the Whigs' relationship with the bankers and fund-holders of the East India Company and was also against the Whigs' interventionist stance in Bengal on matters such as the Education Code which insisted that English become the language of administration and they also opposed the attempt to suppress religious 'idolatry' and practices such as *sati* (widow immolation). Fundamentally, the issue of how far one was to intervene within the colonies was a complex issue not only for the government but also for the evangelic societies who nevertheless maintained their custodianship of the colonies. Early nineteenth century saw another development, which was the response of the Indian intellectuals to the interaction with Britain and Christianity. Ram Mohan Roy wrote one of the very first critiques of religion *Tuhafat-ul-Muwahiddin* in 1802. Although he came close to an atheist stand, he did not deny the existence of God. His concern was a doctrine, which worked in favour of mankind to 'refrain from the commission of evil deeds', that is, he was concerned with the pragmatic role of religion.[24] He along with Devendranath Tagore founded the Brahmo Samaj in 1828 in Calcutta, which propagated monotheism and spoke in favour of socio-religious reform. Bipin Chandra Pal, a nationalist known for his militant stance in the

Congress and founder of the journal *Vande Mataram*, who had lived in the students' Home associated with the *Brahmo Samaj*, in the essay *How I came to the Brahmo Samaj*, highlights how most of the inmates there were preoccupied by the idea of sin and salvation, prayer and divine worship.[25] The engrossment with Hinduism was as has already been stated, started as a conversation with Christianity but that often had its own nationalist aims. This *dialogic*[26] interaction transformed not only the idea of God in Hinduism but also evolved its idea of sin. On the other hand, as Peter van der Veer shows, for the British government 'Race replaced religion as the most important marker of difference, although religion and race were often combined.' It was within this discursive matrix of transformations that 'theatre' in India resided. *Dev Samaj*'s understanding of 'theatre-going' as that which was a path to evil is therefore to be posited in this *heteroglossic*[27] atmosphere within which theatre resided. The existing performance genres like *kathakatha, khemta* came to be seen as crude and vulgar, informed by notions of morality of the time. We have discussed this at length earlier. The Brahmo Samaj, the forebearer of religious reforms in India had its own problems with the theatre. When female performers were introduced onto the Bengali stage, there were huge protests from the Brahmo Samaj and going to the theatre came to be understood as a sin.[28] Therefore the 'house of assembly' that the theatre was, on the one hand was a potential site of visible evil as in the case of Harnam Singh but on the other hand, this potentiality was often used to confront existing social norms. Bipin Chandra Pal mentions that his interest in matters of social reform was actually influenced by the theatre. He writes, 'whatever might be the private character of the actors and the actresses, the plays generally put on the board of these theatres were exceptionally inspiring.'[29] Giribala's coming centre-stage and Binodini's purging the evil off herself were only part of that potentiality that the theatre holds. Talking about this potentiality Victor Turner writes—'shiver... achieved, though, to be a consummation, after working through a tangle of conflicts and disharmonies'—the sins as it were, 'a sense of harmony with the universe is made evident, and the whole planet is felt to be a *communitas.*[30] It was a psychophysical state for the ones taking part in the process of the theatre and at the same time effectively social, as it involved a congregation that unconsciously tended to give in to it. The colonial Government by the late nineteenth century saw this potentiality of a coming together, as theatre and dramatic literature had become a regular pursuit of the native society who had taken to representing the social and the political on stage. In Calcutta, several plays reflecting economic exploitation of the colonial subject which were literally named *darpan* plays or mirror plays were written and staged in the early 1870s. *Nil Darpan* written by Dinabandhu Mitra and published in September 1860 about exploitation of the labourers of the indigo factories by the English planters became enveloped by controversy when it was translated into English by James Long (possibly he just wrote the foreword and Michael Madhusudan Dutt translated it) of the Church Missionary Society and circulated in the name of the Bengal Government soon after. That the news of exploitation reached England became a reason of extreme embarrassment for the colonial government. As part of the punitive measures, the colonial government fined James Long. However the play itself does not criticize the government directly. In fact, the author in the preface to the play wrote: 'The most kind-hearted Queen Victoria, the mother of the people, thinking it unadvisable to suckle her children through maid-servants (possibly East India Company), has now taken them on her own lap to nourish them. The most learned, intelligent, brave and open-hearted Lord Canning is now the Governer General of India... it is becoming fully evident that these (he mentions many other officials) great men will very soon take hold of the rod of justice...'[31]. However the controversy mainly began not only because of the content of the play but also surrounding the missionary activities in the indigo plantation areas. These areas were a potential site for Christian converts but the exploitation of the planters was damaging the reputation of the Europeans. Long's initiative in translating and circulating the play was to highlight the missionary sense of justice as against the planter's injustice.[32] However, more than the justice and injustice done to the native labourers, the government was concerned about any possible revolt from the native population as also the financial loss that the closing down of the indigo plantations might cause to the Government. So it found it fit to punish Long. After this play, the Government became vigilant of the political plays that aimed to critique the English or the Government. In the 1870s when certain political plays, about the Colonial Government's relationship with the native states were staged, the Government argued that 'the acting of such plays at a time of political excitement' could do 'serious harm'.[33] A need to introduce a bill to control dramatic performances was felt. The Dramatic Performances Act (Act No. XIX of 1876) came into force and by December 1876 its operation covered all of India with immediate effect. Within this act any play, pantomime or other drama performed, which the local government found scandalous, defamatory, seditious, likely to corrupt audience members or harmful to the interest of the public, local government, or an officer were to be prohibited and such performance was a punishable offence not only for the makers but also the providers of 'house, room or space' and the spectators of such performance. The play script of every performance or the purport of a pantomime had to be submitted to the concerned authorities. This decision of the Government was met with a lot of protest. Joteendra Mohun Tagore, Secretary to the British Indian Association wrote to the Government asking it to re-consider the decision as, 'the native public regard with apprehension the new law, lest it should have any repressive effect upon the growth of the legitimate drama—a branch of literature which is but struggling into existence. Most of the dramas yet produced are trashy and scarcely worth the paper on which they are printed...'.[34] The Act which also had within its bounds the censorship of any play that could 'corrupt' audience members by promoting immorality or obscenity drew attention of some like W. Bell, the Superintendent and Remembrancer of Legal Affairs who argued about the content of the Act,

> Is it to be a European or a Hindoo standard? A performance which might in the opinion of an English moralist corrupt an English

> audience, might not in the opinion of a Hindoo moralist, corrupt a Hindoo audience. A native nautch for instance, of a certain description strikes a European as an exceedingly immoral performance, but it would not present itself in the same light to a person who had not formed his views of the purity of life from the teachings of Christianity. Mr Leckly, in his most interesting work upon European morals, has pointed out how widely the Christian view of morality differs from that entertained by the purest and most exhalted moralists of Greece and Rome... To me it seems that it would be as dangerous and unjust to force upon a Hindoo our peculiar views of morality as it would be to force upon him our cherished dogmas of religion.[35]

However, the Act was brought into force as it was throughout India on 16 December, 1876. Fundamentally, the colonial government intended to curb any possibility of theatrical excess that was beyond its knowledge especially as it felt threatened post the rebellion of 1857. Theatricality itself was targeted by absolute power that was no more god as JMD suggests where the power to punish was left for the Judgement Day but rather it was replaced by a colonial government that imposed a law of censorship and surveillance to check everything that it did not permit. In India, the regulation set to restrict theatrical excess very consciously aimed at censoring that which the colonial government thought to be of seditious nature. It was not necessarily at par with the Licensing Act of 1737 or the later Theatres Act of 1843 in England that required all new plays in London to be submitted to the Lord Chamberlain and if he thought them to be 'fitting for the preservation of good manners, decorum and public peace' only then were they staged. Nevertheless there would often be opposition to such censorship and in 1907 there was even a suggestion of voluntary system of censorship. In India, however the question of censorship of 'dramatic performances' had far reaching consequences that developed from a sense of insecurity post the revolt of 1857 as also a sense of sovereign power over the colonial population.[36] Given the popularity of some of the plays with a political tone performed in the public theatres run by the colonial native population, the government became alert to their far fetched effect. It was not the moral consequences of these plays that were seen as alarming but rather the question of unjust rule by the British (as portrayed on stage in the play 'Surendra Binodini' in which the ultimate goal was political emancipation from foreign domination) or dishonouring of the ruler (as in the play 'Gajananda O' Juboraj' in which the Prince of Wales being invited to the inner halls of the Calcutta based lawyer Jagadananda Mukhopadhyay's house where he was introduced to the women of the household was ridiculed), which were being censored.

3.3 Theatre, Identity and Colonial Native Society

Theatre's relationship to the question of conduct, in public or in private spaces had been an element of concern for the playwrights and dramatists from the very beginning of the initiation of dramatic writing during the British rule. It was because the question of conduct was seen as directly related to the social status and identity of the class that engaged in dramatic writing in the beginning of the nineteenth century. As has been discussed in the previous chapter, the initial interaction within the colonial space was limited to the native elite and the English ruling class. English education played a significant role in establishing the hegemony of the imperial culture. This has already been discussed earlier. In such a state of affairs that the first play to be written by any native in colonial India was in English is not surprising. The play 'The Persecuted' was written by Reverend Krishna Mohan Bandyopadhyay. It was published in 1831, the same year as Prasanna Kumar Tagore's 'Hindu Theatre' was established. The book begins with a dedication to the 'Hindoo Youth' with 'hope of their appreciating those virtues and mental energies which elevate man in the estimation of a philosopher'. He clarifies later in the preface that his purpose of writing the dramatic text was to expose the 'wiles and tricks of the Brahmin'[37] whose influence the youth needed to get rid of. He thanks the teachers and visiting managers of the Hindoo College and the Calcutta School Society, for under their supervision and guidance he received such an education. It is interesting to observe that the critique here is not only of the Brahmin caste/class that is the uppermost caste and was responsible for imparting education within the larger Hindu society but also it is juxtaposed against English education, which clearly comes across as more just, according to the author. The Brahmins manipulate the trust and faith that their students, the 'shishyo', to be literally translated as disciples have in them as it were, while the English are the 'aware' lot. The plot revolves around a father Mohadeb finding out that his son Bany lal is given to eating beef and drinking alcohol. Mohadeb wants his son not to accept such a fact, as that would make him an outcast and also bring bad name to the family. Bany lal finds this hypocritical as the fact or what he calls the 'truth' is that he has eaten beef and he also drinks. Bany lal looks at such restrictions imposed by the society as superstitions. Bany lal, who clearly represents the author's voice as well as the 'Hindoo Youth' that the play is dedicated to, says while anticipating his father's reaction to his drinking and eating habits:

> ...Am I discovered?—Well—I am not surprised. —I anticipated all that are now transpiring, when first I began to feel hostile to Hindooism. —Such occurrences must happen. When knowledge has begun its march, Hindooism must fall and must fall with noise. Reformation must come on and excite heart-burning jealousies among men... Am I at last to be instrumental in bringing on his (his father Mohadeb's) death? The very thought is misery.—Philosophy! Art thou so weak? Is nature so strongly opposed to thee! —Aye; —but this will not surprise me. I expected this and am prepared for it—prejudice and liberalism cannot long reign under the same roof without a rupture.'[38]

The colonial interactions indeed created a 'rupture' between existing modes of living and the new one that were emerging. For many of the English educated urban youth, what they saw around them was rather fake and hypocritical, often vulgar and indecent. In the play for example the old servant of Mohadeb finds it disturbing that—'They (Hindoo Youth—Bany lal, his friends and alike) say our Krishna was immoral because he had intercourse with his numerous Gopeenees (female friends)!'[39] The play ends with forming a community, of those who were the 'enlightened' against those who were still under the shadows of Hindu superstition. The playwright clearly intended to have a European audience for the piece, which is why he gives a glossary of terms and phrases at the end of the play called 'Notes and Illustrations' or even as footnotes for the European reader to understand. One wonders if he ever thought of staging it! Incidentally also, the old Bengali servant uses the words *Pisanio, Posthumous, Orlando* and *Adam* in one of his speeches. The author explains the inclusion of these names:

> ... in the text means merely a good faithful servant and his master. —In Hindoo tradition instances of this kind are very rare. —The author in consequence availed himself of those names in order to be clearly understood by Europeans. The author surely does not give his OLD SERVANT a knowledge of Shakespeare's characters.[40]

The 'faithful good' servant of course is without any English education and being 'enlightened' is not even expected of him. So the communities at a tug of war were those who were the 'liberal Hindoos' and those of the 'orthodox community'. The author calls out to the orientalists to help them expose the people of this community who take refuge in the sacred texts to fool people, what he calls 'Brahmin craft'. Ultimately, through the play the author and those like him declare, 'I pledge, as long as I live, I will be a devoted servant to the cause of truth and Hindoo reformation.'[41]

From a reformed religious community, the author furthers such a role for the sake of another body—that of the 'country'. He writes:

> Let us handle this sacred cause, and desert it only by our death... Let us prove ourselves dutiful sons of our country by our actions and exertions. Now let us see what strength can ignorance and bigotry bring into the field. Let us mark how feeble is prejudice when rational beings attack it with prudence.[42]

From the very first dramatic text written, the question of identity, more precisely a national identity was at the heart of the theatrical landscape. An inherent contradiction between the earlier modes of livelihood, the notion of knowledge, truth and viability of class/caste domination of the earlier times within the new given conditions of cultural interaction where English education and henceforth associated 'philosophical truth' seemed undisputable to the emerging educated elite. This was an elite because not everyone irrespective of class background was able to receive such an education. At the same time, the urban centres where such educational institutes developed became the hub of this new 'community'. It wasn't any intrinsic property that made the community form itself but these were politico-hegemonic articulations[43] (here following Laclau and Mouffe, hegemony is not necessarily thought of in the negative sense of despotic oppression achieved by one group over all others but rather as historically and politically contingent binding together) of the interactive times where education, social dining, drinking, chatting, writing, publishing, theatre-making-going etc. made such a cohesion possible. Added to the contradiction was a constant tension of the 'Hindoo'/but not so 'Hindoo' dichotomy. One wanted to transform to become another but one did not entirely want to give up on one's historical lineage, hence the call to the orientalists, to a much more glorious 'Hindoo' past as it were. Who are 'we', that are almost like 'you' (the British) but not quite? Early nineteenth century immersed itself into this question for a new emerging civil society that found itself closest in interaction with the British administrative class. We have discussed this in much further detail in the earlier chapters. However, here the people who got left out of such a conglomeration were the 'fools' and the 'hypocrites'. While in 'The Persecuted', the hypocritical Brahmins who had been cheating on other lower castes (not necessarily always lower classes) were the other along with the orthodox conservatives (whereby its not an 'other' formed on the basis of any specific identity but rather a heterogeneity that worked up through an 'articulation' of 'us'), the fools were the other lower orders, like the characters of the old and the young servant who of course belonged to a lower class background. They did not necessarily belong to the other because they did not appear as any conflicting or intellectually challenging group. They were the 'fools' (as Banylal keeps addressing his servant) who just needed to obey, or much better, were inconsequential. However, the logic of a Hindu self never perished from such an identity formation. Whether 'The Persecuted' was ever really performed is not quite known. Like the audience of the 'Hindu Theatre', such dramatic texts, English literature or dramatic performances were always intended for the English educated gentry or the European residents as is evident from the notes to 'The Persecuted'. But for the other section, the community that has been termed the 'orthodox' ones, the elite that could afford to organize performances within their own domestic premises, what remained popular were *half akhrai, bulbul lodai* and other such already existing performance forms.[44] These performances were also often open to the lower sections of the society who were more familiar with them and were not necessarily invited to the 'theatre' performances.

3.4 Public Arena and the Jatra

Amongst those performances that were popular around this period in and around Calcutta was also the *jatra*. *Jatra*'s inherent association with the idea of *bhakti* had rendered it different from some of the other performance forms. This also established *jatra*'s association with religion. We have in short dealt with what *jatra* is in our very first chapter. In order to proceed further we will now deviate our attention to the idea of *bhakti* as this has a significant relationship with what we would be talking about later through this chapter.

Christian Lee Novetzke in the essay '*Bhakti* and its Public' suggests that essentially *bhakti* seeks to form 'publics of reception rather than communities that imply a single cohesive issue or idiom'. So the term cannot be reduced to any individual concepts or something to do with the private realm alone but the idea of *bhakti* always seeks out a public creating a social space of reception. Trying to historicize the term, Novetzke finds in the etymology of the Sanskritic verbal root 'bhaj' the meanings to share, and to apportion. The other meanings of this root are to divide, distribute, bestow, to obtain one's share, to enjoy or possess, to resort to, engage in, assume (as a form), put on (garments), to experience, to practise or cultivate, to choose, to serve and adore. He writes:

> The noun *bhakta* refers to a person (or in some cases a thing) in whom some qualities of bhakti inhere. Thus, a bhakta is someone

> who is devoted, who serves, who is associated with a community, and who is faithful and loyal.[45]

The notion of *bhakti* within the public sphere has not only been an expression of devotedness to a god but it has been used to denote 'a 'movement' of social protest against caste, class, religious, or gender inequities' as early as the sixteenth century. Novetzke argues that historically although no single social movement cohered to the term *bhakti* or its sentiments) innumerable religious communities, practices, bodies of texts etc. can be indicated that invoked *bhakti* as their generative principle. It also cannot be associated with any one religion[46] as it was often co-opted, or rather, given the term's resistance to any heuristic definition could become an envelope term. One of the performative gestures of *bhakti* could be repetition of a word or a phrase. For example when Ramakrishna suggested to the actress Binodini to repeat the name of Hari (an avatar of Krishna), it was in order to perform *bhakti* or bring the feeling of *bhakti* (*bhakti-bodh* where *bodh* could mean sense, feeling, experience etc.) that would purge her from all evil that lay within her as it were. In *jatra* it was common to have performances around one divine being, or a Hindu god or a mythological story. Many audience members/devotees/*bhakta*s would often bend down their heads, or cry etc. feeling a sense of connectedness/oneness as a result of *bhakti-bodh*. This is a very common practice known as *darshan*[47], which is visual contact with the deity. Essentially the *bhakta* within the performative space (or ritual space?)[48] of the *jatra* experiences a divine view of the one he or she is a *bhakta* of, turning it into a holy ritualistic space. Given that the theme of *Chaitanyaleela* was a performance borrowed from the popular *jatra* tradition, and that Ramakrishna belonged to those members of the audience group who were aware of such a tradition, he possibly suggested the road to *bhakti because* like every ritualistic form promises, he saw an evident transformative power in the process. In fact, the name of Chaitanya, Vaishnavite leader of the Hindu *bhakti* tradition has often been associated with the initiation of *jatra*. He would often dress up as a woman and perform the rites of devotion or arouse his *bhakti-bodh* towards the Hindu God

Krishna. These performances have been described as 'anker bidhaney nritya' or roughly translated as 'episodes in the form of dance' in Chaitanya Bhagavat.[49] The form for portraying *bhakti* is not fixed; it is rather anything that a community or an individual feels fit. Novetzke critiques Habermas' argument that the construction of the public sphere often relies upon at least the technologies of modernity or as according to Arjun Appadurai and Carol Breckenridge's study of public culture that it remains limited within the interstices of modern life. He rather uses the definition by Michael Warner which is that of 'a public (that) enables a reflexivity in the circulation of texts among strangers who become, by virtue of their reflexively circulating discourse, a social entity'[50] wherein the object of belief of the public is a fictional one or 'not a physically demonstrable thing, like a state, village, township, or other polity; nor does it exist in a carefully constructed discourse, like the judiciary, a set of laws, or a dogma. The public relies as much on the imagination of each individual as on a collective agreement as its existence. People must believe they are part of the public, and this gives it both its strength and its ephemeral quality'.[51] Finally, he goes on to argue that the formation of a social cohesive body cannot be limited to the study of modernity. He shows that in case of the public, which is distinct from the term popular, and which makes a utilitarian appeal to a majority or the word communal where the individual is subordinated to the whole, 'implies a measure of resistance to homogenous social entities that cause the erasure of the individual'. It, in its experiences or portrayal or being part of the sense of *bhakti,* is neither ruled by dogma nor coercion but made cohesive by a social agreement where participation is suggested by the 'embodiment' of *bhakti* as a prerequisite for its practice. That is to say it needs bodies, which is the epicentre of all happening. According to him it is this symbiotic equation between *bhakti* and its embodied performance within the confluence of which the public is created. He equates it to love and asks if love can be called a social movement and argues that it is 'a locus for the creation of publics, not the formation of a single social or literary movement'. And this power of creation can both hold a negativity or positivity as *bhakti* remains an 'empty vessel'. In nineteenth century Calcutta, *jatra* was slowly becoming devoid of the element of *bhakti,* that is, it became more and more inclined to entertain rather than to persist as the portrayal of *bhakti*. The emphasis in these new *jatra* performances, known as 'shokher jatra' which is roughly translatable as '*jatra* of one's fancy' or '*jatra* which is a hobby' and which is often argued to be influenced by the 'theatre' of the period, was supposed to be vulgar or concerned with the more immediate earthly matters as against the matters of the divine.[52] In Calcutta and around, this kind of 'shokher jatra' groups would be founded by the patronage of the gentry. The growing change of de-deification was often lamented by the traditional *jatrapalakars* or makers/ writers of *jatra*.[53] But at the same time, these *jatra* performances, which were extremely successful[54] in turn influenced many to establish theatres. The popularity of the *shokher jatra* on the one hand and the arrogance of 'knowledge' gained out of English education faced a conflictual situation when the success of performance came into question or even when the question of one's identity was furthered. For instance, given the limited number of seats available at the National Theatre, it was decided that those who were qualified enough to understand acting would be allowed to get a ticket. That is why a lot of the audience started to come with certificates proving qualification.[55] However *jatra*'s association with *bhakti* and also religion was not entirely lost which is why when the Dramatic Performances Act came into existence in 1876, after some deliberation, it was kept outside the purview of the Act. While formulating the Bill for the Act, keeping in mind the consequences of 1857 'mutiny', it was opened for debate. It was admitted in the records of the Legislative Council Proceedings that a section of Indian opinion was against the Bill. One such instance of opposition or rather suggestion was from Raja Narendra Krishna who proposed amongst other things that *jatra,* not only on religious occasions but on other occasions as well be excluded from the purview of the Bill.[56] It was kept out until the question arose much later in the beginning of the twentieth century—but what is *jatra*? The question was asked by L.F. Morshead, Inspector General of Police, Lower Provinces of his Indian subordinates in a letter dated September 15, 1910. He asked, 'Can you tell me precisely what a *jatra* is? The question has arisen, as you know, as to whether steps should be taken to prevent them spreading sedition, but I find myself hampered in considering it for want of a clear definition... They seems to me to have a great potentiality for spreading sedition but there does not appear to be much evidence for saying that they are actually so used.' His subordinates clarified, 'Jatra is an informal dramatic performance, usually quite harmless, without any scenes or a stage. These jatras are usually held on occasions of *pujas* (Hindu religious ceremonies) in the quadrangles of gentlemen's residence for the amusements of guests. It is also held in the open air, when sections of bazar people in Calcutta and elsewhere celebrate their *Barwaris* or common *pujas*. The subjects are usually religious or mythological. The *jatrawallas*, who are usually very poor people, sometimes introduce comical farces, usually at the end of the jatra, to amuse chiefly children and the youth, the subjects being quarrels between two ghosts or between co-wives or between some drunken people etc.'[57] Hence the 'informal' nature of the performance of *jatra*s had kept them away from the purview of any censorship law until 1910.

3.5 Coagulating Peoples, Mutating Identities and the Swadeshi Movement

The phenomenon of coming into form or giving form to communities, distinct from pre-existent social groups only increased with time. As is the case with the youth of the 'The Persecuted' most of these groups, associations, *samiti*, *sangha* (whose names took on any of these words in English or in the regional languages) comprised mostly students of the newly founded educational institutions, a generation that Thomas Babington Macaulay, the member of Supreme Council of India between 1834 till 1838, had in his famous *Minutes on Education* in 1835 called 'Indian in blood and colour, but English in taste, in opinions, in morals, and in intellect.'[58] However there was a growing sense of alienation from the rest of the population which this generation felt was its responsibility to reform. The early *samiti*s or associations were interested in such social reform work as was felt relevant within their context. These associations would often also form themselves into clubs promoting physical exercises, gymnastics, or traditional forms of martial arts which were known as *akharas*, or they could be simply reading and discussion groups or even theatre associations, clubs, some of them *jatra* parties or *jatra dols* (*dol* meaning group). But a sense of alienation persisted among these new communities who tried to sever themselves from the society they belonged to but at the same time were in an ambiguous position when it came to their own identities. If one notes the names of some of these clubs like *Atmonnati Samiti* of Calcutta which means Society for the promotion of self-development or *Swadesh Bandhab Samiti* of Barisal which can be translated as *Society of Friends of One's Own Country* (Swadesh) or simply *Surhid Samiti* or *Society of Friends* or *Friends' Society*, there was a growing need to reach out to a larger public. Initially many of them started as benevolent associations but by late nineteenth century/early twentieth century, they had become politically inclined.[59]

Such social concern was also reflected in the work of the theatre associations. 'The Bagbazar Amateur Theatre' formed in 1867 for example performed plays like 'Shadhobar Ekadoshi' (Married Woman's Widow-Rituals) or 'Biye Pagla Buro' (The Oldie Mad to Get Married) written by the playwright Dinabandhu Mitra who had earlier written *Nildarpan* that was to later transpire into becoming an instigation for the coming of the Dramatic Performances Act. Both these plays performed by 'The Bagbazar Amateur Theatre' were about the condition of women in the society. This theatre group later came to be known as 'The Calcutta National Theatre' and still later 'The National Theatre'[60] when they could form a permanent stage in the house of Rajendralal Pal of Shyambazar. This theatre later became the hub of the meeting of Hindu Mela (1867). Hindu Mela (initially known as Chaitra Mela) was an association that came into existence in 1867, under the initiative of Nabogopal Mitra who was inspired by the article 'Prospectus for the Promotion of National Feeling Among the Educated Natives of Bengal' written by Rajnarain Basu, that Mitra had published in his newspaper *National Paper*. It was an association of the educated middleclass that focused on issues related to socio-political matters of the country without encouraging antipathy towards the ruling class. However this organization was one of the first platforms that spoke about nationalism in a broader perspective of a nation that was 'Bharat'.[61] Singing patriotic songs, reading poems and essays that promoted patriotic feeling was one of the features of the meetings of the Hindu Mela.[62] It also encouraged discussions on social, political, economic and religious conditions of India. In one of its meetings, Ganendranath Tagore, a member of Hindu Mela highlighted, 'One principal positive aspect of the English race is its self-reliance. We have initiated ourselves in the imitation of that positive aspect... so that such self-reliance is established in Bharatbarsha...'.[63] Several national songs were composed during this phase. A song that epitomises how Hindu Mela was invested with glorifying the Indian national question can be shown through one of their most popular songs written by Satyendranath Tagore,

> *Miley shob Bharat shontan,*
> *Ek taan monoh pran;*
> *Gao Bharater josho gaan.*
> *Bharatbhumir tulye ache kono sthan? ...*

> (Together children of Bharat/tuned as one heart and soul/ sing the glories of Bharat/Is there a place in comparison to Bharat?)[64]

An interesting observation has been made by Geeta Chattopadyay in the book *Bangla Swadeshi Gaan* (Patriotic songs in Bengali) that Nishikanta, a professor of Sanskrit language and literature in the Saint Petersburg University, wrote to Rajnarain Basu about how the Russian prince received the songs when Nishikanta sang some of them to him in 1879 from the translated version of collected patriotic songs. What Nishikanta wrote to Rajnarain Basu is worth quoting:

> Alluding to the patriotic songs, His Imperial Highness asked, if such hymns were not prohibited by the British Government, to which, as far as I was aware, I answered in the negative.

He further wrote:

> Apropos, I observed that these patriotic hymns had been mostly composed and sung on the occasions of what we call 'The Hindu Mela': an annual vernal feast which bore much resemblance to the Greek Olypmic Games and which has for its objects, as in the other case, the inculcation and the development of the national spirit of the Hindu race.[65]

A sense of tradition and historicity was being provided to the 'Hindu' thus comparing it to Greek traditions. In the later period, however a Hindu glorious past was more and more invoked in the patriotic songs, as the question of *dashatva* or slavery to other races was believed to have begun with Muslim invasions. As in the songs, it was a common affair to portray socio-political subjects in the theatres (which is why the Dramatic Performances Act was invoked in 1876); however it was limited to the purview of a few circles. In fact, after the implementation of the Act of 1876, and the strict vigilance of the courts where a systematic procedure was followed to avoid probable texts or performances of seditious nature, many writers and theatres stopped involving themselves with such subjects. By the late nineteenth century/early twentieth century however, there was a changed political climate in the Bengal region which necessitated the use of performances as a medium to communicate, not only to the urban educated but also to the ones the new communities felt alienated from.

In 1903, Lord Curzon, the then Viceroy of India proposed the partition of Bengal. At that point of time, Bengal Presidency was one of the larger provinces of British India that included the present day West Bengal, Bangladesh, Assam, Bihar and Orissa. The argument given for the partition was the vastness of this Presidency and for better governance, the need to divide it up. However, the need to divide the Bengal Presidency was seen to control the rising sense of nationalism amongst the Bengalis. Sumit Sarkar notes that already in 1896, the Commissioner of Chittagong Division had mentioned about the political benefits to 'unite the most important part of the Mohammedan population of Eastern India' thus reducing what he called the 'politically threatening' position of the 'Hindu minority in the undivided Bengal Presidency. Even Curzon had mentioned that the last thing that was wanted was any kind of consolidation of communities against the British as was happening in case of the Maratha race in the Bombay Presidency. Hence the initial motive was also 'divide and rule' fearing a Bengali solidarity. As has been already discussed, by the early twentieth century, there was a growing sense of identity that was principally because of social mobility, standard literary language, the print media, theatre etc. Amongst this community there was a growing sense of political disappointment, disappointment over racial discrimination, and economic distress over repeated famines at the end of the nineteenth century and on the other hand, an increasing belief of being a nation. This was based on revivalist attitude over the quest of the past, influenced especially by Hindu nationalist visions as was propagated by writers like Bankim Chandra Chatterjee. These factors were furthermore influenced by international events like Japan's victory over the Russian Empire that took place between 1904-1905, the changing political atmosphere within Russia, the Boer Wars etc. By 1905, when Curzon declared the Bengal partition plan, all groups of Bengal patriots had developed a definite consciousness opposed to the partition. Especially post-1905, most of them supported boycott of foreign manufactured goods and declared economic self-reliance or *swadeshi* (of one's own country). The movement that developed around this point of time, often seen as one of the first movements that saw the self-expression of India as a nationality, came to be known as the *Swadeshi Movement*. On the one hand, there was a willingness to break off from the British empire by some, who thought that British rule was incompatible with national progress and there was the need to prepare to overthrow them and on the other there was the moderate style of petitioning championed by the Indian National Congress founded in 1885. But what all groups increasingly felt during the course of the movement was the need to mobilize all classes of the society because in the beginning, the movement remained confined within the educated few. Since 1905 there was a conscious effort from especially the extremist groups—those that wanted to uproot the British government to mobilize people from the grassroots. As Sumit Sarkar argues, mass involvement in politics made the idea of freedom appear a realizable goal. To augment mass participation, the same platform of the group, *samiti, samaj* was once again used creating 'national volunteers' who would involve themselves in physical and moral training social work during famines and epidemics, propagate swadeshi through lectures, songs, jatras, besides organizing Swadeshi Craft School and boycott of British products. However the idea of a glorious past that had helped create a Hindu national unity had at the same time alienated the Muslim population as a result of which the movement failed to obtain Muslim support. Also the acts of aggression by the extremists and other religious fundamentalists led to riots between the Hindus and the Muslims. However this period remains unique mainly because of the way mass participation was evolved through the use of new techniques and the idea of nationalism for the first time reached beyond the confines of the educated elite. At least a method of approaching people with a perspective of creating a new community, in fact, a national one was attempted. In any case, the proposed Bengal partition, which resulted in a violent upsurge, had to be revoked in 1911.

One of the *samitis* or groups that played a significant role in establishing connection with a wider population was the 'Swadesh Bandhab Samiti' founded by Ashwini Kumar Dutta, a member of the Indian National Congress, at Barisal in present day Bangladesh. Ashwini Kumar Dutta believed that the need of the hour was to bring the masses in immediate contact with the political reality of the country, to make it more aware as it were. He used the school 'Brojomohan' founded by him in 1885 to instil a sense of patriotism amongst his students. In 1889 he founded the Brojomohan College. About him was written, 'He (Ashwini Kumar) began to agitate against the Partition of Bengal even before it took place and in the Autumn of 1905, Lord Curzon was burnt in effigy in the compound of the institution. Throughout the following years Ashwini Kumar was a leader of the agitation in Eastern Bengal, and his institution was a centre of disaffection, with almost all the processions and demonstrations in Barisal beginning or ending in the compound of his college.'[66]

One of the other features of promoting patriotism amongst students was the use of *Swadeshi* songs within school programmes. One such song was:

Kapaye medina koro joyodhhoni
Jagiya uthhuk mrito pran
Jibon-roney jibon daney
Shobarey koro hey aaguyan

(Make the earth tremor with victory call/Let the dead soul awaken/In life-battle life-giving/Take forward everyone)

Essentially, the necessity of an individual to be an active participant within community affairs was one of the main features in such training. If one were not an active participant then it was almost as if he/she had a dead soul (*mrito pran*). The call was to awaken the soul and join the larger struggle of life, in this case, a national life. We will now delve into our case study—the *Swadeshi jatra*.

3.6 Swadeshi Jatra and Vacillating Definitions

What was the reason for the genre confusion and because of what socio-political consequences did L.F. Morshead, Inspector General of Police ask the question—What is *jatra*? To elaborate on this we need to go back to the story of Ashwini Kumar Dutta. Brojomon School started by Ashwini Kumar Dutta had made an immense impact on the youth of the region. One student of his school was Joggeshwar Dey who came to be known as *Charankobi Mukundadas* or *swadeshi jatrawala* or *jonogoner kobi which means poet of the people* so on and so forth. Joggeshwar although influenced by patriotic teachings in Brojomohan School was not really interested in school education as such. He left school after five years of being there and started a humble living by opening a small grocery store. He was at the same time known for being a drunkard and a goon of his region.[67] However he took keen interest in *kirtaniya* (a form of religious singing) and would be a regular visitor to *kirtan* sessions by travelling groups who would be invited by the local zamindars or landholders during religious festivals. He soon joined one such group run by *Vaishnav Bhakta* (Vaishnavite or *bhaktas* of Vishnu) Bireshwar Gupta. As he became a core member of Bireshwar Gupta's group, he opened a small group around his own shop. He was the leader of his group, the principal singer and *mridanga*[68] player. After the death of Bireshwar Gupta, Joggeshwar's (who had by now transformed himself in terms of how he looked, giving up his usual attire and switching over to a white cloth called *dhoti* and a *chadar* or shawl, typical of what Vaishnavites wore) group became a famous *kirtan* group in the region. Meanwhile around 1898, a *kirtaniya* group run by Krishnakomal Goswami came to Barisal and performed the *pala* or episode 'Rai Unmadini' (The Mad Rai or Radha) and *Nimai Sanyash* (Nimai the Renouncer) that became extremely popular in the area. Joggeshwar's group secretly learned up the *pala* and then performed it at various places. Given many similarities between *kirtan pala* and *jatra pala*, Joggeshwar's training at this phase helped him move from one form to the other. Joggeshwar was intent on becoming a successful *kirtan* singer which was why he started reading *vaishnavite* literature and soon under the *abadhuta*[69] named Ramananda Haribolanada converted to Vaishnavism. His name changed from Joggeshwar to Mukundadas which means one who serves Krishna. At this point he wrote several songs in adulation of Krishna that were first published in 1903. Although he was a Vaishnavite, he was also inclined to the sect *Sakta* (of those who were the bhaktas of the goddess Kali). His inclination led him to often visit the temple of *Kali* at Barisal. A regular visitor to this temple was Ashwini Kumar Dutta. Several others, who were active in thinking about ideas of nation and nationality, were visitors here. Mukundadas converted to the Sakta sect. Here it needs to be noted, inspired by Bankim Chandra Chatterjee's novel Anandamath that glorifies the Goddess as the mother of strength and urges a masculine violent Hindu nationalist movement, many groups during the *Swadeshi* movement had changed over to the worship of the Goddess Kali.[70] It was here that the Vaishnavite Mukundadas felt more and more attracted to the strength that the images of *Kali-Durga* manifested and its consequence was his associating himself with the *Swadeshi* ideology. After the announcement of the Bengal partition, when the *Swadeshi* movement was in full swing, Mukundadas got drawn into the movement influenced highly by the leader of the movement in Barisal, Ashwini Kumar Dutta. Ashwini Kumar's conviction that it was necessary to bring in all classes of the society in order to create a '*samaj*' or a larger society made him believe in the *Swadeshi* movement. 'In this country education is spread through *kathakatha*, through sermons, and through songs. Speeches/lectures do not touch the hearts of common people, and if the common people do not accept *Swadeshi*, this movement would not be successful'[71], writes a teacher from Brojomohan School and a historian Surendranath Sen. Ashwini Kumar went on to influence people like the singer of *Jari* Mufizuddin Alam and performers of *Kathakatha* like Hemchandra Mukhopadhyay to add new elements to these popular performance forms such that 'common people' connected with the *Swadeshi* ideology. For that matter here was an attempt in the sense of Laclau and Mouffe to rearrange systems of social co-existence and transform them, as also to hegemonize them to create an identity politics instilled with anti-colonial sentiments, and questions of economic and political self-reliance etc. Mukundadas too got inspired. He started working on his first of what came to be known as *Swadeshi Jatras* in 1906. The problem of working with Mukundadas' work is manifold. One of the primary problems is the unavailability of much evidence of the performances themselves, their changing improvisational nature and of course the immediacy of performance integral to the genre. There would have been a possibility to approach them to some extent given that several performance texts were published because of Mukundadas' enthusiasm about publishing them, and he often was the publisher of these texts. However, even these texts, especially those of the *Swadeshi* period are lost because the colonial government prohibited most of them.[72] Nevertheless, the impact of these performances becomes evident from the Confidential Records of the Political Branch of the Government of Eastern Bengal and Assam. Evidence of several other *Swadeshi Jatras* can be obtained from these records. In an introduction to the collection of these records, Basudeb Chattopadhyay highlights that the proliferation of these *jatra* parties or groups happened as a result of the strict vigilance regarding 'theatre' performances. As has been earlier mentioned *jatra* performances would often be known as *geetabhinoy*[73] or song-acting. Even before Mukundadas' performances made a huge impact at least in propagating the *Swadeshi* ideology, there were several other *jatrawalas* trying to bring about socio-political consciousness. As has been earlier mentioned, the question of *bhakti*, or generating a sense of *bhakti* was interlinked to social questions from a much earlier point. The use of the same keeping in mind the modern political concerns only reinforced the form, and made it once more appear as an effectively working political tool. Hence initially there was not much need felt to move away from the mythological structure because depending on the social concern, the mythological structure evolved its message, which did not need to be static. Here we come across Motilal Roy who formed the *Nabadwip Banga Geetabhinoy Sampraday* (The community of *Geetabhinoy* performers from Nabadwip in Bengal) around the end of the nineteenth century who interwove current socio-political concerns in his *jatrapalas*.[74] However the first performance that came to the notice of the colonial administration was *Matripuja* (Holy Celebration for the Mother) in 1908, not the one Mukundadas prepared in 1906 but that of Gagan Chandra Sutradhar's *jatra* party from Calcutta that performed in Mymensingh in present day Bangladesh. In a letter written to the Chief Secretary by one R. Nathan on December 28, 1908, we come to know that Mukundadas' *Matripuja* had also come under notice. Furthermore from these records we learn that on December 30, 1908 it was highlighted that a note was to be sent to Magistrates and Superintendents of Police and also to Commissioners with an introductory note which said:

> Recent reports indicate that one of the most effective means of promoting seditious feelings lies in the representation of jatras, songs, and dramatic pieces. The reports also show that among the most popular and at the same time most objectionable of these compositions is one entitled Matripuja which, though its representation in different places presents various features, seems on the whole to be essentially the same...[75]

In another record (File No. 410 of 1909) we see that there was an investigation to ascertain the 'history of the *Jatra* parties', and at least two palas, *Matripuja* (being played since the partition of Bengal) and *Danabdalan* or House of the Devil (being played since eight years) were of concern. In the same record, we come across the Court order from Mymensingh, a verdict of the case between the King-Emperor versus Gangan Chandra Sutradhar and Nabin Chandra De who created the *Jatrapala Danabdalan* in which they were to show cause why they were not to be fined for performing Matripuja and Danabdalan respectively. It elaborates the story of Matripuja saying that it,

> describes a contest between the gods and demons in heaven, in which the demons (*Asuras*) are represented as rulers and the gods (*Debagan*) as the persons ruled. Owing to the oppression of the demons, the gods ultimately rise against them and drive them out...[76]

The note that elaborates on the story shows that throughout there are references to Hindu mythological elements transposed to current nationalistic concerns. For example the note highlights:

> The gods fought for their motherland, personified as a woman of great beauty and dignity, and now and again appeared in the stage weeping for the gods, whom she called her children, and who were suffering so unjustly from the oppression of the demons.'[77]

The names of political figures such as Surendra Nath Banerjee and Ashwini Kumar Dutta were also mentioned. Ashwini Kumar becomes a physician in heaven in the *pala*. Similarly the name of Bankim Chandra Chatterjee who composed the song Vande Mataram made popular by the *Swadeshi* movement is also used. As Bankim Chandra means a moon in a bending attitude, his name becomes an epithet for the god Krishna who apparently 'composed a sweet song in honour of the Mother'.[78] At the same time, the *pala* spoke about *bideshi* or foreign made goods that needed to be discarded. The note concludes that,

> The appearance of this new form of jatra in these days of agitation has some political significance. At least the people generally understand it to be so, though the story is based on a very old book of Hindu mythology and apparently there is nothing wrong in the play.[79]

Nabin Chandra De was discharged, as *Danabdalan* did not carry such overtones of political matters. However the British administration became cautious about any cultural text that was called *Matripuja* because of the seditious sentiment that any document with such a name might spread. Hence when Mukundadas' *Matripuja* was being performed there was excessive vigilance about it. His *Matripuja* deviated from Gagan

Chandra Sutradhar's version. In fact, it did not take the route of the mythological at all. In Mukundadas, the story is about a Deputy Magistrate who eventually leaves the slavery and drudgery caused by the British and wants to join the *Swadeshi* movement. His wife tells him to stop serving the British government but he throws his wife out of the house. He later comes across a fortuneteller, a fallen woman and a few cloth sellers who tell their stories of how they got converted to the *Swadeshi* doctrine. Influenced by these meetings, the Deputy Registrar changes his mind and converts to the *Swadeshi* doctrine. It was often said during the early phases of 'theatre's' interaction with the natives, that while 'theatre' was something one saw, 'jatra' was something one listened to. The songs within a *jatra*, and the musical tonality of dialogues, often made one identify it with an 'opera'. Pulak Chanda in *Jagaroner Charan Mukunda Das O Tar Rachanashamagra*, a compilation of Mukundadas related documents argues that it was not really the storyline but the songs of Mukundadas' *pala*s that made an impact on the members of the audience. Although initially his *pala*s were not being readily accepted, soon they, especially the songs of Mukundadas' *jatrapala*s became extremely popular. *Swadesh Bandhab Samiti* of Barisal that was run under the leadership of Ashwini Kumar Dutta at this point would help Mukundadas' *jatra* party to schedule performances and look after other managerial aspects of the group. In fact, Ashwini Kumar at this point was seen as the 'patron and employer of this seditious and ribald anti-British sedition monger.'[80] From May 1907 onwards, any kind of public gathering around *Swadeshi* activities had become impossible due to government restrictions, and *jatra* was the only way to reach out to people. From one of the police records of January 24, 1907 we come to know, 'The party enacts pieces written in support of the Swadeshi movement and in ridicule of the government, and in their repertoire there is a play which caricatures the resignation of Sir Bampfylde Fuller[81], and another representing the gradual conversion of an anglicized deputy magistrate to the Swadeshi cause'[82]. The police continued to remain vigilant about Mukundadas' activities but could not directly take action as *jatra* remained outside the purview of the Dramatic

Performance's Act. It found another way of dealing with *Swadeshi Jatra*. It invoked article 144 which prohibited unlawful assembly. Hence in order to stop Mukundadas' performances, an injunction would be ordered. But nevertheless, every time there would be news about such an order, Mukundadas would move to the next police jurisdiction to perform. In this way, he collected around thirty-seven injunctions that aimed at stopping his performances.[83] Mukundadas came to be known as the *Swadeshi* Minstrel. His songs would be literally dialogues with the mother figure who was the embodiment of the nation, and at the same time with the Goddess Kali. Mukundadas as we discussed earlier belonged to the *Sakta* sect. They would also be hymns about the Mother. These songs were informed of the *bhakti* tradition and hence could directly connect with an audience that was increasingly becoming aware of the political situation. In this case, the medium used was a familiar one, not only because of the form used but also the sentiment that it evoked. Mukundadas sang,

Bhoy ki moroney rakhitey shontaney
Matangi meteychhe aaj shamar rongey...

(Why fear death, to save her children/Mother Goddess is celebrating the warring colours today)

or

Mayer naam niye bhashan tori
Jedin dubey jabey re
Sedin robi chandra dhrubo tara
tarao dubey jabey re...'

(The boats that sail in the name of the Mother/The day they would sink/That day the sun, moon and the stars/They would also sink)

or

Omol anondey nach bir chhondey
Bol re Kali maiki joy
Chheler dakey pagolini jagibey re kundalini
Ki bhoy- ki bhoy- ki bhoy
Har har bom bom om om om om,
Anohey ano re proloy
Koti kontho-jontrey bharater mohamontrey
Bighoshito koro jogonmoy ...

(In Great joy dance in beats O' courageous/Say victory to Mother goddess Kali/By the call of the son the mother will be awakened/What fear what fear what fear/*Har har bom bom om om om om/* Bring o' bring destruction/In millions of throat-machines the great words (mantra) of Bharat/Call out all over the world)

However these songs especially because of the Hindu imagery and other symbolical references that were constantly made, became alien to the Muslim community. Although Mukundadas did not propagate communal politics as such; rather he would sing songs of religious harmony and the need of the hour to fight against the British together; explicit Hindu bearings were not able to strike the right chord with the people of other religious communities. He sang,

Ram Rahim na juda kor bhai
Monta khati rakh ji
Desher kotha bhab bhai re
Desh amader mataji
Hindu musulman ek maier shontan
Tofat keno koro ji..

(Don't separate Ram and Rahim/Keep the heart pure/The country is our Mother/Hindu Musulman are the sons of the same mother/Why do you differentiate?)

But given the class and caste consciousness which were inherent in these songs, they became acceptable to the majority of the population. He sang,

Amra bhai baul charan mukti mantra chhariye berai
Garo shautal bagdi methor, neta achhey oder bhitor
Matri montrer shadhok tara, tarai Bharat korbey shadhin...[84]

(We are *baul* singers spreading the *mantra* of freedom/*Garo shautal bagdi methor* (all different castes and tribal communities) the leader is in them/They are the *shadhak* (spiritual practitioners), they will make Bharat (India) free)

At the same time, there was criticism of the gentry, the *babu*, who were complete slaves of the British administration as it were. He sang,

Babu bujhbey ki aar moley
Kadhey shada bhoot chepechhey, ek dam dofa sharley
Chhilo dhaan gola bhora, shet idurey korlo shara

Do you know[85]*, bangali babu*
You head firangir booter toley...

> (*Babu* will you understand after death/The white ghost is sitting on your shoulder, and has done its job/There were stores full of rice grain, the white rat destroyed it/*Do you know* Bengali *babu*/ Your head is below the foreign ghost)

Finally it was on the basis of four songs out of fifty-three songs of *Matripuja* that were published that a charge sheet was prepared against Mukundadas, which were considered of seditious nature. About him the detective department in its compilation of facts wrote:

> He...became a *jatrawalla*, and toured the country with his company of strolling singers. In 1909, he was convicted and sentenced to one year's imprisonment for publishing a book of seditious songs and to two years at a separate trial, for singing seditious songs in public; his appeal against these convictions was dismissed by the Session Judge of Bakarganj in March.[86]

Mukundadas was kept in a jail in Delhi in fear that he might influence his inmates in the jails of Bengal. In August 1911 he was released. He once more went back to making *jatrapalas* and this time his focus became the society (his pala Samaj), rural India (his pala *Pollisheba*), and duties of citizens (his pala *Karmakhetra*) etc.

The genre confusion had to come to an end. Although *Mukundas* was a primary figure who brought the question of 'jatra' into the official discourse, the proliferation of *jatra* groups all over Bengal, and their capacity to question power and mobilize political opinion, fundamentally functioned as any other performance having transformative powers. In this case its association with *bhakti* brought forth messages close to its people, changed what *jatra* meant within the official discourse. It was no more a religious form that was singularly aimed at spreading religious dogma. The Government became vigilant about the possibilities that *jatra* held. It began to collect information about the rural *jatra* parties. Enquires were made in nine different districts of Bengal. The entire process came to an end in 1910. In a circular issued on July 28, 1910, the Chief Secretary to the Government of Eastern Bengal and Assam wrote:

> I am desired to say that the Lieutenant-Governor has considered, in consultation with his legal advisers, the procedure that should be followed to prevent the performance, by jatra parties or others, of plays of objectionable character or containing objectionable passages.[87]

It was also noted that it was required to remain vigilant about performances by *jatra* parties and 'On the information thus obtained, the Local Government will proclaim obnoxious plays under section 12(I) of the Press Act (1910), and issue orders with respect to them under section 3 of the Dramatic Performances Act, 1876.'[88] Although it was suggested that the local police should note the *jatra* parties of their area and be present to see what they were performing, and it was highlighted that,

> The provisions of the Dramatic Performances Act, 1876, although they may be applied in the case of certain towns[89] in the manner indicated in the first portion of this paragraph, are not, it is feared, suitable for application in mofussil areas, since the Lieutenant-Governor is advised that jatra parties do not perform in ordinary circumstances in places which are public places within the meaning of section 3, or places of public entertainment within the meaning of section 10 of the Act. Such entertainment usually take place in the local *Kalibari*[90], in some private house, or possibly in an unenclosed space open to all. A further difficulty arises from the application of section 12 of the Act, as almost all *jatra* parties in the mofussil are given during or in connection with religious festivals. The Lieutenant- Governor is advised that action under the Act would almost invariably be met by an allegation that the performance was in honour of one or other of the deities of the Hindu pantheon.[91]

The question of *jatra* was a difficult one for the British Government to address. It not only brought forth questions of form but also questions about public/private, religious/secular, entertainment/ritual etc. I would like to argue that it brought forth some very important questions about modernity within the Indian subcontinent. The question of identity that was being addressed, was dialogic in nature and was never a homogenous one. It was not entirely acquired as Benedict Anderson would like to argue. National identity was constantly perforated with elements and concepts very rooted to their own grounds, not immediately translatable as it were. They were to transform by themselves according to the need of historical conjunctures. However, there lie inter-connectable patterns in how they appear. What makes one give *jatra* a new genre status or what makes them think of theatre as *bilati jatra,* depend on these underlying principles which appear I would argue only under moments of historical transitions, events, and transformations. Genres face crisis and come back stable on the grounds of their principal truth. Here the very ability of performance to be transformative, to hold possibilities of politics and create political communities transforming social identities as it were, becomes evident. The concern of JMD of theatre's potential as an evil, and Harnam Singh's, Giribala's or even Binodini Dasi's personal journeys cannot be detached from the larger coming to terms with, evolving, transgressing and transforming into becoming something new. And here our case study shows that it is not limited to a narrow understanding of theatre but rather depends on what I have elsewhere termed the *archigenre* of theatre. This is what holds the possibility of bringing together the coming new—it also holds the possibility of converting even a space of absolute religiosity into that which JMD labelled as the *House of Satan*.

REFERENCES

1. Jeffery Cox, *Imperial Fault Lines: Christianity and Colonial Power in India, 1818- 1940* (Stanford University Press, 2002), 66.
2. Kenneth W. Jones, *Arya Dharm: Hindu Consciousness in Nineteenth Century Punjab* (UCLA, Berkley, 1976), 115-119.
3. *Unique Fruits or The Unique Higher Life or Sri Dev Guru Bhagwan Part I: Shewing the wonderful unique changes wrought in the souls of fit persons through the unique light and power of Shri Dev Guru Bhagwan* (Printed and published by Sriman Amar Singh, Jiwan Press, 2nd Edition, 1921), 62-63.
4. Victorian morality played a significant role in creating the colonial subject. Ideas about immorality insofar as they were sexual behaviour of a certain kind, use of a certain kind of language (In 1856 books with obscene images and erotic elements

were banned in India by the colonial government), addiction to alcohol (the Temperance Movement of England and America played a significant role in shaping the movement against alcohol in India. In 1863 was formed the Bengal Temperance Society. Brahma Samaj also participated actively against alcohol drinking), and women's behaviour and clothing were informed by Victorian debates about the moral and the immoral.

5. Antonin Artaud, *The Theatre and its Double,* Trans. Mary Caroline Richards (Grove Press, New York, 1958), 96.
6. As quoted by Partha Chatterjee, A Religion of Urban Domesticity: Sri Ramakrishna and the Calcutta Middle Class. In *Subaltern Studies VII: Writings on South Asian History and Society,* Partha Chatterjee and Gyanendra Pandey (eds.) (Oxford University Press, New Delhi, 1992), 63.
7. A form of chanting/singing devoted to God.
8. *Maa* is a way of addressing mother in Bengali often also used lovingly for women (almost with asexual undertones)
9. *Amar Katha o Ananya Rachana* (New Rainbow Lamination, Kolkata, 1416 Bengali year), 42-43.
10. For a detailed study see Sumit Sarkar, 'Kaliyuga', 'Chakri' and 'Bhakti': Ramakrishna and His Times', *Economic and Political Weekly,* Vol. 27, No. 29 (July 18, 1992)
11. We discuss this later in detail.
12. Partha Chatterjee, A Religion of Urban Domesticity: Sri Ramakrishna and the Calcutta Middle Class. In *Subaltern Studies VII: Writings on South Asian History and Society,* Partha Chatterjee and Gyanendra Pandey (eds.) (Oxford University Press, New Delhi, 1992), 47.
13. English and Dutch missionaries had already formed educational institutes in Bengal by private or collective effort by the early nineteenth century. Bhabatosh Dutta, *Banglar Jagoroney Missionary-der Daan.* In *Unish Shotoker Bangalee Jibon o Shonskriti,* Swapan Basu and Indrajit Choudhury (eds.) (Pustak Bipani, Kolkata, 2003), 93.
14. American Mission Press [Calcutta, 1842?], available in the General Reference Collection of the British Library, London, UK, 12.
15. *The Calcutta Christian Observer,* Vol. 1, June to December 1832 (Baptist Mission Press, Calcutta 1832), 144.
16. Apparently the British actor David Garrick had sent his assistance for the establishment of the theatre *Old Playhouse* run by amateurs in Calcutta; Amal Mitra, The English Stage in

Calcutta, *circa 1750, Sangeet Natak,* April-June (Sangeet Natak Akademi, New Delhi, 1988), 17.

17. Capital letters as used by the author
18. Ibid.
19. Ibid.
20. The Battle of Plassey which was won by the British East India Company in 1757 over the Nawab of Bengal and his French allies established the stronghold of the Company in Bengal.
21. Amal Mitra, *The English Stage in Calcutta, Circa 1750,* 16.
22. Peter van der Veer, *Imperial Encounters: Religion and Modernity in India and Britain* (Princeton University Press, New Jersey, 2001), 18.
23. Queen Victoria and India, 1837-61, *Victoria Studies*, Vol. 46, No. 2, Papers from the Inaugural Conference of the North American Victorian Studies Association (Winter, 2004), 267.
24. K.N. Panikkar, *Culture and Consciousness in Modern India: A Historical Perspective* (People's Publishing House, New Delhi 2003), 7.
25. *Bipin Chandra Pal, How I Came to the Brahmo Samaj,* Ed. Verinder Grover (Deep and Deep publications, New Delhi, 1993), 529.
26. Mikhail Bakhtin uses the term *dialogic* in the contest of literature where a text is continually in dialogue with other texts and authors subsequently transforming itself and also the other texts with which it is in a dialogue. I call it dialogic as it also changed the understanding of Christianity for some apart from relaxing the position of the colonial government about the Hindus. William Adam, a father of the Baptist Mission who came to India in 1817 gave up his belief in the Trinity due to his interactions with Raja Rammohun Roy (Bhabatosh Dutta, 93)
27. The co-existence of distinctive varieties within a single text. See *The Dialogic Imagination: Four Essays*, M.M. Bakhtin, Michael Holquist (eds.), Caryl Emerson and Michael Holquist (trans.) (University of Texas Press, Austin, 1981).
28. Bipin Chandra Pal, 530.
29. Ibid.
30. Dewey, Dilthey and Drama; Victor Turner in *The Anthropology of Experience*; ed. Victor Turner, Edward M. Brunner (University of Illinois Press, 1986), 43.
31. As quoted in *Acts of Authority/Acts of Resistance: Theatre and Politics in Colonial and Postcolonial India* by Nandi Bhatia (Oxford University Press, New Delhi, 2004).
32. For a detailed study see *Acts of Authority/Acts of Resistance: Theatre*

and Politics in Colonial and Post-colonial India.

33. *Persecution of Drama and Stage,* Pulin Das (MC Sarkar and Sons Private Limited, Calcutta, 1986), 7.
34. Judicial File 183, Proceedings 91-92, February 1877, West Bengal State Archives, Kolkata.
35. Judicial File 214, Proceedings 31-37, September 1876, West Bengal State Archives, Kolkata.
36. See Pulin Das, *Persecution of Drama and Stage.*
37. The Persecuted or Dramatic Scenes: Illustrative of the Present State of Hindoo Society, in *Calcutta* by Baboo Krishna Mohana Banerjea (A. Monriro & Co.'s East Indian Press, Calcutta, 1831).
38. Ibid., 4.
39. Ibid., 2.
40. Ibid., 36.
41. Ibid., 34.
42. Ibid.
43. Laclau and Mouffe in the book *Hegemony and Socialist Strategy: Towards a Radical Democratic Politics* writes that an articulation is any practice establishing a relation among elements such that their identity is modified as a result of the articulatory practice. Which is to mean that unlike in identity politics where subjects are pre-given to representation, 'politico-hegemonic articulations' rather 'retroactively create the interests they claim to represent'. Whereby any essentialist logic of social identities is dislodged, highlighting the fact that they donot pre-exist their social articulation. *Hegemony and Socialist Strategy: Towards a Radical Democratic Politics* (Verso, London, New York, 2001).
44. Subir Raychoudhury et al. (ed.), 19.
45. Chritian Lee Novetzke, Bhakti and Its Public, *International Journal of Hindu Studies*, Vol. 11, No. 3 (December 2007), 257.
46. Like in the case of Sufism which branched from Islam
47. See Diana L. Eck, *Darsan: Seeing the Divine Image in India* for further details
48. See more on these debates: Erika Fischer-Lichte, *Theatre, Sacrifice, Ritual: Exploring Forms of Political Theatre* and also Richard Schechner, *From Ritual to Theatre and Back: The Structure/Process of the Efficacy- Entertainment Dyad..*
49. Dr Md. Manowar Hussain, *Jatra: Deshprem o Samajchetona* (Pustak Biponi, Kolkata, 2011), 12.
50. Bhakti and its Public, ibid. 261.
51. Ibid.
52. Dr Md. Manowar Hussain, 17.

53. Ibid., 22.
54. Some of the well known jatrapalakars of the time being Ramchand Mukhopadhyay, Gopal Udey.
55. Subir Raychoudhury et al. (ed.), 21.
56. The Dramatic Performances Act of 1876: Reactions of the Bengali Establishment to Its Introduction by Manujendra Kundu, *History and Sociology of South Asia* 7(I) (Jamia Millia Islamia and Sage Publications, 2013), 79-93.
57. *Folk Theatre and the Raj: Selection from Confidential Records*, Introduction by Basudeb Chattopadhyay (West Bengal State Archives, Higher Education Department, Government of West Bengal, 2008), iv-v.
58. http:// www. columbia. edu/ i t c/ mealac/ pritchett/ 00generallinks/macaulay/txt_minute_education_1835.html
59. Hiren Chakrabarti, *Political Protest in Bengal: Boycott and Terrorism 1905-1908* (Papyrus, Calcutta, 1992).
60. See Chapter I for the debate around calling it 'The National Theatre'.
61. Geeta Chattopadhaya, *Bangla Swadeshi Gaan* (Delhi University, Delhi, 1983), 9.
62. Ibid., xi.
63. Ibid., 11.
64. Bankim Chandra Chattopadhyay, an ideologue of Hindu nationalism who inspired the later *Swadeshi* movement and wrote the song *Vande Mataram* (I praise the Mother) which was popularized by the Congress (came into existence in 1885) and also *Vande Mataram* itself became a slogan for the nationalist struggle.
65. Ibid., 13.
66. As quoted by Pulak Chanda, *Jagaroner Charan Mukunda Das o Tar Rachanashamagra* (Dey's Publishing, Kolkata, 2011), 23. From *Political Trouble in India (1907-19011)* by James Campbell Ker, Mahadeb Prasad Saha (eds.) (Editions India, Kolkata, 1973).
67. Ibid., 24.
68. A percussion instrument used for *kirtan* singing.
69. A mystic or saint.
70. For further details see Tanika Sarkar, Birth of a Goddess: 'Vande Mataram', Anandamath, and Hindu Nationhood, *Economic and Political Weekly*, Vol. 41, No. 37, (Sep 16-22, 2006).
71. As quoted by Pulak Chanda, 26.
72. Ibid., 14.
73. See Chap II.

74. Basudeb Chattopadhyay, vii.
75. Ibid., 6.
76. Ibid., 13.
77. Ibid., 18.
78. Ibid., 19-20. This epithet, for the purposes of the book, has been given to the popular and "Krishna", who is a prominent personage in the story.
79. Ibid., 24.
80. Pulak Chanda, 31.
81. Lieutenant Governor of the newly formed province of Eastern Bengal and Assam.
82. Basudeb Chattopadhyay, 33.
83. Ibid.
84. It needs to be mentioned here that he did not necessarily write all these songs himself, many of them were picked from other writers and compiled in his repertoire.
85. Note the use of English.
86. Pulak Chanda, 37.
87. Basudeb Chattopadhyay, 122. 88. Ibid., 123.
89. Dacca, Chittagong, Guwahati.
90. Temple of Goddess Kali.
91. Introduction; *Folk Theatre and the Raj: Selections from Confidential Records*, 125-126.

4

The Commune- ist Air—The Case of the IPTA Central Squad

4.1 The Coagulating Communities at the Beginning of the Twentieth Century—A Case of 'Rowing'

The House of Satan continued with its search for a *homo nationalis* through the early twentieth century. With time it became more assertive of an identity that it wished to establish. However, the collectives, the sociables, and the groups that were largely associated with its functioning had not changed much in terms of the configuration of such congregations. In urban spaces it continued to be spearheaded by a certain educated section of the society although an increased mass base of the anti-colonial movement as a whole, provided impetus to the performance of the working groups. While reforms remained the primary agenda in this age of associations, the primary search through most narratives remained a search for the common being. And mostly that was the national common being. It was more like throwing one's hand out in darkness not knowing what one wants—a substance-less-substance. 'Rowing' should we call it through the unknown? Is that how it can be most appropriately defined? An interesting take on such a quest of the substance-less-substance can be seen in the play by a performance collective that was formed in the Calcutta University around the Second World War. It was the Youth Cultural Institute (YCI). One play that it performed at the Ashutosh Hall in Calcutta was called 'Politicians take to Rowing' written by Jolie Kaul, a member of the YCI. She writes that what she aimed at was reaching out to a larger community given the hypocricy and confusion around the political situation of the time.[1] In this interesting take, a farce on a common being, a notice is sent to the Fuhrer from India, about a rowing challenge amongst four. The Fuhrer, Hitler has no idea about how to row. He discusses his problem with Benito Mussolini. They come to the conclusion that rowing is something practised by the 'decadent students of Oxford and Cambridge'. However he could not refuse the challenge because that would mean that his Aryan culture lacks something. So he calls upon Joseph Goebbels to order a truce with England because England knew rowing and they could teach the Germans. Goebbels was to take this message to Winston Churchill who was the Prime Minister of the United Kingdom at the time. However he had to explain to Churchill that it was because of the Jews that the Germans forgot rowing. Meanwhile, Goebbels practises the sport and all of them meet for the competition. Lord Linlithgow, the then Viceroy of India becomes the moderator. The representatives from India who come to the rowing competition are Chakravarti Rajagopalachari—a leader of the Indian National Congress in the Madras Presidency; Lord Linlithgow introduced him as 'He is the only member of the working committee who is working seriously for a compromise'; the next was Mahatma Gandhi who is introduced by Linlithgow as a saint-politician and that he has had 'several talks with him already in which we have both understood each other perfectly but not arrived at any settlement'; the next is Subhas Bose, 'the Congress President of the All India Forward Bloc; the next one is 'Mr Hindu Mahasabha Savarkar' and finally Jinnah whom Linlithgow introduces as the one 'who has devised a brilliant scheme to keep India under the British as a dominion'. However even before the competition could start, chaos begins when Adolph Hitler declares himself as the leader of his team. Churchill clearly has a problem with that. Mussolini takes Hitler's side but the debate remains unresolved. On the other hand, in the Indian side, while Rajagopalachari begins with a compromise, Subhas Bose says the essential thing was leadership and he would make the compromise if made the leader. Savarkar goes on to argue 'Our ancient munis and rishis could have won this race by pure spiritual power. We Hindus have no unity amongst ourselves; that is the cause of our downfall and we have actually gone and included a Muslim in our crew', while Jinnah argues for minority reservation and wants fifty percent Muslim representation in rowing. Although Linlithgow tries to intervene and says 'you must never agree together but you must have perfect unity amongst yourselves'. However the Indian representatives become quiet when Mahatma Gandhi threatens them with a hunger strike. The farce remains unresolved.[2] The author Jolie Kaul, an active woman member of the cultural movement of the Calcutta University leaves several questions open. That a sport could become the motivation for a union turned the entire political scenario into a ridiculous situation where no one had an idea about the purpose—neither the Indian side nor the European. The question of the purpose, the reason for why the fight, is ridiculed not only within the national context as it were but also the international one. This question continued to haunt the cultural movements of the time.

4.2 The Commune-ist Air

In this last section of the research project, we would look at a case-study, which is slightly different from the previous two studies in conjuncture. Here theatre is no longer only an external force or a tool for communication but rather here theatre itself evolves the possibility of being together not as such in everyday but by moulding the very nature of every day's being. Here the 'common', which from mere mimicking had evolved to the assertion of a political self, has now begun the exploration of a name-community. By a name-community, I mean to say a community that finds itself in language—a community with an identifiable meaning. A meaning that was being defined and further defined every time without having become an essence of utterance itself. In its attempt of consciously discovering, through performing life and theatre, it became political. This belief system of a possible new, in living as the common, not so much as ordinary, but as a system in itself that believes in a common goal of discovery, brought together the people of the Indian People's Theatre Association's Central Squad who formed a commune. This chapter is concerned with its form, which was explicitly 'commune-ist'. Commune-ist is in this context a certain lifestyle in a commune, which becomes a belief system, such that the suffix '-ist' has been added to the word commune. (Here it could be highlighted that the suffix '-ist' is often used to signify a certain adherent of a belief system, practice, ideology etc.) Before moving to a study of the Central Squad, I would like to lay down a theoretical framework such that our later study is facilitated and as the meaning of the term commune-ist unfolds, it stands distinctively against the word communist with which it has phonetical affinity.

4.3 Commune

The word 'commune' immediately emits several connotations. It suggests a community, the common or even communism. Its historical significance lies in the way the idea of the commune has been implemented with political intent. The commune has been seen as that which dissolves the nation-state but at the same time as lacking 'statist capacities'. Functionally, its ability to overturn, that which is normative, makes the idea of the commune appealing. However, this revolutionary character of the commune is only relevant in conjuncture, for example in case of the Paris Commune. So then, what exactly is a Commune? Is it when a group of people consciously, live together? Karl Marx explains otherwise. In *Grundrisse: Foundations of the Critique of Political Economy,* he asserts that forms of social life that may appear quintessentially irreparably divided and individuated are actually communal.[3] Hence for him, the process of a commune might not involve an *act* insofar as an *act* could be understood as an action consciously taken forward by an agent but rather he identifies the 'original' commune in the Asiatic, ancient, Germanic and Slavonic forms as pre-capitalist mode of living. He discusses it in terms of social relations of kinship/clan where it comes to exist as a result of 'the communality of blood, language, customs'. The commune comes to represent itself, subjectively, as a unity in which property rights reside.[4]

In this form of commune, according to him, surplus labour

performed, predominantly on communal land, is appropriated by the entire clan. This sort of a commune and related form of subsistence has often been called 'primitive communism'. On the other hand, talking about the Paris Commune, Marx talks about 'self-government'. 'It is the people acting for itself by itself' he says.[5] The Paris Commune that came into existence on May 28, 1871, following the defeat of France in the Franco-Prussian War is seen as, 'the reabsorption of the state power by society as its own living forces instead of as forces controlling and subduing it, by the popular masses themselves, forming their own force instead of the organized force of their suppression—the political form of their social emancipation... This form was simple like all great things.'[6] Although essentially the two forms of communes discussed here highlight 'communality' that is they share-in-common something, for example land, space etc., but at the same it emphasizes *being*-in-common,—a 'substanceless substance'.[7] This 'substance-less substance' has been the 'thing' of curiosity also for anti-colonial movements, when *being*-in-common required to be emphasized, as against difference or even beyond the common something[8]. Mahatma Gandhi in the context of the Indian anti-colonial struggle clarifies his position in this regard in the *Hind Swaraj*, which he himself translated into English as Indian Home-Rule, a small booklet written in 1909 in the form of a dialogue between two characters, The Reader and The Editor. When asked by The Reader what he has to say to the nation, Gandhi asks, 'Who is the Nation?' and subsequently answers 'it is only those Indians who are imbued with *real love*[9] who will be able to speak to the English... without being frightened, and only those can be said to be so imbued who conscientiously believe that Indian civilization is the best and that the European is a nine days' wonder.'[10] However, his nationalistic commentary on the Indian civilization is not limited to the idea of 'real love' for it alone; rather it is impregnated with the idea of *swaraj* or self-rule. *Swaraj* is not only political *swaraj* or self-government but also individual *swaraj* or self-mastery. Regarding the idea of village *swaraj* he writes: 'My idea of village *Swaraj* is that it is a complete republic, independent of its neighbours for its own vital wants, and yet interdependent for many others in which dependence is a necessity.'[11] It is an idea, which is similar to what Marx calls the 'original' commune. But associated with this idea explicitly in case of Gandhi is the idea of self-governance. To experiment with his method, Gandhi started seven *ashrams*, two in South Africa and five in India, in the beginning of the twentieth century that were spaces of self-governance for him. They were spaces of social emancipation as Marx claimed in case of the Paris Commune. About the ashram is written:

> With members drawn from many castes, classes, religions, occupations, regions, and languages, *ashrams* provided retreats to those who wished to join a community dedicated to a new form of life, a life of simple living, service, and political activism.[12]

He called such mode of life as *Satyagraha* or holding firmly to truth, where *satya* means truth and *agraha* means insistence or holding firmly. The followers of this path were called the *Satyagrahi*. During the independence movement of India these *ashrams* played an instrumental role in creating public opinion especially amongst masses. A *Satyagrahi* was in that sense a commune-ist who performed experiments with truth[13] in a rather self-disciplining manner.

4.4 Transforming a Thought-form to a Material one- I: Life in a Commune- the Case of IPTA CS

Coming back to the context of the commune in the light of the Indian People's Theatre Association's Central Squad (IPTA CS), we need to highlight that this space of the commune that functioned for a very short period of 4-5 years, was an act of performing out of a space where social relations were reinvigorated within the historical conjuncture of an anti-colonial movement. On the one hand, it was proclaimed as the 'Gandhian Ashram with pluses'[14] by the General Secretary of the CPI, Puran Chandra Joshi (P.C. Joshi) who had formed it as according to the already existing CPI commune, while on the other hand, it was criticized as the model of 'primitive communism' by Rajani Palme Dutt of the Communist Party of Great Britain.[15] This chapter highlights how the space of the Central Squad commune not only aimed at a 'communality' that was based on borrowed principles from the Communist

Party of India but also constantly responded to anti-colonial upsurge within the surroundings of which it functioned in creating and performing the '*being*-in-common'-ness and at the same time traversed the realm of the 'unavowable' to use Maurice Blanchot's term when it was finally disbanded by the CPI itself.

On June 1, 1943, the formation of the Indian People's Theatre Association or IPTA was declared at the first national conference of the Communist Party of India (CPI). But the Central Squad of the IPTA came into existence a little later when a group of performers of the IPTA Bengal Squad came to perform at Bombay to collect money for the Bengal famine in mid-1944. It was rather on the request of some of the members of the Communist Party of India and some performers from the Indian ballet dancer Uday Shankar's troupe, that the Central Squad was founded. According to P.C. Joshi, it was to achieve more 'professional expertise' in the cultural work for 'freedom' not only from the British but also from various societal norms within the wider panorama of world politics that the Central Squad was started. The men and women in the squad were mostly from student politics as was the case in most such efforts. Some members lived in the commune with their families. Such a commune had already been started by the CPI even before the IPTA CS came into existence. The CPI had its headquarters at Bombay which was also known as the PHQ or the Party Headquarters. It was set up for the party members at Raj Bhawan in Bombay, renting two floors following the direction of the party general secretary P.C. Joshi. N.K. Krishnan writes:

> On the first floor were the offices of the members of the Polit Bureau, P.C. Joshi, G. Adhikari and B.T. Ranadive, offices of the party secretarial staff and the typists' section as well as the editorial offices of the Party organ, People's War which was being published in the five languages, English, Hindi, Urdu, Marathi and Gujarati. On this floor was also housed the library and the press cuttings section. The second floor housed the common kitchen and dining hall, the common room for reading newspapers, lounging and gossiping, and residential rooms including a room each for four families, and last but not least the dark room of that talented photographer of the party, Sunil Janah.[16]

A second smaller building in Khetwadi Main Road in Bombay was set up where some party members were given accommodation. Between 1942- 47, sixty members were staying there speaking different languages, working tirelessly and with a great spirit of comradeship'[17]. After the formation of the IPTA Central Cultural Troupe or Squad, a similar commune in the 'Gandhian *ashram with pluses'* fashion as P.C. Joshi claimed, was set up at Andheri. According to Dina Gandhi, a member, the bungalow at Andheri 'surrounded by gardens' in Bombay in which the troupe lived and where the commune functioned was given[18] to the Central Squad by the uncle of Gul Bardhan who was a sympathizer of the party. 'As soon as you entered the premises, you were in a big field and adjoining that there was a lawn as well as a swing' writes Rekha Jain.[19]

Among the female members of the squad in the first year of its functioning were:

- The two sisters, Dina (Gandhi) Sanghvi who later became Dina Pathak (1922- 2002) and Shanta Gandhi (1917- 2002) from Gujarat and associated with the students' movement as also the cultural movement in Bombay; Shanta Gandhi was also at the Uday Shankar India Cultural Centre at Almora for sometime;[21]
- Gul (Zaveri) Bardhan (1928-2010) who was also a Gujarati, born and brought up in Bombay who later joined the student's movement there and was about to join Uday Shankar's Centre at Almora when it closed down;
- Reba (Roy) Roychoudhury (1925-) who was part of the student's movement as also of the Mahila Atma Raksha Samiti (MARS, a society started for the security of women in the wake of the Bengal Famine in 1942) at Rangpur (now in Bangladesh) and later joined the Bengal Squad. She was also the sister of Benoy Roy of the Central Troupe About her the first souvenir of the CS said 'She is an accomplished singer, but now does more of dancing';
- Preeti (Sarkar) Banerjee (1922-2014) who was a student activist at Rajshahi (now in Bangladesh) and later joined MARS there was also the cousin of Reba and Benoy Roy;

- Rekha Jain (1924-2010) was the wife of the party member Nemi Chandra Jain. She also was part of the Cultural Squad in Bengal;
- Leila Sayyad (- 1988), married to P. Sundarraiya who later came to be known as Leela Sundaraiyya was a bank accountant associated with the Congress and later Bombay Cultural Squad, Kisan Sabha[22] and the women's movement;
- Ruby (Gauri according to brochure) Dutt (1935[312]-) was the sister of the famous Kalpana Dutt of the Chittagong Armory Raid fame and sister-in-law of P.C. Joshi, later married to P.C. Joshi (Junior), the economist.
- Parvati Krishnan (1919-2014) who was a party member, Secretary of P.C. Joshi was the manager of the troupe who lived in the Party HQ with her husband, N.K. Krishnan and child.[23] She was also the announcer for their programmes and was especially well-known for her commentaries in English.
- Usha Dutt whose name was included in the first brochure of the programme of the IPTA CS but was later removed from CS.[24]

Among the male participants of the troupe were

- Shanti Kumar Bardhan was 'one of the dance tutors at Uday Shankar's Cultural Centre at Almora. Feeling that for dancing to be vital, it must go to the people, he joined the Indian People's Theatre Association in 1944 and became the Director of the newly formed Squad.'[25]
- Abani Das Gupta was 'a leading musician in Uday Shankar's Cultural Centre. He also joined the IPTA at the same time as Shanti Kumar and is the Music Director of the Squad'[26];
- Sachin Shankar 'is a cousin of Uday Shankar. He came to Bombay to join a film company, but on seeing the work of the Squad, he felt that his place was with them. He helps Shanti Kumar and also dances in many items;'[27]
- Benoy Roy 'from Bengal was a Trade Union worker who took to composing songs for the people on the struggle for liberation. He was a leader of the Bengal IPTA squad

that toured Punjab, Maharashtra and Gujarat and raised two lakh rupees for the People's Relief Committee. He now composes some of the songs and also sings and dances.'[28]

- Dashrathlal 'from Bihar was a Tramway worker and is a well-known figure in the Trade Union Movement in Calcutta. He was also a member of the Bengal Squad led by Benoy Roy. He now composes songs for the squad;' (ibid)
- Nagesh 'comes from Karnatak. For many years, a political worker in Bombay, he worked in the Bombay IPTA from the time of its formation. He does both dancing and singing'; (ibid)
- Appuni 'is a peasant boy from Malabar. He worked in the Kisan movement and joined the squad to serve those very kisans with whom he had worked'; (ibid)
- Prem Dhawan 'is from the Punjab where he has worked in the student movement. He has a deep knowledge of Punjab folk melodies and composes many of the Hindi songs that you will hear'; (ibid)
- Sushil Das Gupta 'is the brother of Abani and joined the squad very recently. He is one of the musicians'; (ibid)
- K.M. Reddy 'comes from Andhra. His love for music was aroused when he was studying at Shantiniketan. He intended to be a journalist, but decided finally that the best way to serve the people was by joining the IPTA and making use of his magnificent voice'; (ibid)
- The second souvenir of the CS has the addition of Ravi Shankar about whom the souvenir says 'One of the foremost of the younger musicians in our country today. He had his training under Ustad Allauddin Khan and was for many years with Uday Shankar's troupe. He joined the Central troupe in August last year (1945-2012[29]) and is now the music director of the troupe';
- The others whose names were not in the first souvenir were Nemichand Jain—'a young Hindi writer who joined the troupe recently and works with the music section and also composes songs';
- 'Narendra Sharma from the United Provinces, like Sachin,

has come to us from Almorah. He also assists Shanti Kumar in his work';

- 'Gangadharan is from Malabar and has had some years' training at the Kalamandalam started by the poet Vallathol. He is a recent addition to the troupe and belongs to the dance group';
- Hasan[30] 'comes from Gujarat. He is part of the dance group and is also responsible for stitching all costumes and curtains';
- 'Guniyal Javeri is from Gujarat and has been in the IPTA movement for the last two years';
- 'Bahadur Hussain is a nephew of Ustad Allauddin Khan. Plays sarod under training of Ravi Shankar';
- 'Noda Chand (or Nader Chand) is from Calcutta. Recently joined, plays several instruments';
- 'Vasu Deo Bhalaban, Marathi boy from Bombay recently joined music group';
- 'Debanshu Mukherjee, a student of Vishnudev Chaterjee from Calcutta. Recently joined the music section.'[31]

Many of the members lived with their families, for example Abani Das Gupta lived with his wife who was in charge of the kitchen of the commune and their daughter called Silu, Rekha Jain with her husband Nemi Jain and daughter Reshmi (who was later sent back, as it was being difficult for Rekha Jain to work with her being around[32]). When Ravi Shankar joined the troupe, he lived with his wife Annapurna, daughter of Ustad Allauddin Khan and son Shubho. The families had separate rooms for themselves, whereas the women stayed in one room and the men in other shared rooms.

At the commune, life was disciplined and focused mainly on the work of the troupe. Gul Bardhan writes in a memoir about her days in the IPTA:

> Our first class would begin at seven o'clock in the morning. We would exercise till nine o'clock and then break for one hour for breakfast and cleaning the house. From ten to one we would again practise till lunch break. In the afternoon from four o'clock, after tea, we learnt new movements and practised compositions. We would break for tea again at six for half an hour and then continue

> till nine or ten at night. In a sense our routine was fixed by the kitchen bell.[33]

Preeti Banerjee, another member notes that the ones who were in the music group would get up a little earlier for regular riyaz (rehearsal):

> ...the moonlight would still be there when I would wake up ...Reddy...Ravishankar... his wife (Annapurna)... Sushil would sit on the swing and do the riyaz of his flute.[34]

The members would often sit back, after the rehearsals were over at night, to help in the making of the costumes and other accessories necessary for the performances. Pictures of their activities in the commune such as costume making etc. were published in the magazine called People's Age which was the mouthpice of the CPI. It became necessary to render the private activities public in order to establish its significance as work for the nation. In one such newspaper report published in the People's Age on January 13, 1946, Balraj Sahni, a member of the IPTA wrote:

> Typical of the spirit of bold experiment which characterizes the IPTA are the costumes. As the curtain went up on the dress rehearsal I was struck by their glamour. The patterns are entirely new and the colours extraordinarily pleasing. It took Chittoprasad (the artist whom all readers of People's Age know quite well already) two months to design them. Incredible as it may sound these costumes are mostly made of gunny cloth...The IPTA has neither the means nor the desire to go to the blackmarket for silks.[35]

However according to Preeti Banerjee, not only gunny but also other materials were used.[36] After lunch during the break period women would help in kitchen work. Holidays were very rare during their stay at the commune and especially during the period when a 'show' was to be held soon, the performers would hardly get time to breathe. However, Gul Bardhan, writes:

> ...once in a while we would get a holiday and I would run to Bombay to see three films one after another in the four-anna section. And at twelve o'clock at night I would stealthily climb a tree and enter the bungalow. Abani[37]-da used to visit us around ten o'clock to see whether the whole group was in bed or not. So I used to arrange the bed beforehand in such a way that it looked

as if someone was sleeping in it... Other members would go and spend their five rupees (the monthly allowance was 40 rupees according to most of the members of which one had to pay for food separately) on a good meal.[38]

The rituals of every day were carefully choreographed in order to meet not only the needs of the performances but also to create national subjects as the nation was still being defined. The entire process was voluntary. The banalities of life gained significance in order to establish the significance of not only what was being done as having importance in national life but also to purge theatre and dance of the prejudices that were attached to them mainly within the middle class urban population. The details of every day were linked to ethical issues of social significance. The public discussion of such details aimed at collapsing the gap between the performer/activist/revolutionary and the masses. It was in the manner of the Gandhian ashram that life was being performed in order to create democratized spheres of public interaction especially against Colonial government.[39] Hence Rajani Palme Dutt's comment of a 'primitive commune' in this context seems to be quite contradictory.

Within the scope of this research, it would not be possible to discuss the several processes of the Central Squad which re-contextualised the everyday life of the Central Squad performers from mundane inconsequential activities to vital work, something worthwhile. However to highlight the transformation that was happening, I would like to quote from an interview of Preeti Banerjee. In an interview with Dhruv Gupta she notes:

Before this we had done different kind of work outside—we were not used to staying inside the house and practicing for hours. Joshi (the general secretary of the CPI) had told us then—now your true work is to play the *tanpura* (stringed musical instrument) and devote your time to *riyaz* and rehearsing your steps.'[40]

The *riyaz* or rehearsal was not only for a good 'show' but as P.C. Joshi said, for them it was also 'true work'—a work that would eventually lead them somewhere—they were not sure exactly where—but a place and time which would become as true as their work in their present. And this nostalgia for the truth—a future of their own gave them the impetus to deal with their difficult lifestyle 'inside', an 'inner domain'—which dislodged or rather subsumed any form of closure and opened up the space for a metamorphosis, transformation, innovation, reorganization, restructuring or revolution. However, at this point it should not be assumed that this is what exactly happened. On reading about the IPTA CS performances and the narratives of the CS, one finds how the re-contextualization transformed into textualization of those very narratives and performance modes that once held the potential of a revolution. Let us now look at the performances of the IPTA CS.

4.5 Transforming a Thought-form to a Material one- II: Performances of the IPTA CS

The Bengal Squad that came to perform in Bombay in mid-1944 had the sole purpose of socio-political good in mind. In fact, several cultural organizations had come to exist whose vision was a new culture for a new nation, India. Ali Sardar Jafri recalls the *Progressive Writers Association* (PWA) movement which took inspiration from 'Iqbal's tremendous line—*Uttho Meri Duniya ke Garibon ko jagado* (Arise and wake the poor of my world)', had a 'wide spectrum'—'Sajjad Zaheer was a Communist, Prem Chand was a Gandhian. But the common rallying point was the freedom movement'.[41] PWA was founded in November 1935 in London 'when after the disillusionment and disintegration of years of suffering in India and conscious of the destruction of most of our values through the capitalist crisis of 1931, a few of us emerged from the slough of despond of the cafes and garrets of Bloomsbury and formed the nucleus of the Indian Progressive Writers' Association'[42], although the first meeting was held in Lucknow, India, in April 1936. Writers in different parts of the world like in Paris, London, Brussels and Madrid, during this period were getting together to assert their view about fascism and war. In their 1935 meet at Paris were present Gorky, André Gide, Romain Rolland, EM Foster, and André Malraux among others. From this meet of the writers arose the need to form branches in different parts of the world. In 1936, in the second meet of the *International Writers' Congress,* Mulk Raj Anand was the representative from India.[43] Under similar circumstances was formed the Youth Cultural Institute in Calcutta. Initially some students of the Calcutta University, at the end of 1939, planned to organize a research group for research and popularizing various socio-economic and political problems of different countries. When this could not materialize, among the group, some students on their own accord wrote and staged dramas in English especially for performance before the members of the Calcutta University Rowing Club. Inspired by the popularity of their work they contemplated a permanent cultural movement on the lines of the PWA. PWA along with the YCI became the forerunner of the IPTA movement. The formation of the IPTA as has been mentioned earlier, was formally declared in the first All India Conference of the CPI after the ban on it by the colonial government was lifted as a result of the CPI's support to the Allied group whose part was Britain in the Second World War. European modernism, 'living newspaper' form of theatre of China which was anti-imperialist in nature, 'living newspaper' form used in America in support of Roosevelt's 'New Deal' programme influenced the formation of various cultural squads which believed that the 'richness' of the folk forms of India could do the same work of mobilization as 'living newspaper' theatre forms in China and America were doing and also strive for the new like European modernism. Such work of these cultural squads was being supported by the left in India in the early 1940's.[44] 1940s were also a period when the whole of Bengal Presidency was hit by one of the worst famines that the region had ever seen due to black-marketeering during the Second World War. The horror of death in the streets of Calcutta forced people to act demanding a right to live and a total retreat by the colonial government, which allowed this to happen. It became necessary to unveil the inhuman attitude of the colonial government which failed to treat its colonial subject at par with its subjects in England. Thus during this period, we find several cultural forms depicting the gruesome deaths in a way that made the horror look real. Sunil Janah's photographs of the corpses being sniffed and eaten by dogs, piled on the banks of ponds, lying in the fields brought this reality to the *people*, an instance of which one could experience at Wellington

Square in Calcutta. Sunil Munshi, a member of the CPI recalls[45] 'American and English soldiers did not dare to enter here' which 'was the limit' of their exploit. Zainul Abedin's, Somnath Hore's, and Chittaprasad's paintings similarly visually narrated the stories of death.[46] Rekha Jain recollects her experience during this period and how she joined the cultural movement in order to mobilize people and collect funds for famine relief:

> When in 1943 we reached there (Calcutta), the whole of Bengal was in the clasp of the famine. Beggars (who were essentially farmers) would come out from here and there, and their voices saying 'phen dao, mago phen dao' (give us some water in which rice has been boiled) would resonate from all directions. One in hunger would take one's last breath on the platform of the streets. A strange smell would float in the air making one anxious. The experiences that many have had with those who were famine stricken were even more heart rending. During this time when the intellectuals of the FSU (Friends of Soviet Union) would meet at the office, their main concern would be how to give some relief to the famine stricken. What programme could be adopted such that enough funds could be collected. I met a lot of writers, singers, actors to discuss this crisis... Benoy Roy (later to join IPTA Central Squad), Jyotirendra Moitra wrote many songs on this occasion and these songs were composed and a group was formed which would sing these songs of the famine. Nemi (Nemi Chandra Jain, husband of Rekha Jain) and I were included in this group. When this group would move across various localities singing these songs, I saw men and women would collect to listen to our songs in the streets, in the galleries of their houses and throw bundles of rice, pulses, money in our *jhola* (bags for money collection). It was during this time that some friends prepared a dance called 'Bhukha Bangal' (Hungry Bengal) and a play in Bengali called 'Jaban Bandi'. This dance and drama used to affect the audience so deeply that they would contribute very generously. A lot of money was collected. In view of the dreadfulness of the famine, this feeling was not enough, therefore from the experience of these performances it was decided that such performances should be organized even outside Calcutta, so that the people of other regions also have some impression of the destruction of the Bengal famine and thus money could be collected.[47]

It was in view of the success of 'Bhukha Bangal' and 'Jaban

Bandi' which was translated to Hindi and named 'Antim Abhilasha' (there are anecdotes which say these performances collected more than one lakh rupees only from Punjab during this time) and the performances of the Bengal Squad invited to Bombay in mid-1944 to collect money for famine relief[48] that P.C. Joshi, the general secretary of the CPI during this period, decided to initiate a cultural process that would mobilize political action of the masses. Sunil Munshi who was then a member of the All India Students' Federation, a students' wing of the CPI remembers:

> A meeting was called at the Red Flag hall[49], we went to the AISF (All India Student's Federation) working committee (meeting). In the AISF working committee Joshi told us, 'you all come in the evening, just come and watch what we are doing for you, you must learn from what you see and participate in this movement'. So we went to the Red Flag Hall. The team was getting ready at the Red Flag Hall, which later came to Bengal as the IPTA squad. He said what you could not do, they will. They will collect money, inspire people, they will involve them in anti-famine relief work. If you can do nothing more, do this much, which is to collect audience for them, so that they can perform well, that they can go everywhere—arrange for that. This is your duty for the Party. (S Munshi in interview with me)

P.C. Joshi mentions in a memoir of Balraj Sahni that although these performances had vigour and had opened up new horizons what they inevitably suffered from was 'amateurishness'. He writes about the IPTA :

> What made the IPTA really well-known then and famous later was their choir of patriotic songs from all the languages of India together with folk songs with a social content and moving tunes... We had deliberately adopted the policy of young Left intellectuals with cultural talent, to learn, perform and popularize the folk heritage of the various parts of our vast and ancient land...[50]

However as P.C. Joshi notes that it was to achieve 'professional expertise' in the 'work of the nation' that the Central Squad was founded. Hence not the content alone but the aim of the Central Squad, as was chalked down by the General Secretary P.C. Joshi lay in edging out the formal aspects of the performances. The congregation that created the IPTA Central

Squad hence comprised of many experts in dance, music etc., who did not necessarily agree with the ideological inclinations of the Communist Party but agreed to join the Central Squad on the grounds that the group had already acquired some name in its work for the nation and also substantially contributed to the anti-colonial movement. Shanti Bardhan, the choreographer of the Central Squad, who was already a trainer at the Uday Shankar India Cultural Centre, and Abani Dasgupta, a musician again from the Uday Shankar India Cultural Centre, who joined as the music director of the Central Squad and who was later joined by the ace *Sitarist* Ravi Shankar therefore became names associated with the IPTA Central Squad in order to give it the professional expertise it required. Here it needs to be mentioned that 'Uday Shankar India Cultural Centre' at Almora was opened by Uday Shankar, a ballet dancer himself, with the aim of creating a modern school for dance and music training. He had been immensely inspired by the idea of giving a national form to the performing arts of India. With the financial support of some friends, independent sponsors[51] and the money he collected from performances world over, he founded the 'Uday Shankar India Cultural Centre' at Almora, which started functioning from March 3, 1940, modelled on the Dartington Hall in England. Uday Shankar appointed stalwarts of the dance forms like Kathakali, Bharata Natyam, Manipuri and also of music in his centre. Rabindranath Tagore was striving to do the same in Shantiniketan and Rukmini Devi Arundale was reviving Bharata Natyam at Kalakshetra that she founded in 1936. According to Sudhi Pradhan, Uday Shankar's work was also informed in the 1940s by the 'floating news' of 'his Bengal's[52] dying people'. He collected money for the Bengal Famine through his performances at Delhi. Influenced by the socialist maxim that had given rise to socialist realism in Russia and other modernist cultural movements in Europe like German Expressionism (the influence of which becomes apparent in Shankar's film *Kalpana),* whose experiences he had gathered during the extensive tours in Europe, he had earlier created the ballet 'Labour and machinery'. In Delhi in one of his performances through a symbolic use of the sickle he tried to portray that the socio-economic problem in India was essentially that linked to the peasant and farmers. 'Janajuddho' the mouthpiece of the CPI on November 23, 1943 reports:

> ...the world famous dancer Uday Shankar is going to Bombay along with his troupe. His manager has informed the leadership of Bombay IPTA that he is going to present his dance in front of the working class with nominal charges of tickets. Most of the money collected from the ticket sale will be given to the IPTA—the IPTA will spend this money on the victims of the Bengal famine... We hope that the efforts of a world class artist like Uday Shankar would inspire other artists.

Such presentations also brought him criticisms such as—Uday Shankar has left 'throne of the pure golden art' and has become a socio-political 'propagandist'.[53] However, when due to lack of funds the Almora centre had to be shut down, Shanti Bardhan, Abani Dasgupta and many others joined the IPTA Central Squad and it could also be argued that they brought along the aesthetics of the ballet form that Uday Shankar had by now mastered.

4.6 'Spirit of India'

IPTA's rationale could be identified by its most invigorating slogan 'People's theatre stars the People'. This slogan in its humanistic passion created the new social icon of the national 'people'. Typical to any performative ritual, the first performance of the first season of the IPTA CS started with the 'Call of the Drum'.

The souvenir for this performance claims it to be and I quote– 'Dance of Invocation for the Youth of India, rousing them to patriotism'. This was followed by the song composed by Ravi Shankar 'sare jahan se achha'- a 'people' better than any other 'people' as it were; 'hum bulbulein hain us ki, woh gulsitah humara' or we are its nightingales and it is our garden abode. The claim to difference lay in the very beginning of proclaiming the *being*-in-common within the abode or home. The difference was not only claimed by declaring it, but also establishing it – a process of exclusion/inclusion inherent to the ideology of nationalism. 'She died of hunger' – a solo dance in classical style portraying the sorrow of a peasant of Bengal who arrives home to find that his wife and companion has died of hunger acts as

Call of the Drum: 'Shanti as the nation's drummer: Sachin and Dina portray rallying of the nation's youth' (*People's War*, Jan 21, 1945)

a newspaper report of the events that were taking place in Bengal. The Bengal famine of the early 1940's was known to be a man-made famine whereby more than six million people died only in Bengal. The exploitation of the people by the British was one of the key elements to affirm difference and declare the British rule as illegitimate. *Being*-in-common was performed in tabloid form depicting the various forms of cultural life of the different folks of India. According to Sunil Munshi who was among the audience at some of the performances of the IPTA Central Squad, the performances were a collection of items one after the other, not necessarily interlinked by any logic of narration.[54] The aesthetic of these tabloids were borrowed from the picture tabloids, which were published in the magazine of the Communist Party of India regularly.

These picture tabloids highlighted the lives of 'working class', 'peasants' and 'real people' of India. Thus based on an originary principle of the idea of a nation a collection of performances of communities which borrowing from Etienne Balibar one could call 'primary' were presented.[55] 'Lambardi Dance'—A simple folk dance of the Lambardis, a gypsy tribe living in Hyderabad State, 'Dhobi Dance'—A folk dance commonly seen among the Dhobis of Andhra, 'Collective Farmers' Harvest Dance'—This incorporates folk dances and music of more than one province of the Punjab, of Bengal, of Andhra and of the UP, 'Ramleela'— 'The troupe present a scene from the story of Ramchandra in a folk form very commonly seen in the UP villages, of the first season and 'Sentry Dance'—The guards in the Frontier Provinces as they dance together at night in peace time. 'Gajan'—folk dance of Bengal in which Shiva and Parvati, with their followers compete in dancing, 'Khadaun'— A classical form of dancing with intricate foot-work, with wooden sandals and 'Chaturanga' of the Northeast and Bengal, 'Holi'—A glimpse of the colour festival in UP... of the second season, were incorporated as ethnographic tabloids. The aim was to create a singular narrative interweaving 'communities of location' or networks of relationship formed by face to face interaction within geographically bounded area to 'communities of interest' or networks of association that are predominantly characterized by their commitment to a common interest. In this case an interest of identifying a nation in the *communality* or sharing-in-common of diversity that in turn created that 'substanceless substance' of *being*-in-common.

'The Lambadi– a tribal folk dance'
(*People's War*, Jan 21, 1945)

'Ramleela as performed in the UP villages' (Ibid)

Gandhi-Jinnah phir miley: 'Gandhi-Jinnah meeting – the full story in ballet' (Ibid)

'Chathurang: Classical Dance of Tippera (Bengal). A form now dying out, but being revived by the troupe' (*People's Age*, Jan 6, 1946)

'Gajan: A folk dance of rural Bengal, with a ballad relating the story of Shiva and Parvati. A moment during the competition between Shiva and Parvati, with Shiva depicting the mood of 'terror'' (Ibid)

'Holi: The popular harvest dance in the villages of the United Provinces' (Ibid)

4.7 'India Immortal'

From 1945 onwards IPTA CS came to be known as the Central Cultural Troupe. Now a Squad can be understood as a crew, squadron or cadre (a term made famous by communist use) that performs a function, and brings a certain action to its completion whereas a troupe is one that is a band, an ensemble, that performs, but that performance is not guided by any function that it consciously carries forward. By the beginning of the second season of the CS performances, the activistic fervour had been eclipsed by a need '(to give) fillip to creative activity'[56], although it continued to maintain its *historical* tour of the new 'people' even in its second season. Both the ballets, *'Spirit of India'* which the souvenir records 'is a ballet based on the story of India since the advent of the British' of the first season and *'India Immortal'*—'gives a picture of India from the earliest times to the present days touching momentous events that form the landmarks in the cultural history of India' were demonstrations of—a journey towards a 'people' *to be*, from a 'people' *that has been*. IPTA CS performances exemplified a federation of *people(s)* whose icon or 'star' is the 'people' itself, meaning that the supreme power of representing lies in the hands of this 'people' that it stars.

'India Immortal: Ballet depicting the story of our country and our people from early times to the present days, the background of our rich cultural heritage and the growing unity of our people to end foreign rule' (*People's Age*, Jan 6, 1946)

But compared to the first season of its performances, in the second season this 'people' does not remain a common 'man' anymore but becomes the 'artist' who invokes not 'man' but a higher power in order to craft the 'people' using his artistry through 'intricate' work. But in both cases, the objective is naturalized by a historical logic of a 'spirit' of India and then a more self-determined 'immortal' India that imbibed its determination from a 'glorious' historical past.

> *Aj shonabo ki kahini srihina bharatbhumir*
> *Sampode shourjey chhilo jar sreshtho ashon dhoronir*
> *Shatto nyayer deep jalilo buddho namey raj tonoy*
> *Kabir hetha hindu muslim Milan-bani bilay*
> *Raja Ashok badshah Akbarer raj ki hoe smaran*
> *Shanti shukh o nyay dharmey sharthak proja palon.* (Spirit of India)[57]
>
> (What story would I tell you about the once beautiful land of Bharat (India)/Wealth and valour had made it the best in the world/Buddha lit the candle of truth and justice/Kabir spread the word of Hindu-Muslim unity/Does one remember the rule of Raja Ashoka and Badshah Akbar/The rule over the subjects was based on peace, happiness and the *dharma* of justice)

This tendency of giving form to the 'substance-less substance' in the name of a spirit or an inner being of a certain locatable people on the basis not only of 'real love' as Gandhi would have it but also on the basis of creation of difference, a dual creative process of not any dialectical movement but rather an obsession with an almost photographic tabloid-like form, shifted the concerns of the IPTA CS commune. Many members not only of the CS but also of the CPI went through a phase of doubt about the role of such a commune.[58] This phase of doubt could be somewhat identified from the ballets of the two seasons. The narrative of *The Spirit of India* of the first season was borrowed from the earlier famine plays like 'Nabanna' (New Harvest) and 'Antim Abhilasha/Jaban Bandi' (Last Wish). In that sense it was more of a narrative that was still under the effect of a historical reflex that motivates the other famine narratives. But at the same time, this performance of the CS was one of the first few performances that hints at a glorious 'past' of a united India but even then that 'past' remains limited to 'tales of heroism' alone, rather than the representation of any pre-existent cultural monumentality. The narrative ends leaving the possibility of an act to change the existent modalities of 'being'. Apart from the famine narrative that the IPTA had been using successfully in mobilizing relief funds as well as anti-colonial sentiments, the performances in this season included *They Must Meet Again* whose theme was directly taken from the CPI's agenda of 'sovereign national constituencies' elected by universal suffrage on the basis of linguistic regions (modeled on the Russian Leninist model of mini-nationalities) and electing in their turn an all-India Constituent Assembly, with each region or 'nationality' retaining a right to secession.[59] The narrative of a singular history in *The Spirit of India* at the wake of a demand of 'sovereign national constituencies' hence becomes a representation of the agenda of CPI, as it was at this point that CPI also demanded for such 'constituencies', which in turn would elect 'an all-India Constituent Assembly'. With these performances when the IPTA CS had gained much popularity, Ravi Shankar and many others of Uday Shankar's Almora Troupe joined the group. During this phase, the second season ballet of the CS was produced which was called *Immortal India*. It 'gives a picture of India from the earliest times to the present days touching momentous events that form landmarks in the cultural history of India. It starts from early worship of the Himalayas and passes through past impacts of culture to modern times.' The obsession with a national culture increases in the performances of the second season of the CS giving it a monumentality that it did not have earlier. Both Ravi Shankar, the director of music in this season, and Shanti Bardhan the director of dance in the season mention 'our rich cultural heritage, handed down from generation to generation'[60] in the notes written for the brochure by them. In this ballet, a worker dreams of 'puja' and 'invocation dance' in the Himalayas, rivers-land-harvest, Buddhists-Muslims-Chaitanyas—'all our people flourish together'. A magician charms this *people* with his magic flute. 'Traitor plans against the Nawab with the Magician—Nawab is overthrown and the crown given to traitor—traitor and magician together rob the people... Individual revolts of the people against this oppression are suppressed by the magician—the people rise once again in an attempt to revive their own culture.' The ballet ends with the black marketeers and hoarders 'devour(ing) the food and cloth themselves and dance(ing) in frenzy—the dream (of the worker) is shattered—one woman with a child in her arms rises alone questioning whether life will always be dark... but the answer is heard that the people will unite, will rise and will fight to be free.'[61] Thus a singular narrative driven by the existence of a 'national culture' and shared experience of exploitation, by the foreign 'magician' runs along the linear thread of fictional/real accounts.

4.8 Communism in India and the Commune-ist Air

At this point, it is necessary to note that the Communist Party of India was in the beginning known to be a foreign conspiracy organized by Moscow.[62] The founder of the Communist Party in India, Naren Bhatacharji (alias Manabendra Nath Roy or M.N. Roy) had come in contact with the Bolshevik Mikhail Borodin when he was in Mexico in 1919 and was helping to found the Communist Party in Mexico! In 1920, in the Second Congress of the Communist International (Comintern) he met Lenin and got into a controversy regarding the role of the Communists in the Colonial World. According to Lenin, 'the colonial bourgeoisie competed with the imperialist bourgeois class in terms of control over the colonial market, control over resources and liberalization of the legal and juridical context for the economic activity of imperialist interests. As the indigenous bourgeoisie could not escape these conditions of its economic existence, it was likely, thought Lenin, that political organizations which would represent their interests would periodically press for an intensification of nationalist struggle; but once concessions were extracted, put brakes on militancy. Dualism, therefore, meant a patterned behaviour, which was not contradictory in the sense of being merely disorderly or without a rational design. It indicated a deliberate strategic oscillation between a politics of confrontation and politics of compromise.[63]... (M.N.) Roy's understanding of dualism was wholly different. For him, it meant an application of the model that Marx had applied to the European bourgeois classes. The historical career of the bourgeoisie will show a progressive phase, though marred by compromises; but it will eventually arrive at a final political crisis in which the bourgeoisie would betray the national movement. Dualism simply referred to the existence of these two stages in the political biography of the bourgeois class. Nevertheless, despite certain differences with Lenin, the Comintern admitted Roy's intellectual eminence and he was entrusted with the leadership of the communist movement in India.'[64] In October 1920, M.N. Roy, Abani Mukherji and some *muhajirs* (Khilafat enthusiasts who later had crossed over through Afghanistan into Soviet territory) like Mohammad Ali and Mohammad Shafiq founded a Communist Party of India in Tashkent! Its headquarters was shifted to Berlin in 1922 when hopes of penetrating India had faded. There the fortnightly *Vanguard of Indian Independence* and *India in Transition* (in collaboration with Abani Mukherji) were published. Several other groups during this period were turning to Marxism like the old Berlin group headed by Virendranath Chattopadhyay, Bhupendranath Dutt and Barkatullah who founded the India Independence Party in Berlin. Under Rattan Singh, Santokh Singh and Teja Singh Swatantra, a section of the Ghadr movement who were in exile also turned to Communism. A large section who had become disillusioned by the Non-Cooperation movement[65] and Khilafat movement[66] like S.A. Dange in Bombay, Muzaffar Ahmad in Calcutta, Singaravelu in Madras, and Ghulam Hussain in Lahore had started to give shape to communist groups. By the end of 1922, through emissaries like Nalini Gupta, Shaukat Usmani and M.N. Roy started to establish secret links with these groups.[67] However soon Lenin's view of *contextuality* as raison d'être of nationalities whereby 'self-determination'[68] of such nationalities become an obvious imperative for the very existence of such nationalities directed the fate of the communist movement in colonial India. With the popularity and acceptance of Lenin's method which resulted in the dissolution of the Comintern in 1943 as also localization of dialectic as against Marxian universal of class struggle, P.C. Joshi, the General Secretary of the Communist Party of India argued in the party organ *National Front* in April 1939 that the 'greatest class struggle today is our national struggle' of which Indian National Congress was the 'main organ'.[69] Therefore, communist movement in India remained national in character. However between 1942-1945 the CPI received a serious setback as a popular political movement as a result of the continuous tension that it faced due to the contradictions of nationalism's localized logic and communism's universal dialectic. While British policies during this period of war remained extremely repressive and reactionary, Britain also happened to be an ally of the socialist state Soviet Russia, when Hitler invaded Russia. After a lot of hesitation, in January 1942 the CPI lined up with the international communist movement calling for support to the anti-fascist 'people's war' 'even while reiterating the standard Congress demands for independence and immediate national government. But such a dual position of both support of war, whose effects were directly making an impression in India in terms of socio-economic consequences, and also, antagonism towards the colonial rule of the same British government, no more remained a precondition for support to the national movement. On the one hand it helped lift the ban on the party, making it easy for the party to work and on the other hand, made the party extremely unpopular. The performances of the IPTA CS and the call for 'unity' in order to form a national community on the grounds of the existence of a singular linear past in the post-war situation was a strategy also to win back the people it had lost during the war years. Preeti Banerjee remembers:

> In 1942 the party made a huge mistake—during the movement (Quit India[70]), our cultural movement could break that isolation... the isolation due to the position on 'people's war' could be overcome because of our cultural effort.[71]

Thus through a coalition of histories the CS created a performance of paradox whereby on the one hand it upheld the liberal democratic rhetoric of nationalism through the use of linear narratives and on the other hand highlighted issues that were thought to be in alignment with the Marxist universal logic of a classless society. The huge success of the IPTA CS performances of the first two seasons was not merely due to its complete potential to represent a national culture that the national bourgeoisie aimed for, or due to the sincere socio-economic issues that these performances often talked about in concurrence with the CPI's often chaotic agendas, but more fundamentally it was a result of a *communitas* that it created for itself. By *communitas* is meant 'a direct, immediate and total confrontation of human identities'[72] whereby it (the *communitas)* allows performance to 'play' with the audience's fundamental beliefs, without producing immediate rejection. For it is 'the ludic nature of the audience's role that allows it to engage with ideological difference, that allows rules to be broken (via authenticating conventions) while rules are kept (via rhetorical conventions). This paradox links theatrical performance to carnival and other forms of public celebration...'[73] The IPTA CS performances thus became unique in their successful juggling with different 'identities' and 'ideologies'. P.C. Joshi writes:

> The Central Troupe of the IPTA was just coming into its own not only politically, professionally and organizationally, but also earning a reputation for attempting something unique and distinctive in our cultural life. It is then, during the end of 1947, that a sectarian offensive inspired by the incorrigibly Left comrade Ranadive was put into operation through the good-hearted but narrow-minded treasurer, Ghate. As the treasurer, he complained that too much of the central funds were being wasted in cultural work by subsidizing the IPTA troupe while its earnings were nominal.[74]

Gul Bardhan remembers this period:

> In 1946 we did an all-India tour and went to Lahore with *India Immortal...* The left in the party felt that the Central Squad was a white elephant. 'So much money is spent and they won't even work for Party propaganda (apparently they were asked to do a performance on the two nation theory, which was not even the CPI's agenda, but what is possible is that they were asked to do a performance on 'sovereign constituent nationalities' as against a federal system that the Congress had proposed)... So, after a very successful all-India tour with *India Immortal,* the Party disbanded the Central Squad. During our tour we received a lot of appreciation everywhere we went and because of our work a large number of intellectuals and artists came closer to the Party and many became Party supporters. But the Party did not realize that. When we returned to Bombay, we were told that it had been decided to disband the Central Squad. Naturally the sword first fell on Shanti Bardhan and four others who were not party members. They had to leave. There was no debate or discussion.

> So Shanti-da, Ravi Shankar, Abani-da, Sachin and Narendra Sharma left together. All the members of the Central Squad felt very sad and sorry about the whole thing. We felt that this was absolutely wrong but we were too young to speak against the leadership.[75]

One of the reasons for the party's high-handedness regarding this issue was its newly found self-confidence. After the war years, especially after the victory of Soviet Russia over the fascist powers, CPI could move on from its 'people's war' line to more populist regional agendas in order to recover from the damage that their party line had caused them in terms of popularity during the war years. They pioneered the Kisan Sabha movement, trade union activities, in providing leadership to the Telengana[76] movement in Hyderabad, Tebhaga[77] Movement in Bengal, movements in Kerala etc., which ultimately resulted in their emerging as 'the principal contenders of the Congress in several provinces' in the election of 1946.[78] But at the same time, continuous attacks on the communists with regard to their earlier anti-Quit India movement and 'people's war' positions, bitterness resulting from the trials of the Indian National Army (INA) war prisoners (who under the leadership of Subhash Chandra Bose asked for the help of Japan, an ally of Germany in liberating India), and condemnation of their violent actions against the government by the Congress and mainly by Gandhi, often created isolations (in spite of their position of a Congress, Muslim League and Communist united leadership against the imperial forces). It resulted in a ghetto-like mentality amongst many of the CPI members and this also created the need to shield itself more sternly even in their involvement with the CS as they dictated the terms with frequent 'do this, edit that'[79] vigilance.

After the IPTA CS was disbanded, Shanti Bardhan, Ravi Shankar, Sachin Shankar and Narendra Sharma joined the 'Indian National Theatre' of the Congress where they produced *Discovery of India* conceptualized by Jawaharlal Nehru. The rest of the troupe continued with their work at Andheri and produced a third season of performances in 1946-47. Preeti Banerjee recalls:

> I have forgotten the names of the items, actually these are

> memories of long ago (the interview was taken in 2010), although I remember the names of the ones that we performed earlier – those of 45- 46... the songs would be composed by Benoy-da (Benoy Roy), others would add folk tunes of different regions—Dashrathlal would add folk tunes of Bihar, Prem (Dhawan) those of Punjab. Benoy-da would write the songs and the Hindi ones would be written by Prem... These were not performed for many days though.[80]

The third season of the performances was more propagandist in nature. The two main ballets of this season *Naval Mutiny* and *Kashmir* were directly conceptualized from the party's position on the Royal Indian Navy (RIN) mutiny in Bombay on 18-23 February 1946 and its agenda of forming 'sovereign constituent assemblies'. In her interview with Dhruvo Gupta taken in 1988 she recollects:

> ...we had prepared a ballet on the RIN mutiny in Bombay. We would begin with the song *Jana Gana Mana* (this became the national anthem of India after Independence). The British Government had banned all the items of this season including *Jana Gana Mana*. The song 'Vande Mataram' would be allowed. We would secretly perform the ballets by changing their names. Nobody would rent us auditoriums... we made our own stage within the compounds of the house at Andheri, where we would perform the ballets. We would invite the Navy personnel.

Reba Roychoudhury[81] mentions some other items they performed in this season like 'Gandhi-Jinnah Phir Miley' on the talks between Gandhi and the Muslim League leader Jinnah on the issue of separate nation state formations and 'New Village' where a village woman kills an exploitative feudal lord and 'Collective farm'. The use of communist propaganda became apparent not only in the contents used during this period but also in the apparent use of communist symbols. For example, in the ballet called 'New Village', one of the songs explicitly refers to the red symbol.

> *... Hindu Muslim bhed mitaiboi shob mil korboi kamoa*
> *Beet gayi hai sab durdinwa*
> *Ek shonge jiiboi ek shonge morboii*
> *Chahe jae poranwa*
> *Kisan Sabha ke baat manbei kor bai shob kahanwa*

> *Hum uraibei lal nishanwa*[82]
>
> (...we shall destroy the clash between the Hindu Muslims, together we shall diminish it/The bad days are gone/We shall live and die together/Let our lives leave us/We shall listen to Kisan Sabha and do as has been said/We will fly the *Red symbol)*

Although for some time the CPI financially supported their work, within a year of disbanding the CS, the remaining members were asked to go back to their own regions and 'use whatever you have learnt' (Reba Roychoudhury talking about what P.C. Joshi had told them) in their work at the regional IPTAs.

4.9 Freedom and the Question of a National Theatre: Are They Contradictory?

IPTA CS had lost its earlier vigour in its third season of performances as the day of liberation of India from the rule of the British government approached nearer. When Dhruvo Gupta asked Preeti Banerjee the reason behind this she replied:

> ...I think it was not the failure of the IPTA alone—rather our failure in everything—the private ego had become more important than the collective, the fall within the group, one should see it adding to all of these.

According to Shanta Gandhi—

> ...the entire IPTA period movement was basically based on humanism, a humanism of a very left orientation. Marxism had played a very leading role. People connected with the Communist Party that had been the driving force in this and it was through these people that the movement was linked up with the people's movements like Kisan movement, Trade union movement, students' movement, women's movement... there was no difference of goal in getting the British out...This was not possible after Independence...[83]

When the independence of the Indian sub-continent happened —in a 'tryst with destiny', and it finally became free on August 15, 1947 from the clasp of the imperial rule which set the ball of a 'federal democratic republic' rolling into the court of the subcontinent. Although it existed earlier but now it experienced *freedom* in its free corporeal existence or in the form of a 'free people', as if the desire of a *being*-in-common got articulated. However insofar as this articulation is an experience, which is sense, data, cognition and also feelings and expectations that come to us verbally as also in images and impressions whereby they refer to an active self—to a human being who not only engages in but also shapes an action[84]—the experience is personal. But in case of something like the freedom of a 'people', this experience is both shared, as through the idea of one 'people' and at the same time through an individual. It is both within and without. For the individual who is consciously a constituent member of the one idea 'people', the shared experience becomes a necessary social precedence to remain within the community of the 'people'. In society, the experience of freedom however, is essentially linked to the empirical existence of signs of freedom in the form of social liberties—as identifiable categories. For a 'people' who were once colonized, therefore freedom is liberation from the colonizer followed by subsequent social liberties—which are fundamental expectations of these free 'people'. Therefore freedom in itself when understood as a shared experience of national freedom is not a revolutionary idea but rather a developmental idea where freedom comes through socio-economic developments. In the wake of August 15, 1947, the 'people' of India had similar expectations. Although it was aware of the existing socio-economic disparities, at the same time, the fact that imperial rule was over which was an empirical truth, the expectation that it was thereby *free* now onwards thrilled the entire population as Jawaharlal Nehru the first Prime Minister of the country declared—'At the stroke of midnight hour, when the world sleeps, India will awake to *life and freedom.*' For the IPTA, which had till now created for its audience a *national culture* that acted as a cohesive agent, the sudden slogan of 'yeh azadi jhoota hai' (this freedom is a lie) under the aegis of the CPI was a betrayal insofar as freedom was visible in terms of empirical evidence. The IPTA thus not only lost its popularity amongst its own audience. Ultimately once the CPI realized that the CS of the IPTA had acted as the voice of the same 'people' it (CS) aimed to create—which was a 'one people' of India which had identified itself as the withdrawal of imperial power happened from the centre of governance, the CPI called CS off and asked its members to go back to their own regions. Possibly the CPI expected the audience of the CS to be with it till a free India, in the communist sense was achieved. It is not surprising that only a few months later in March 1948, the CPI was banned by the *free people*'s government. The members of the CS disillusioned by the entire episode and disintegrated themselves from the commune to go into various modes of living. Dina Pathak when asked about the link of the IPTA with the Communist Party said:

> I would say only this much that the forces which were linked to life, their activities for life, IPTA's association with them was in those activities... Our anti-British feeling gave a revolutionary touch to our work.[85]

For Dina Pathak, who had promised her father that in Bombay she would not join any political party, work for 'life' was possible through participation in the IPTA movement. The 'revolutionary touch' that she talks about was the thought of *freedom* when freedom itself did not get defined as an empirical existence but was believed to be possible once the British left. Shanta Gandhi remembers:

> ...a vital element of this movement and because there was no difference of goal (with the Communists) in getting the British out, people of all shades, of all liberal thoughts, all combined and joined hands in this.[86]

Therefore, the IPTA's principal aim was *freedom* that was believed could be achieved by the removal of the British by an equal sharing of this responsibility in the path towards *freedom*. Thus one could say *freedom* was conceived of as emancipatory for all. If freedom was emancipatory for all then why did the IPTA fail to rejoice in the freedom it achieved—a freedom it had aimed for? Is Communist freedom separate from the freedom of a 'federal democratic republic'? Is proletarian freedom different from the 'people's' freedom? These questions arise when one tries to understand the failure of the IPTA after 'freedom' was achieved from the colonial power. Preeti Banerjee thinks:

> ...all sections have to be covered. Can anything be achieved only

> with rigid politics? Nothing exists like that.' See what CPM (Communist Party of India Marxist which started to fall in West Bengal after a continuous rule of three decades under which the IPTA West Bengal functioned after it came to power) has done. Is IPTA functional anymore? They don't know how to call everyone.[87]

Preeti Banerjee raises the question of *freedom for all*—an equal freedom or a *freedom shared equally* by all. For the post- colonial people, the word 'freedom' remains meaningful as long as it is opposed to 'subjugation' or the word 'colonial'. It is purely a political category whereby freedom is understood by the exchange of power from the foreign inhabitants to the native inhabitants. But nevertheless, the philosophical freedom leaves its 'trace' in that thought as 'a certain un-constrained-ness, or a certain *liberality*, the principal characteristic of which is an ability to make everything possible.'[88] For the Marxist, freedom is the recognition of necessity—the subjugation of freedom to necessity—insofar as necessity predestines existence—'We are condemned to be free'; Sartre arrived at this idea from the unique fact that 'subjectivity—which names the substantial self that is supposed to have the power to support itself and to secure its identity—cannot keep itself afloat. The floundering of subjectivity does not mean that human beings, as weak and poorly equipped vessels, are not strong enough to actualize what they desire. With such a conception of human fragility, Sartre arrived at the formula...' But this very formula has its genealogy in the Hegelian conception of *dialectic* whereby any present state of affairs is in the process of being negated, changed into something else. For Marx, the agent of this change is the proletariat class. This man-nature dialectic and the attainment of the 'new' every time is what Sartre calls condemnation to freedom. Therefore, in Marxism *freedom* can never be achieved but is itself a process that holds in it the 'trace' of a philosophy of freedom—which is all possibility. Here lies the contradiction between the conception of *freedom* for the colonized subject for whom freedom is an achievement and the communist subject for whom it's an ongoing process. Thus IPTA CS's failure lay in the contradictions on which it was built, and this same contradiction led the members of the IPTA towards two distinct paths post-independence although both carried the 'trace'.

Aware of the developmental possibilities in *free* India, Shanta Gandhi declares, '...it would have been better if this movement born in a much more organized way served as a closer link or with an organizational link with the Akademis when they came into existence...' (in interview with Pratibha Agarwal). Aparna Dharwarkar in her book on theatre in post-independence India notes, 'With the reoriented cultural politics of the first decade of independence as a backdrop, the Sangeet Natak Akademi's 1956 drama seminar marks a symbolic end to the theatre movement of the 1940s...'[89] In this seminar the need to disassociate theatre from a specific political programme was felt along with rethinking it comprehensively in relation to the remote and proximate past. Among the participants of this seminar were the erstwhile members of the IPTA like Shombhu Mitra, Dina Pathak, and Nemi Chandra Jain among others. 'Some of the seminar's most vocal and influential spokesmen, Mulk Raj Anand, and the actor Balraj Sahni (both associated with the PWA and the IPTA respectively)... argue(d) that colonial and late-colonial theatre institutions are no longer usable and they anticipate a future theatre radically unrelated to its colonial past.' The developmental projects in the post-independence India continued, as a concrete cultural policy was being formulated in the years after 1947. National School of Drama (NSD) was set up by the Sangeet Natak Akademi in 1959 as one of its constituent units. While some of the members joined hands with the Congress government in post-independent India, others joined the regional branches of the IPTA. Reba Roychoudhury who remained associated with the CPI and the IPTA, in an interview with Khaled Choudhury remembers that after returning from Bombay in February 1947 along with Benoy Roy and Preeti Banerjee, she joined 'the party' as a 'whole timer'. She recalls:

> It was decided that I have to teach the dances of the central ballet troupe (CS). I started teaching *Ramlila, Holi, Kashmir, Lambardi,* and *Call of the Drum* with a lot of enthusiasm... Simultaneously the rehearsals for *Shahider dak* went on. Benoy became the secretary. We started preparing for travelling all over East Bengal, North Bengal and Assam'. After Independence, 'The line of

> Indian People's Theatre Association, changed. In a general body meeting Hemango Biswas[90] said that till now we were trying to grow our paddy plants but now we have to sow the seeds.[90]

For all these performers of the CS, the experience of life had changed after the political independence of India. For some, it was a path that followed from the achievement of freedom of the nation; for some others this freedom remained 'a lie' and they fought back in the name of the 'party'. But when both 'life and freedom' are seen as opposed to colonial repression as is evident in Nehru's speech, they become significant as against 'struggle and subjugation' within that same colonial context. So there can be a 'struggle for freedom' within that context but can the same be possible after attainment of independence? Is 'life' in the *free* state a struggle or growth? If utopia is understood as 'a new earth and a people that does not yet exist'[91] then the 'struggle for freedom' can be understood as the struggle for that utopia—*for a people yet to be and a land yet to exist.* But once it is declared that the struggle has now converted to the 'life' that was being sought, this might create a momentary awe for that 'life'; but at the same time it is the end of the thought of the utopia. In the Marxist sense, utopia is the reason for radical change, the kind of change that sweeps all resistances, although the achievement of a radical change is possible which is the revolution, but as Mao suggests, contradictions would exist making the sweeping of 'resistances' an eternal process. Therefore, in Marxist thinking, utopia cannot exist, and life is a continuous struggle towards the thought of the utopia—utopia in that sense is the 'essence' of existence.

IPTA CS had set out to form a *national community* through the use of the narratives of real/fictional, linear/tabloid-esque paradoxical understandings of history. The efficacious objective of the CS in the multiplicity of contextualities and ideologies driven both by nationalism and universalism at the same time did succeed in creating a huge support base among the people, which I have called the *communitas* borrowing from Victor Turner. But in itself, the troupe of the CS could not remain a 'community' as a result of the very clashes that created a *communitas* for them. For *being-in-common* is no product that can be created but rather a process. The commune-ists who once believed in the possibilities of a space that encouraged such a process gave up. The commune ceased to exist. As a more concrete image of the nation appeared, which was not an alternative space but rather a space free of those elements of difference, which was the British—the raison d'être of the coming together as it were, the political struggle for a togetherness not in terms of mere numbers or 'series' as Sartre would call it but as a performing community was abandoned. The commune-ist air in colonial India that once held possibilities of questioning power, in the form of performing banalities and *living* or rather *acting* everyday out while performance for an audience was rehearsed, was cast aside as in a new-India, the commune was replaced by the nation that had already discovered itself as it were.

REFERENCES

1. Jolie Kaul, *YCI: Smriti* (Bohurupi, Nabanna Smarak Shankha, 1969), 34.
2. The play text is available at Natya Shodh, the theatre archive based in Kolkata, India.
3. Jack Amariglio, Subjectivity, class and Marx's Forms of the Commune (Special Issue on the 'Common and the forms of the Commune, *Rethinking Marxism*', Vol. 22 No. 3, July 2010), 330.
4. Amariglio, *Subjectivity, Class and Marx's Forms of the Commune,* 333. 'Marx does not privilege the idea that the direct producer of surplus is an individuated, labouring subjective entity over a subjectivity in which, or through which, the commune/clan is the unity to which the term direct producer can be applied. The notion of a direct producer, or worker, is seen as a historical product.'
5. Karl Marx, *On the Paris Commune* (Progress Publishers, Moscow, 1980), 130.
6. Ibid., 153.
7. Special Issue on the *Common and the Forms of the Commune...,* 308.
8. For Maurice Blanchot this could be the simple absence of conditions which he calls the negative community. *The Unavowable Community*, Trans. Pierre Joris (Station Hill Press, New York, 1988). Agamben sees the possibility of politics in this absence, something that rejects all identity and every condition

of belonging. The Coming Community, Trans. Michael Hardt. In *Theory Out of Bounds*, Vol. I (University of Minesota Press, Minneapolis, London, 2009).

9. Italics mine.
10. *Hind Swaraj*, as published in Gujarat columns of *Indian Opinion*. (11th and 18th Dec., 1909), 66.
11. *Harijan* 76 (26-7-1942), 308-9.
12. Lloyd I. Rudolph et al. *Postmodern Gandhi and Other Essays: Gandhi in the World and at Home* (The University of Chicago Press, Chicago and London, 1967), 152.
13. For Gandhi 'Truth' is not merely an opposition to a lie but rather it is a principled position. Ashram—Experiment with Truth, Raghavan Iyer, ed. *The Essential Writings of Mahatma Gandhi* (Oxford University Press, New Delhi, 2012), 283.
14. *A Dedicated and Creative Life* (Vikas Publishing House Pvt. Ltd., 1974), 59.
15. Ram Rehman quotes the incident from Sunil Janah's unpublished autobiography in the 14th P.C. Joshi Memorial Lecture delivered by him on 'Sunil Janah, Photographer and P.C. Joshi: The Making of a Progressive Culture' in 2010.
16. N.K. Krishnan, *Testament of Faith: Memoirs of A Communist* (New Delhi Publishing House, New Delhi, 1990), 128-29.
17. Ibid.
18. Rented according to Rekha Jain, Shantida–My Mentor, Gul Bardhan, ed., *Rhythm Incarnate: Tribute to Shanti Bardhan* (Abhinav Publications, New Delhi, 1992).
19. Ibid. 60.
20. Interview with Pratibha Aggarwal on 28th August 1984.
21. Kisan Sabha was the name of the peasants' front founded in 1936 at the Lucknow session of the Indian National Congress. It demanded the abolition of the existent feudal system and other oppressive taxes on the peasants. Although founded by the initiative of the left inclined individuals of the Congress, it came fully under the control of CPI in 1942 around the time CPI was fully legalized.
22. Although this is the recorded year but her original date of birth according to her husband P.C. Joshi (junior) was around 1930-31.
23. Parvathi Krishnan in interview with M. Allirajan and Subha J Rao, *The Hindu*, January 13, 2003.
24. Apparently although P.C. Joshi had asked her to join CS, she was removed by Benoy Roy, Usha Dutt, *Ora, Amra, Era;* Sova

Sen (Thema, Kolkata, 2000), 64.

25. Sudhi Pradhan (ed.), First souvenir of the CS, *Marxist Cultural Movement in India,* Vol. I (National Book Agency Pvt. Ltd., 1979), 380.
26. Ibid.
27. Ibid.
28. Ibid.
29. According to a report by Balraj Sahni in *People's Age* published on January 13, 1946.
30. 'Kathiawari Muslim youth, who was working as a tailor's apprentice before the IPTA noticed his talents and took him in'-ibid.
31. Sudhi Pradhan (ed.), 389.
32. In interview with Pratibha Agarwal.
33. Gul Bardhan, What a Tremendous Movement it was..., *Seagull Theatre Quaterly,* Issue 7 (October 1995), 40.
34. In interview with me on May 4, 2010 at Kolkata.
35. IPTA Central Dance Troupe's Programme and Tour, Balraj Sahni, *People's Age,* Sunday, January 13, 1946.
36. In an interview with me on May 4, 2010 at Kolkata.
37. Abani Dasgupta was a musician of the Central Squad. *Da* is a way of addressing the older men (often in the sense of brother but not necessarily).
38. 'What a Tremendous Movement it was...', Gul Bardhan, *Seagull Theatre Quarterly,* Issue 7, October 1995, p. 40.
39. However, it would be too far fetching to argue that all social normatives were questioned in the space of the commune. Heteronormative binaries were often not only unaddressed but rather in daily banality of activities, reinforced. I have in mind the accusation of Reba Roychoudhury, a performer of the Central Squad, in her autobiography '*Jibaner Tane Shilper Tane*'. She wrote about an occasion where she felt discriminated against by the General Secretary P.C. Joshi for not being good looking enough (not being of 'fair' skin like Preeti Banerjee).
40. Dhruv Gupta, Charer Doshok: Uttal Shomoy, *Anushtup,* Vol. 4, Anil Acharya (ed.), (1988) 5. (Translation from Bengali mine.)
41. In interview with Iqbal Masud, *Indian Express,* Bombay, June 6, 1992.
42. Mulk Raj Anand, On the Progressive Writer's Movement, In *Marxist Cultural Movement in India,* Sudhi Pradhan (ed.).
43. Sudhi Pradhan, Bharater Marxbadi Sanskriti Andolaner Prothom Joog, *Gananatya* (Dec 1989).

44. In Bharatiya Gananatya Shangher Itihas, *Epic Theatre* (April- May 1978).
45. In an interview taken by me on August 14, 2009 at Kolkata.
46. In February 1944, the Calcutta Karukala Sangh organized an exhibition of Representations of the Destitutes. This included works by Adinath Mukhopadhyay, Indu Gupta, Bimal Majumdar, Shaila Chakraborty, Anil Mukhopadhyay and woodcuts by Ramendranath Chakraborty . Similarly many other visual artists, writers represented them in their work. For a detailed study see *A Matter of Conscience: Artists Bear Witness to The Great Bengal Famine of 1943,* Nikhil Sarkar, trans. Satyabrata Dutta (Punascha, Calcutta, 2003).
47. Nemiji ke Sath Mera Natyanubhav, Rekha Jain, *Rangkarm 2006-* The Annual Magazine of IPTA, Raigarh (2006) 1-2. (translation from Hindi is mine).
48. P.C. Joshi, A Dedicated and Creative Life, in *Balraj Sahni–An Intimate Portrait,* P.C. Joshi (ed.) (Vikas Publishing House Pvt. Ltd., 1974), 63.
49. At Bombay
50. *Balraj Sahni—An Intimate Portrait* by P.C. Joshi in *A Dedicated and Creative Life,* ed. P.C. Joshi (Vikas Publishing House Pvt. Ltd., 1974), 63-65.
51. That included Alice Boner, Michael Chekhov, Mr and Mrs Leonard Elmhirst, John Martin, Jawaharlal Nehru, Sir Ferozkhan Noon, Sir Chinubhai Madhavlal Ranchhodlal, Romain Rolland, Sir William Rothenstein, Leopold Stokowski, Mr Whitney and Lady Daphne Straight and Rabindranath Tagore.
52. Uday Shankar is a Bengali
53. Sudhi Pradhan, 'Gananatya Sangho o Uday Shankar', *Gananatya,* (October 1977).
54. Sunil Munshi interviewed by me at Kolkata on August 14, 2009.
55. See Balibar, 25.
56. Ravi Shankar in the Second Souvenir of IPTA CS, Sudhi Pradhan (ed.), *Marxist Cultural Movement in India: Chronicles and Documents, 1936-1947* (National Book Agency Pvt. Ltd., Kolkata, 1979), 383.
57. Sudhi Pradhan (ed.), *Marxist Cultural Movement in India: Chronicles and Documents, 1936-1947* (National Book Agency Pvt. Ltd., Kolkata, 1979), 379, 386.
58. *Gananatya Katha,* Sajal Roychoudhury (Mitra and Ghosh Publishers Pvt Ltd, Kolkata, 1990), 37.
59. Talking about the party classes held to inform the members with

the ideology oft he party Ravi Shankar writes—'Those days I don't know why the members of the squad would be very harsh while talking about Nehru (Jawaharlal Nehru)... Then one day I remember Rajni Palme Dutt came to speak in one of the meetings. That day I had some work for a film that I was doing. I could not be there for the speech. But when I came back I heard everything. He came and said you are making a mistake. You are not understanding what Nehru is trying to do... and similar other things he said. He actually praised Nehru a lot in the meeting. When I returned in the evening I heard a different tune from everyone. Everyone had suddenly got used to praising Nehru. I am saying this because I would find the vacillation of their love for things very strange.' (*Raag Anuraag*, Ravi Shankar, Ananda (Dec 2006), 127. (Translation from Bengali mine)

60. The CPI had made its positions clear earlier in 1942 in an article 'National Unity Now' published in *People's Age* on August 8, by asserting that the Muslim League leadership was 'playing an oppositional role vis-à-vis imperialism in a way somewhat analogous to the leadership of Indian National Congress itself...'
61. Pradhan, 383. 61. Ibid. 388.
62. Sarkar (2006), 247.
63. Comintern and the National and the Colonial Questions as quoted by Sudipta Kaviraj in *The Heteronomous Radicalism of M.N. Roy*. In *Political Thought in Modern India,* Thomas Pantham and Kenneth L. Deutsch (eds.) (Sage Publications, New Delhi, 1986).
64. Kaviraj (1986), 220-221.
65. This was a movement initiated under the leadership of Mahatma Gandhi to resist the British Government in the 1920s.
66. Khilafat Movement was started to create pressure on the British Government in order to protect the Ottomon Empire after WWI
67. Sarkar (2006), 247-248.
68. When in the early twentieth century, the question of 'self-determination' was often raised in the context of the colonial society, Rosa Luxemburg argued that in any class society to speak of self-determination for the people would ordinarily mean the 'self-determination' of the ruling classes. In *The National Question: Selected Writings,* Rosa Luxemburg (Aakar Books, Delhi, 2009).
69. Sarkar (2006), 374.
70. It was a civil disobedience movement started in August 1942 asking the British Government to leave India.
71. In interview with me Preeti Banerjee talking about their performances in New Delhi recalls, 'Sarojini Naidu used to watch

our programme everyday. She used to specifically like the depiction of the history of India'. In Dhruvo Gupta, *Charer Doshok Uttal Shomoy*, Vol. 4, Anil Acharya (ed.), Anustup (1988), 8.

72. From Ritual to Theatre, Victor Turner, *Performing Arts Journal*, New York (1982), 47.
73. Kersaw, *The Politics of Performance: Radical Theatre as Cultural Intervention* (Routledge, London and New York, 1992), 28.
74. P.C. Joshi, *A Dedicated and Creative Life*, 69.
75. Bardhan (1995), 42.
76. The Nizam of Hyderabad wanted an independent status as was enjoyed by the princely states during the independence of India. A movement was created called 'Join India' in order to include Hyderabad within the Indian nation against the Nizam's wish. Peasants joined the movement under the leadership of CPI who wanted the abolition of the feudal system. In 1948 the Government of India with the help of the Indian Army assimilated Hyderabad into the nation in an operation called 'Operation Polo'.
77. The Tebhaga Movement was initiated by the Kisan Sabha in order to increase the share of crops of the peasants from the landowners. Tebhaga which literally means one third share was their demand that they would give to the landowners against the half of the crop share that they gave.
78. Sumit Sarkar (2006), 426.
79. Ravi Shankar (2006), 127.
80. In interview with me on May 4, 2010 at Kolkata.
81. In her interview with Khaled Choudhury (from the collection of Natyashodh Sansthan, Kolkata)
82. Sajal Roychoudhury, Gananatya Katha, 45.
83. In interview with Pratibha Agarwal on August 28, 1984 (from the collection of Natyashodh Sansthan, Kolkata).
84. Edward M. Bruner, 'Experience and its expressions', in *The Anthropology of Experience*, Victor W. Turner et al. (ed.) (University of Illinois Press, 1986).
85. In interview with Pratibha Agarwal.
86. Ibid.
87. In interview with the author in 2010.
88. For Hume, Freedom is not a property of human subjectivity. It does not distinguish human beings from other things – in that sense freedom is of/for all. The idea of freedom in its retreat from any discourse leaves a trace of itself. This freedom or liberality as he calls it expends itself, in the 'gentle force' called

'the imagination' and the imagination, true to its word, makes possible for the soul to perceive anything. In A *Treatise of Human Nature* by Hume as discussed by Peter Fenves in the Foreword to *The Experience of Freedom,* Jean Luc Nancy (Stanford University Press, California, 1993).

89. Reba Roychoudhury, *Jibaner Tane Shilper Tane,* 34.
90. Ibid.
91. Gilles Deleuze et al., *What is Philosophy?* (Colombia University Press, 2003), 108.

'For a free India of brother peoples' (*People's Age*, January 1946)

Epilogue: Indian Theatre: What Are We Talking About?

I. On the Question of the Vitruvian Man

How perfect can the *I* be? An *I* that enunciates an origin, an *I* that in the very act of being said, exists; an *I* that is overpoweringly dominant over all other 'I's. It leaves one without existence if one does not belong in the *I*. *I* does not exist without being acknowledged by an 'I'. *I* is what has been written before and after it. *I* aims at perfection. *I* is a political being in this assertion. *I* is watched as *I* walks by an empty stage. *I* and its partner who has been watching *I*—*we* a 'group', *we* are together in our will; our choice to be within the same spatio-temporal reality. We have created that which is called theatre (should we say for a lack of a better word). But *you* want to know if *we* exists? Then 'you' must as well exist! But *we*'s political assertion is in the fact that *we* is better than *you*—or does *we* need not qualify? *I* belongs with its partner in an empty space as much as *you* does with its. And their existences could also parallelly run, as they remain alienated—in this case in a positive way. Can there be one more game this time—of not becoming the *Weltmeister*? For say, Carl Schmitt, such a game is not possible. He would prefer that the political 'enemy'—the other group—be 'the other, the stranger; and it is sufficient for his nature that he is, in a specially intense way, existentially something different and alien, so that in the extreme case, conflicts with him are possible.'[1] Hence the political lies in the realm of a distinction and comprehension of friend-enemy. But then, have we still not seen enough animosity? Like we discussed earlier, a 'group' and its origin in the sense of Sartre is the effort of assembled individuals to dissolve the *seriality* which to Sartre is a negation of praxis, that exercises its own counter-finality through inertia without as such having an author but however given that it was produced by man, it creates its own rationality, who then is alienated within it, theoretically free and sovereign but in reality 'powerless'. Here I would argue that this is what encompasses the colonial mind to break out and create its own logic. Therefore to see any anti-colonial struggle not as emancipatory by itself would be wrong—however the question could be for whom? We have tried to discuss certain such coagulations that tried to break off. Now coming back to Mr Schmitt, if a 'group' essentially suggests a certain enmity for the sake of its own survival, for there could be *x* number of 'groups' which are not necessarily the 'State' unlike in case of Schmitt, then coercion becomes inevitable. Or to go by Schmitt, within the State, any other force, to put in his words 'the political power of a class or of some other group', if that hinders the State's activities, then the political entity is destroyed. But in such cases, he gives the power to the 'decisive entity' that can take control over the critical situation – the 'exception'. So by Schmitt's definition, a state by definition must be coercive if it has to be so. Now here comes our proposition. In case of theatre, which we have already decided to call thus for the lack of a better word, a 'group' in the Sartrean sense gets coagulated. But how does such a group exist under the panorama term State? Will the State not be a decisive break from the liminal path that the theatre treads? For the State must be decisive, but can the theatre be so? Would that not be contrary to theatre's basic instinct of conjoining and constituting freely? The story of IPTA CS, I think tells us of such a fate. For the Vitruvian Man—the obsession with perfection and keeping proportion of even diversity can be the work of the State but not of theatre. It cannot afford to be proportionate for the sake of its own freedom—its *liberality*.

The Indian State after independence from British colonial rule made such a blunder, although with utmost sincerity of welfare. The looming question of a national theatre like the other national this and that became exigent. In April 1956, nine years after India had cast off colonial rule, a drama seminar was organized by a national academy founded in 1953 aiming at 'managing' culture of the nation. In the words of the then Chairman of the Sangeet Natak Akademi, it was charged with 'preservation and development of the great arts of music, dance, drama and film'. It had also organized the film seminar in 1955, the music seminar in 1957 and the dance seminar in 1958. As it becomes very clear from the welcome address of the Chairman P.V. Rajamannar, the preoccupation of the drama seminar was the 'nation's culture'. He tries to extend the logic of its might to the times of the 'Ancient Hindus'.[2] We have already seen the genealogy of such a discourse lies in the orientalist writings that later went on to shape a pan-national 'Indian' identity. Whether it was the *Swadeshi* movement which in any case was coloured by Hindu nationalist ideologies or even the performances of the IPTA CS, the 'national' imagery continued to be coloured by a linear narrative logic that found its discovery in the ancient Hindus. The tone of the seminar was set by a motto upholding decolonization. The drama seminar's director Sachin Sengupta pointed out:

> Current drama in our languages, usually witnessed in urban areas, received baptism and benedictions from foreign priests of culture. But even then, they could not be altogether un-Indian, like the anglicised Indian who fails to be totally un-Indian. Neither did our artists apishly copy the Western drama, nor was it forced on us. It came and captured the imagination of our artists who were too liberal and too progressive to refuse to welcome what was astoundingly powerful and alluringly beautiful. But to assimilate an art which had reached its peak in the glorious days of Elizabethan England, which was also Shakespeare's England, was no easy job for a people in bondage who had drifted far away from the glorious days of the Guptas, the days of Kalidasa, the days of India's material and cultural expansion... For three hundred years (during the period of colonial rule), India saturated herself with bhakti-rasa and with the spirit of self-surrender to the eternal lilas of the divine dispenser... Once more, the people's arts grew anew and played an important role in the making of India...In the closing years of the nineteenth century, India's dramatic artists came in touch with Western forms of drama. It is erroneous to believe that there had been a complete break of Indian

> dramatic tradition when Westerners appeared in the field. There had never been a total break... All these the Seminar will try to clarify.[3]

The question of continuity and fighting back any cultural domination were indisputably put forward all through the seminar. At the same time, there was an attitude towards 'building drama and theatre anew'.[4] While the so-called 'folk' performances were seen as unadulterated, the emphasis was to study the Sanskrit drama extensively in order to give shape to 'Indian theatre'.[5] It is no surprise that post-independence such an urge was felt because a discourse of the roots in the 'folk' had already taken shape in pre-independent India, whose political assertion was most pertinently put across by the IPTA. And we have already seen that with the performances of the IPTA CS. In post-independent India the question of the origin continued to haunt as one searched for the 'really Indian'[6] identity. Habib Tanvir, the theatre director who was for a while associated with the IPTA movement and is often associated with the controversial 'theatre of the roots' movement in post-independent India puts it eloquently in an article called 'Theatre is in the Villages' published in 1974. He writes:

> It must now be realized that the vehicle provided by urban theatre forms borrowed from the West is totally inadequate for effectively projecting the social aspirations, way of life, cultural patterns and fundamental problems of contemporary India. The true pattern of Indian culture in all its facets can best be witnessed in the countryside. It is in its villages that the dramatic tradition of India in all its pristine glory and vitality remains preserved even to this day. It is these rural drama groups that require real encouragement. They need to be given an environment conducive to their fullest growth. On the other hand, it is not until the city youth is fully exposed to influence from folk traditions in theatre that a truly Indian theatre, modern and universal appeal and indigenous in form, can really be evolved.[7]

The question of the 'real Indian', where he comes from, what he defines continued to be pertinent within a discourse that became more about identity and less and less about the 'group', which we have called theatre. Hence the Vitruvian Man as an ideal for a national model, as is the case with the drawing by

Chittoprasad, in a headgear and dhoti (the white cloth worn as pants) became what was being sought after. It was essentially about being represented equally (while the women remain onlookers in the process). The transformation of a thought form of an egalitarian nation of 'brother people' is hence evidently aimed at material manifestation within the brother groups that could in turn maintain their unique position within such a representative model. However, the glitch was the role of the State which seeked to represent those that were worthy of representation[8]—creating vacuums, a sense of alienation now and then. The playwright, theatre critic, and academic Govind Purushottam Deshpande puts an interesting point forward in this regard. We discuss that in our next section.

II. Theatre and Thiyetar or 'Yes, I Only Have One Language, Yet It Is Not Mine'

In an article published in 1995 in the Seagull Theatre Quarterly called 'Is There, Or Should There Be, A National Theatre in India?' Govind Purushottam Deshpande or GPD as he was popularly known poses the question of a national theatre rather differently than merely bracketing it within the 'theatre in the past' or 'theatre of the villages' discourses although he begins by saying—'Nobody can have any objection to national theatre per se.'[9] However at the same time he destabilizes any possibility of having a singular idea of the national theatre and challenges the ground on which such attempts are made. He sees the problem of associating the word 'national' with an epistemological one where such an association happens through an a priori definition of the term 'national'. He diverts the question from how one defines 'national theatre' to '...is it necessary to define national theatre?'[10] Borrowing from Nietzsche he calls anything like a 'national theatre', 'a semiotic concentration of an entire process'. He sees such a project of definition in post-colonial states as a result of domination of 'distorted cultural nationalism' or even 'religious fundamentalism'. Historically, the roots of both religious fundamentalism as well as cultural nationalisms can be found in the orientalist theatre history writings. Although often not apparent, in creating the imagery of an 'other' it visualized a community that was to later define itself in the same parameters as the 'Indian'. We have discussed these issues especially in the first chapter. When 'theatre', that involves drama and the auditorium space became the identifying quality of that which came to be known to the natives as 'thiyetar', instilled a pan-collective pride in a nation as it were, the need to define it by the nation became imperative to suit its representation in the world as a 'meister'. But this happened within the context of the collective—by rightfully representing it (it became a question of arithmetic—who all are being represented); GPD in this context writes:

> Of course, an arithmetical exercise of determining what is Indian national theatre is always possible. But a bit of Bengal, Maharashtra, Tamil Nadu, plus folk, plus ancient tradition, plus *Natyasastra* all wrapped up into an enormous package tied with saffron ribbon—doesn't work. They don't add up. The beauty of Indian theatre lies in the fact that we are all Indians because we don't add up to being Indian.[11]

'We' as us who belong in our free will to become a 'group' do not need to add up to anything. Even today the debates around the question of a national Indian theatre remain clouded by problems of representation. In a seminar organized in 2008 by the India Theatre Forum at Ninasam, Heggodu, in a way to undo the drama seminar of 1956, which was called *Not the Drama Seminar*, these questions came up again—of representation and under-representation, of 'truly Indian' and 'western'. Both these binaries bring us to the question of the 'I'. Has theatre—the term we used for the lack of a better word, not been established as shared time and space? It even entails some kind of *connect*, be it the one which is built as described by the theory of *rasa* or by Aristotelian catharsis or even communitas as Victor Turner proposes. In all cases whatever the nature of the *connect*, some kind of association is felt within this shared space and time—a phenomenological study would only help us speculate about their natures—but the truth of a *connect* still remains in all cases —a *connect* that is developed from the space of the *free*—a *liberality* that does not bother about representation or under-representation, Western or Indian so far as it can create the experience of the *connect*. Of course, from this fundamental rather basic instinct of that which we called the theatre arises politics of identity, questions of survival, *bhakti* etc.—but can that decide *a priori* the human tendency to come together in space and time and to connect? Can we allow a 'decisive entity' as Schmitt puts it stop this urge? Can we even give it the name 'theatre' which is rather understood as a borrowed phenomenon as it were? Are we then not depriving some people of their urges to coagulate? Or are we facing an epistemological error here? We probably need to answer this question as a 'group' ourselves. Jacques Derrida in what I would call autobiographical ranting over a similar question on language or rather of expression, in the book 'Monolingualism of the Other or the Prosthesis of Origin' which he writes from his position of being a Francophone Maghrebian, whereby he is a monolingual French speaker but the language is 'not his own' writes:

> Since the prior-to-the-first time of pre-originary language does not exist, it must be invented. Injunctions, the summons (*mise en demeure*) of another writing. But, above all, it must be written *within* languages, so to speak. One must summon up writing inside the given language. From the cradle to the grave, that language, for me, will have been French.
>
> By definition, I no longer know how, and have never been able, to say that it is a good or a bad thing. It just happened that way. Lastingly (*à demeure*).
>
> The obscure chance, my good fortune, a gift for which thanks should be given to goodness knows what archaic power, is that it was always easier for me to bless this destiny. Much easier, more often than not, and even now, to bless than to curse it. The day I would get to know to whom gratitude must be rendered for it, I would know everything and I would be able to die in peace.[12]

This I read as the ranting also of a post-colonial subject. As a humanities researcher who grew up in a post-colonial situation, studied in a university that was symbolic of post-colonial determination, where the medium of study was always English, the erstwhile colonizer's language, I have not known any other language for research. Until while studying abroad, this time in Germany, I was repeatedly reminded of not being a 'native speaker'. Who is this 'native speaker'—if I have known only my colonizer's language since the time I do not remember of, going back in fact before me? Is it my accent, or my grammatical mistakes that undo such an identity for me? Does the 'native speaker' speak not without errors or accent? Or is it my postcolonial fate? Should I just find out my 'native language' to claim my position as also a 'native speaker'—a language I have not learnt how to think critically in—a language that would ever remain translational for me. From this very personal perspective of my fate regarding language, can be seen the question of that which we decided to call theatre for lack of a better word. I will not elaborate further.

III. Once More 'The National Question'—The Present Perils of it

Post-colonial determination also could mean reclaiming the past, and re-inventing something that one is the original possessor of—for example a 'native language'. In case of India, 'theatre's' inclination towards drama because of reasons we have already discussed, —the emphasis when it came to classification was given to its linguistic varieties apart from that which came to be known as traditional theatre or folk theatre. Although like we discussed in Chapter 3 taking *Swadeshi Jatra* as our case study, these forms were never static and were in constant dialogue with their times. However even if we look at the papers discussed during the drama seminar of 1956, we see one of the major concerns regarding representation was that of linguistic representation as also their underrepresentation. In fact, even in 2008's 'Not the Drama Seminar', the question of linguistic representation was brought to the fore not ignoring the emphasis on drama especially in the case of the 1956 seminar! The polemics of such a debate are that, firstly the emphasis continues to remain drama, secondly, representation by the State will always bring forth considerations of 'national worth' whereby discrimination is bound to follow, and thirdly, any national entity which is the decisive entity tends to think in terms of unitary numbers, howsoever diverse that might be and especially the case of India is a good one. From the nineteenth century onwards as British power took administrative hold of colonial India, Hindi which became more and more Sanskritized and often ignored other versions of its dialects came to be popularly known as the language of the *jati, desh, janta* and speaking that language came to be considered as 'desh-seva' or serving the nation. This nationalist emphasis on a particular language as the 'national language' or the language of the *jati* or community or public during the colonial period was over the 'official language' which was the colonizer's tongue or the Persian and Arabic influenced Urdu language of the earlier Muslim rulers which used to be the dominant vernacular of North India in the nineteenth century. However, given the variety of other languages that were still spoken in the subcontinent and for several other factors a normative and critical discourse emerged. Hindi was not stipulated as the 'national language' in post-independent India, but an official one along with English, although the constitution suggests promoting the language as possible. Today, this debate is back to the fore with a leader of the State who proclaims himself as a Hindu nationalist in power. That he has already made officials to communicate with him in Hindi has complicated the situation given the multi-lingual nature of the country.[13] A linguistic emphasis for that which we here have called theatre, and a national theatre will definitely take on this complexity of language politics that already exists. In fact, in the 2008 'Not the Drama Seminar', Sanjay Upadhayay an actor-director emphasizes on this saying that Hindi theatre could have been the 'national theatre'.[14] 'The national question' for theatre brings about dangers of such a normative idea taking hold of the issue. May be we need to be weary.

IV. Towards Not a Nationalist but a Contextual Definition or What Do We Call That Which We Have Called Theatre?

As we have already discussed earlier, 'theatre' the term that was borrowed from English continued to be used, as it is, only slightly differently, as *thiyetar* if you will. The implication of it is not significant because of the displacement that occurred during colonial rule, but rather on its relevance for that which has come to be known as 'Theatre and performance studies' in India. What kinds of classification and genre distinction best suit the context of the theatre scenario in India need to be kept in mind without delineating it from its historical development.

And at the same time, keeping in mind that merely borrowing theoretical concepts from 'Theatre and performance studies' disciplines from anglophone countries might not be useful for a country that needed to rename, re-contextualize and understand anew many of its existent forms. A *jatra* is not 'theatre' and neither is it 'performance' as we understand in the anglophone context. How to sustain meanings of such terms while remaining aware of any nationalistic claims would not be an easy task given the present historical juncture we are part of. It is here that I think we need to push ourselves for the basic understanding of and around these terms—a walk towards philosophy of these terms might show us the direction.

REFERENCES

1. George Schwab (trans.), *The Concept of the Political* (The University of Chicago Press, Chicago, 2007), 27.
2. *Indian Drama in Retrospect* (Sangeet Natak Akademi and Hope India Publications, New Delhi, 2007), 12.
3. Ibid., 18-19.
4. Adya Rangacharya, 34.
5. See Aparna Dharwadkar, *Theatres of Independence Drama, Theory, and Urban Performance in India Since 1947* (University of Iowa Press, Iowa city, 2005) for further a much detailed study of the drama seminar.
6. As put by Mulk Raj Anand during the drama seminar.
7. *Social Scientist*, Vol. 2, No. 10 (May, 1974), 33.
8. See Carl Schmitt.
9. Govind Purushottam Deshpande, Is There, or Should There be, a National Theatre in India? Anjum Katyal (ed.) *Seagull Theatre Quaterly*, The Seagull Foundation for the Arts, Calcutta (August 1995), 3.
10. Ibid. 4.
11. Ibid.
12. Patrick Mensah (trans.), *Monolingualism of the Other* or *the Prosthesis of Origin* (Stanford University Press, Stanford, California, 1996), 64.
13. http://www.thehindu.com/todays-paper/tp-in-school/modis-push-for-hindi-irks-regional-parties/article6134455.ece.
14. Sudhanva Deshpande et al. (ed.), *Our Stage: Pleasures and Perils of Theatre Practice in India* (Tulika Books, New Delhi, 2009), 49.

Bibliography

Agamben, Giorgio. *Remnants of Auschwitz: The Witness and the Archive*. New York: Zone Books, 1999.

_____. *State of Exception*. Chicago and London: The University of Chicago Press, 2003.

_____. *The Coming Community: Theory Out of Bounds*, Vol. 1, Michael Hardt (trans.). Minneapolis, London: University of Minesota Press, 2009.

Anand, Mahesh. *Rekha Jain*. New Delhi: Rashtriya Natya Vidyalaya., 2010.

Armitage, David. *The Ideological Origins of the British Empire*. Cambridge, 2000.

Artaud, Antonin. *The Theatre and its Double*, Translated by Mary Caroline Richards. New York: Grove Press, 1958.

Austin, J.L. *How to Do Things with Words*. Oxford, New York: Oxford University Press, 1976.

Azmi, Saukat. *Yaad ki Rehguzar*. New Delhi, Allahabad, Patna: Rajkamal Prakashan, 2006.

Badiou, Alain. *Logics of World: Being and Event II*, Alberto Toscano (trans.). Continuum, 2009.

_____. *Manifesto for Philosophy*. Albany NY: State University of New York Press, 1992.

Bagchi, Amiya Kumar. *Capital and Labour Redefined: India and the Third World*. Gurgaon: Anthem Press, 2002.

Bakhle, Janki. *Two Men and Music: Nationalism in the Making of an Indian Classical Tradition*. New Delhi: Orient Longman Pvt. Ltd., 2008.

Bakhtin, M.M. *The Dialogic Imagination: Four Essays*, Michael Holquist (ed.), Caryl Emerson and Michael Holquist (trans.). Austin: University of Texas Press, 1981.

Baller, E. *Communism and Cultural Heritage*. Moscow: Progress Publishers, 1984.

Balme, Christopher B. *Decolonizing the Stage: Theatrical Syncretism and*

Post-colonial Drama. New York: Oxford University Press, 1999.

Banerjee, Brajendranath. *Bengali Stage (1795-1873)*. Calcutta: Ranjan Publishing House, 1943.

Banerjea, Baboo Krishna Mohana. *The Persecuted or Dramatic Scenes; Illustrative of the Present State of Hindoo Society in Calcutta*. No. 13, Calcutta: Messrs A. Monriro & Co.'s East Indian Press, 1831.

Banerjee, Sumanta. *Unish Shotoker Kolkata o Saraswatir Itor Santan*. Kolkata: Anustup, 2008.

Bardhan, Gul (ed.). *Rhythm Incarnate: Tribute to Shanti Bardhan*. New Delhi: Abhinav Publications, 1992.

Basu, Swapan and Choudhury, Indrajit (eds.). *Unish Shotoker Bangalee Jibon o Shonskriti*. Kolkata: Pustak Bipani, 2003.

Beasley, Chris. *What is Feminism?*. London: Sage Publications, 1999.

Benjamin, Walter. *Illuminations*. London: Pimlico, 1999.

Berlanstein, Lenard R. *Daughters of Eve: A Cultural History of French Theatre Women from the Regime to the Fin de Siècle*. Harvard University Press, 2001.

Bhaba, Homi. *The Location of Culture*. London and New York: Routledge Classics, 2007.

Bharucha, Rustom. *Rehearsals of a Revolution: The Political Theatre of Bengal*. Calcutta: Seagull, 1983.

_____. *Theatre and the World: Performance and the Politics of Culture*. London: Routledge, 1993.

_____. *The Politics of Cultural Practice: Thinking Through Theatre in an Age of Globalization*. New Delhi: Oxford India Paperbacks, 2005.

Bhatia, Nandi. *Acts of Authority/Acts of Resistance: Theatre and Politics in Colonial and Post-colonial India*. New Delhi: Oxford University Press, 2004.

_____ (ed.). *Modern Indian Theatre: A Reader*. New Delhi: Oxford University Press, 2009.

Bhattacharya, Malini. *Gananatya Andolan O Natyakalar Rupantar Bhabna: 1942-1947*. Kolkata: Pratikshan Publications, 1990.

_____ . *The Indian People's Theatre Association: A Preliminary Sketch of the Movement and the Organization 1942-47*. New Delhi: Sangeet Natak Akademy, 1989.

Blanchot, Maurice. *The Unavowable Community*, Pierre Joris (trans.). New York: Station Hill Press, 1988.

Bose, Vishnu. *Babu Thiyetar*. Kolkata: Srishti Prakashan, 2001.

Breckenridge, Carol A. and van der Veer, Peter (eds.). *Orientalism and the Post-colonial Predicament: Perspectives on South Asia*. Philadelphia: University of Pennsylvania Press, 1993.

Brooke, Peter. *The Empty Space*. New York: Touchstone Books, 1968.

Brown, A. Claude. *The Ordinary Man's Guide to India*. London: Cecil Palmer, 1927.

Busteed, H.E. *Echoes from Old Calcutta: Being Chiefly Reminiscences of the Days of Warren Hastings*. London: Francis and Impey; Calcutta: W. Thacker and Co. and Shimla: Thacker, Spink and Co. 1908.

Butler, Judith. *Gender Trouble: Feminism and the Subversion of Identity*. New York: Routledge, 1999.

Byrski, M. Christopher. *Concept of Ancient Indian Theatre*. New Delhi: Munshiram Manoharlal Publishers Pvt. Ltd.,1974.

Chakrabarti, Hiren. *Political Protest in Bengal: Boycott and Terrorism 1905-1908*. Calcutta: Papyrus, 1992.

Chakrabarty, Dipesh. *Provincializing Europe: Post-colonial Thought and Historical Difference*. Princeton and Oxford: Princeton University Press, 2000.

Chakraborty, Gargi. *P.C. Joshi: A Biography*. New Delhi: National Book Trust, India, 2007.

Chakraborty, Renu. *Communists in Indian Women's Movement 1940-1950*. New Delhi: People's Publishing House, 1980.

Chakraborty, Uma. *Pandita Ramabai: A Life and a Time*. New Delhi: Critical Quest, 2007.

Chanda, Pulak. *Jagaroner Charan Mukunda Das o Tar Rachana-shamagra*. Kolkata: Dey's Publishing, 2011.

Chatterjee, Partha. *The Partha Chatterjee Omnibus*. New Delhi: Oxford University Press, 1997.

Chatterjee, Partha and Pandey, Gyanendra (eds.). *Subaltern Studies VII: Writings on South Asian History and Society*. Oxford and New York: Oxford University Press, 1992.

Chatterjee, Sudipto. *The Colonial Staged*. Calcutta: Seagull Books, 2007.

Chattopadhaya, Geeta. *Bangla Swadeshi Gaan*. Delhi: Delhi University, 1983.

Chattopadhyay, Kamaladevi. *Towards a National Theatre*. Published for the All-India Women's Conference by Aundh Pub. Trust, 1945.

Choondal, Chummar. *Christian Theatre in India*. Trichur, Kerala: Kerala Folklore Academy, 1984.

Choudhury, Darshan. *Bangla Theatrer Itihaas*. Kolkata: Pustak Bipani, 2007.

_____. *Unish Shotoker Natyabishoy*. Kolkata: Pragya Bikash, October 2007.

CPI. *Class Struggle and the Problems of National Unity*, Party Education Series. 3, Communist Party of India (Marxist), December. 1996.

_____. *Constitution of the Communist Party of India*. Communist Party Publication, January 1972.

Cox, Jeffery. *Imperial Fault Lines: Christianity and Colonial Power in India, 1818-1940*. California: Stanford University Press, 2002.

Eck, Diana L. *Darsan: Seeing the Divine Image in India*. New York: Columbia University Press, 1996.

Das, Pulin. *Persecution of Drama and Stage*. Calcutta: MC Sarkar and Sons Pvt. Ltd., 1986.

Dasi, Binodini. *Amar Katha O Ananya Rachana*. Kolkata: New Rainbow Lamination, 1416 (Bengali year).

Dasgupta, Hemendranath. *The Indian Stage*, Vol. 1. Calcutta: Metropolitan Printing and Publishing House, 1934.

Davis, Tracy C. *Actresses as Working Women: Their Social Identity in Victorian Culture*. London and New York: Routledge, 1991.

Deleuze, Gilles and Félix Guattari. *What is Philosophy?*. Colombia University Press, 2003.

Derrida, Jacques. *Demeure: Fiction and Testimony*. California: Stanford University Press, 2000.

_____. *Monolingualism of the Other or the Prosthesis of Origin*. Patrick Mensah (trans.). California: Stanford University Press, 1996.

Deshpande, Sudhanva, Akshara, K.V. and Iyengar, Sameera (eds.). *Our Stage: Pleasures and Perils of Theatre Practice in India*. New Delhi: Tulika Books, 2009.

Devi, Tandra. *Village Theatres: The Foundations of Indian National Theatres*, Foreword by Nandalal Bose. Tandrashram; Kashmir: Tandra Devi Publications, 1938.

Dewar, Douglas. *Bygone Days in India with Eighteen Illustrations*. London: The Bodley Head Ltd., 1922.

_____. *In the Days of the Company*. Shimla, London and Calcutta: Thacker, Spink and Co., 1920.

Dharwadker, Aparna Bhargava. *Theatres of Independence: Drama, Theory, and Urban Performances in India Since 1947*. New Delhi: Oxford University Press, 2005.

Dhingra, Baldoon. *A National Theatre for India*. Bombay: Padma Publications, 1944.

Dictionary of Indian Biography. New York: Haskell House Publishers Ltd., 1906.

Dutta, Abhijit. *Glimpses of European Life in Nineteenth Century Bengal*. Calcutta: Minerva Associates (Publications) Pvt. Ltd., 1995.

Dutta, Krishna. *Calcutta: A Cultural and Literary History*. New York: Interlink Books, 2003.

Dutt, Michael Madhusudan. *Madhusudan Rachanabali* (Collected works of Michael Madhusudan Dutt). Kolkata: Sahitya Sansad, 2012.

Eden, Emily. *'Up the Country' Letters Written to Her Sister from the Upper*

Provinces of India; Richard Bentley. London: New Burlington Street Publisher, 1867.

Engels, Friedrich. *The Origin of the Family, Private Property and the State*. New Delhi: People's Publishing House, 2009.

Fanon, Franz. *The Wretched of the Earth*. London: Penguin Books, 2001.

Fischer-Lichte, Erika. *Theatre, Sacrifice, Ritual: Exploring Forms of Political Theatre*. USA & Canada: Routledge, 2005.

_____. *History of European Drama and Theatre*, Jo Riley (trans.). London and New York: Routledge, 2002.

Forbes, Geraldine. *Women in Modern India*. Cambridge: Cambridge University Press, 2009.

Foucault, Michel. *Foucault Live: Collected Interviews, 1961-1984*, Syvère Lotringer (ed.). Los Angeles: Semiotext(e), 1996.

_____. *The Archaeology of Knowledge and the Discourse on Language*, A.M. Sheridan Smith (trans.). New York: Pantheon Books, 1972.

_____. *The Politics of Truth*. Los Angeles: Semiotext(e), 1997.

Fromm, Erich (ed.). *Socialist Humanism: An International Symposium*. New York: Anchor Books, 1966.

Gale, Maggie B. and Stokes, John (eds.). *The Cambridge Companion to the Actress*. Cambridge University Press, 2007.

Gandhi, Mohandas Karamchand. *Hind Swaraj*, as published in Gujarat columns of Indian Opinion. 1909.

_____. *The Village Reconstruction*, Anand T. Hingorani (ed.). Bombay, Bharatiya Vidya Bhawan, 1998.

Genette, Gerard. *The Architext: An Introduction*, Jane E. Lewin (trans.). Quantum Books, 1992.

Ghatak, Ritwik. *On the Cultural 'Front'*. Calcutta: Ritwik Memorial Trust, 2000.

Ghosh, Ajit Kumar Bangiya. *Lokosanskriti Kosh* (*Encyclopedia of Bengali Folklore*), Barunkumar Chakraborty (ed.). Kolkata: Aparna Book Distributors, 2007.

Ghosh, Manmohan (trans.) *The Natyasastra: A Treatise on Hindu Dramaturgy and Histrionics, Ascribed to Bharata Muni*, Vol. I (Chapters I-XXVII). Kolkata: The Royal Asiatic Society,1950.

Gokhale, Shanta. *Playwright at the Centre: Marathi Drama from 1843 to the Present*. Calcutta: Seagull Books, 2000.

Guha, Ranajit (ed.). *Subaltern Studies IV: Writings on South Asian History and Society*. New Delhi: Oxford University Press, 1999.

Guha-Thakurta, P. *The Bengali Drama: Its Origin and Development*. London: Trench, Trubner and Co., 1930. reprinted Westport Connecticut: Greenwood Press, 1974.

Gupta, Swarupa. *Notions of Nationhood: Perspectives on Samaj, c. 1867-*

1905. Leiden: Brill, 2009.

Habermas, Jürgen. *The Structural Transformation of the Public Sphere—An Inquiry into a Category of Bourgeois Society*. Cambridge Massachusetts: The MIT Press, 1991.

Habib, Irfan. *Essays in Indian History: Towards a Marxist Perspective*. New Delhi: Tulika Books, 2002.

Hobsbawm, Eric J. (ed.). *The History of Marxism: Marxism in Marx's Day*, Vol. 1. New Delhi: Selectbook Service Syndicate, 1982.

Horrwitz, E.P. *The Indian Theatre: A Brief Survey of the Sanskrit Drama*. London: Blackie and Sons Limited, 1912.

Hussain, Md. Manowar. *Jatra: Deshprem O Samajchetona*. Kolkata: Pustak Bipani, 2011.

Jones, Kenneth W. *Arya Dharm: Hindu Consciousness in 19th Century Punjab*. Berkley: UCLA, 1976.

Joshi, P.C. (Junior). *Marxism and Social Revolution in India and Other Essays*. New Delhi: Patriot Publishers, 1986.

Joshi, Puran Chandra. *For the Final Bid for Power!: The Communist Plan Explained*. Bombay: People's Publishing House, 1947.

_____ (ed.). *A Dedicated and Creative Life*. New Delhi: Vikas Publishing House, 1974.

Kak, Shakti and Pati, Biswamoy (eds.). *Exploring Gender Equations: Colonial and Postcolonial India*. New Delhi: Nehru Memorial Museum and Library, 2005.

Kalekar, Hiranmay (ed.). *Independent India: The First Fifty Years*. Delhi: Oxford University Press, 1998.

Kapur, Geeta. *When was Modernism: Essays on Contemporary Cultural Practice in India*. New Delhi: Tulika Books, 2000.

Keith, A. Berriedale. *The Sanskrit Drama: Its Origin, Development, Theory and Practice*, First Indian edition. Delhi: Motilal Banarasidass, 1992.

Kersaw, Baz. *The Politics of Performance: Radical Theatre as Cultural Intervention*. London and New York: Routledge, 1992.

_____. *Theatre Ecology: Environments and Performance Events*. Cambridge: Cambridge University Press, 2007.

Khokar, Mohan. *His Dance, His Life: A Portrait of Uday Shankar*. New Delhi: Himalayan Books, 1983.

Kidambi, Prashant. *The Making of an Indian Metropolis*. Hampshire England: Ashgate Publishing, 2007.

Krishnan, N.K. *Testament of Faith: Memoirs of a Communist*. New Delhi: New Delhi Publishing House, 1990.

Laclau, Ernesto and Mouffe, Chantal. *Hegemony and Socialist Strategy: Towards a Radical Democratic Politics*. London and New York:

Verso, 2001.

Lehmann, Hans-Thies. *Postdramatic Theatre, Karen Jürs-Munby* (trans.). Oxon: Routledge, 2006.

Levi, Sylvain. *The Theatre of India*, Vol. 2, Narayan Mukherji (trans.). Calcutta: Writer's Workshop, 1978.

Lukacs, Georg. *History and Class Consciousness: Studies in Marxist Dialectics.* London: Merlin Press Ltd., 1971; Reprinted Delhi: Aakar Books, 2015.

Luxemburg, Rosa. *The National Question: Selected Writings.* Delhi: Aakar Books, 2009.

Majumdar, Neepa. *Wanted Cultured Ladies Only! Female Stardom and Cinema in India, 1930's-1950's.* Urbana and Chicago: University of Illinois Press, 2009.

Marcuse, Herbert. *Soviet Marxism: A Critical Analysis*. England: Penguin Books, 1958.

Marx, Karl and Engels, F. *On Colonialism*. Moscow: Foreign Languages Publishing House; Reprinted Delhi: Aakar Books.

_____. *The Manifesto of the Communist Party in Selected Works.* Moscow: Foreign Languages Publishing House, 1951.

Marx, Karl. *On the Paris Commune*. Moscow: Progress Publishers, 1980.

McClintock Anne, Mufti, Aamir and Shohat, Ella (eds.). *Dangerous Liaisons: Gender, Nation and Postcolonial Perspectives*. Minneapolis: University of Minnesota Press, 1997.

McClintock, Anne. *Imperial Leather: Race, Gender and Sexuality in the Colonial Context*. New York and London: Routledge, 1995.

McNay, Lois. *Gender and Agency: Reconfiguring the Subject in Feminist and Social Theory*. Cambridge: Polity Press, 2000.

Meduri, Avanthi (ed.), *Rukmini Devi Arundale (1904-1986): A Visionary Architect of Indian Culture and the Performing Arts*. New Delhi: Motilal Banarsidass, 2005.

Mehta, Kumudini Arvind. *English Drama on the Bombay Stage on the Late Eighteenth Century*, Phd thesis submitted to Bombay University in March 1960 (Bombay University Thesis Section).

Mitra, Amal. *Kolkatay Bideshi Rongaloy*. Kolkata: Prakash Bhavan, 1374 (Bengali year).

Moody, Jane and O'Quinn, Daniel (eds.). *The Cambridge Companion to British Theatre, 1730-1830*. Cambridge: Cambridge University Press, 2007.

Munshi, Vidya. *In Retrospect: War-time Memories and Thoughts on Womenॆs Movement.* Kolkata: Manisha, 2006.

Nancy, Jean Luc. *The Experience of Freedom.* California: Stanford University Press, 1993.

_____. *The Inoperative Community*, Peter Connor and Lisa Garbus (trans.), Theory and History of Literature, Vol. 76. Minneapolis and Oxford: University of Minnesota Press, 1991.

Negri, Antonio and Michael Hardt. *Empire*. London: Harvard University Press, 2000.

Nehru, Jawaharlal. *Letters From a Father to His Daughter*. New Delhi: Oxford University Press, 2006.

_____. *Soviet Russia: Some Random Sketches and Impressions*. Bombay: Chetana, 1949.

Padia, Chandrakala and Saxena, S.K. (eds.). *Feminism, Tradition and Modernity*. Shimla: Indian Institute of Advanced Study, 2002.

Pal, Bipin Chandra. *How I Came to the Brahmo Samaj*, Verinder Grover (ed.). New Delhi: Deep and Deep publications, 1993.

Pandey, Anupa. *Concept of Drama: Bharata and Aristotle, The Natyasìastra Tradition and Ancient Indian Society*. Jodhpur: Kusumanjali Prakashan, 1993.

Panikkar, K.N. *Culture and Consciousness in Modern India: A Historical Perspective*. New Delhi: People's Publishing House, 2003.

Pantham, Thomas and Deutsch, Kenneth L. (eds.). *Political Thought in Modern India*. New Delhi: Sage Publications, 1986.

Phelan, Peggy. *Unmarked the Politics of Performance*. London and New York: Routledge, 2001.

Pradhan, Sudhi (ed.). *Marxist Cultural Movement in India: Chronicles and Documents (1936-1947)*. Calcutta: National Book Agency, 1979.

Ranciére, Jacques. *The Politics of Aesthetics: The Distribution of the Sensible*, Gabriel Rockhill (trans.). Continuum, 2004.

Rangacharya, Adya (trans.). *The Natyasastra*. New Delhi: Munshiram Manoharlal, 2003.

Ray, Nisith Ranjan and others (eds.). *Challenge: A Saga of India's Struggle for Freedom*. New Delhi: Peoples Publishing House, 1984.

Raychoudhury, Subir and Mazumdar, Swapan (eds.). *Bilati Jatra Theke Swadesi Thiyetar*. Kolkata: Dey's Publishing, 1999.

Reinelt, Janelle G. and Roach, Joseph R. (eds.). *Critical Theory and Performance*. Ann Arbor: The University of Michigan Press, 2005.

Riceour, Paul. *Time and Narrative*, Vol. 1, Kathleen McLaughlin and David Pellauer (trans.). Chicago: University of Chicago Press, 1984.

Rolland, Romain. *People's Theatre*, Rathin Chakraborty (trans. & ed.). Kolkata: Natyachinta Foundation Trust, 2006.

Roychoudhury, Sajal. *Gananatya Katha*. Kolkata: Mitra and Ghosh Publishers, 1990.

Sampat, Vikram. *'My name is Gauhar Jaan!' The Life and Times of a Musician*. New Delhi: Rupa Publications India Pvt. Ltd., 2011.

Sangari, Kumkum and Vaid, Sudesh (eds.). *Recasting Women: Essays in Colonial History*. New Delhi: Zubaan, 2009.

Sangeet Natak Akademi. *Indian Drama in Retrospect*. Gurgaon: Hope India Publications, 2007.

Sarkar, Sumit. *A Critique of Colonial India*. Calcutta: Papyrus, 1985.

_____. *Modern India 1885-1947*. Madras: Macmillan India Ltd., 2006.

_____. *Writing Social History*. Delhi: Oxford India Paperbacks, 1998.

Sartre, Jean Paul. *Colonialism and Neocolonialism*. London and New York: Routledge, 2001.

_____. *Critique of Dialectical Reason: Theory of Practical Ensembles*, Vol. 1, Alan Sheridan-Smith (trans.). London, New York: Verso, 2004.

Savarese, Nicola. *Eurasian Theatre: Drama and Performance Between East and West from Classical Antiquity to the Present*, Richard Fowler (trans.). Holstebro, Malta, Wroclaw: Icarus Publishing Enterprise, 2010.

Schmitt, Carl. *The Concept of Representation*. London: University of California Press, 1967.

_____. *The Concept of the Political*, George Schwab (trans.). Chicago: The University of Chicago Press, 2007.

Schwartz, Vanessa R. *Spectacular Realities: Early Mass Culture in Fin-de-siècle Paris*. Berkeley: University of California Press, 1999.

Sen, Manikuntala. *Sediner Kotha*. Kolkata: Nabapatra Prakashan, 2003.

Sen, Sova. *Ora, Amra, Era*, Kolkata: Thema, 2000.

Shankar, Ravi. *Raag Anuraag*. Kolkata: Ananda, 2006.

Singh, Lata (ed.). *Play-house of Power*. New Delhi: Oxford University Press, 2010.

Stocqueler, Joachim Hayward. *The Memoirs of a Journalist*, published at the Offices of the Times of India, Bombay, 1873.

Tagore, Rabindranath. *Char Odhay*. Kolkata: Vishwabharati Grantha Bibhag, 1809 (Bengali year).

Tagore, Satyendranath. *Bambai Chitra*. Kolkata: Adi Brahma Samaj Jantra, 1296 (Bengali year).

Tse-tung, Mao. *On Contradiction*. New York: International Publishers, 1953.

Turner, Victor W. and Bruner, Edward M. (eds.). *The Anthropology of Experience*. Urbana and Chicago: University of Illinois Press, 1986.

Turner, Victor. *From Ritual to Theatre*. New York: Performing Arts Journal Pub., 1982.

Unique Fruits or The Unique Higher Life or Sri Dev Guru Bhagwan Part I: Shewing the wonderful unique changes wrought in the souls of fit persons through the unique light and power of Shri Dev Guru Bhagwan. Jiwan Press, 2nd edition, 1921.

van der Veer, Peter. *Imperial Encounters: Religion and Modernity in India and Britain*. New Jersey: Princeton University Press, 2001.

Vieira, Mónica Brito and Runciman, David. *Representation*. Cambridge: Polity Press, 2008.

Wacha, Sir D.E. *Shells from the Sands of Bombay Being My Recollections and Reminiscences 1860-1875*, Bombay: The Indian Newspaper Co. Ltd., 1920.

West Bengal State Archives. *Folk Theatre and the Raj: Selection from Confidential Records*; Introduction by Basudeb Chattopadhyay. West Bengal: Higher Education Department, 2008.

Wheeler, J. Talboys. *The History of India from the Earliest Ages*, Vol. III: Hindu, Buddhist, Brahminical revival. London: Trübner & Co., 1874.

Williams, Raymond. *Keywords: A Vocabulary of Culture and Society*. New York: Oxford University Press, 1983.

_____. *The Politics of Modernism*. New York and London: Verso, 1989.

Wilson, H.H. (trans.). *Select Specimens of the Theatre of the Hindus*, Vol. 1, 2nd edition. London: Parbury Allen and Co., 1835.

Woolf, Virginia. *Three Guineas, A Harvest Book*. Harcourt Inc., 1966.

Yajnik, R.K. *The Indian Theatre: Its Origins and its Later Developments Under European Influence with Special Reference to Western India*. London: George Allen and Unwin Ltd., 1933.

Yuval-Davis, Nira. *Gender and Nation*. New Delhi: Sage Publications, 1997.

Magazines and Newspaper articles

"In interview with Iqbal Masud." *Indian Express*. Bombay (6 June 1992).

"Parvathi Krishnan in interview with M. Allirajan and Subha J Rao." *The Hindu*. (January 13, 2003).

"Queen Victoria and India, 1837-61" *Victoria Studies*, Vol. 46, No. 2, Papers from the Inaugural Conference of the North American Victorian Studies Association (Winter, 2004).

A. Basu, Dilip Kumar. Thankamma, Catharine and Banerjee, Paramita. Agamben, Giorgio. "The Thing Itself." Trans. Juliana Schiesari, *SubStance*, Contemporary Italian thought, Vol. 16, No. 2, Issue 53 (1987).

Ahmed, Siraj. "The theatre of the civilized self: Edmund Burke and the East India trials." *Representations*. Vol. 78, No. 1 (Spring 2002).

Amariglio, Jack."Subjectivity, class and Marx's–Forms of the Commune." Special Issue on the Common and the forms of the Commune, *Rethinking Marxism*, Vol. 22, No. 3 (July 2010).

Bardhan, Gul. "What a Tremendous Movement it was..." *Seagull Theatre Quarterly*, Issue 7 (October 1995).

Bhattacharya, Bandana. "Bharate Nari Jagaran," *Cholar Pothey*, Vol. 2 (June 2009).

Bhattacharya, Malini. 'In search of new roles.' *Theatre India: National School of Drama's Theatre Journal*, No. 2 (Nov. 2000).

Carlson, Marvin. "The Resistance to Theatricality." *SubStance*, Special Issue: Theatricality, University of Wisconsin Press, Vol. 31, No. 2/3, Issue, 98/99 (2002): 238-250.

de Man, Paul. "Literary History and Literary Modernity." *Theory in Humanistic Studies. Daedalus*, Vol. 99 No. 2 (Spring, 1970).

Deshpande, Govind Purushottam. "Is there, or should there be, a national theatre in India?" In Anjum Katyal (ed.) *Seagull Theatre Quarterly*, The Seagull Foundation for the Arts, Calcutta (August 1995).

Forbes, Derek. "Our theatrical attempts in this distant Quarter: the British stage in eighteenth century Calcutta." *Theatre Notebook* (June 2007).

Gupta, Dhruv. "Charer Doshok: Uttal Shomoy," Anil Acharya (ed.). *Anushtup*, Vol. 4 (1988).

Hansen, Kathryn. "Parsi theatre and the city: locations, patrons, audiences." *Sarai Reader* (2002).

Harijan, 76 (26-7-1942): 308-9.

Jain, Rekha. "Nemiji ke sath mera natyanubhav." *Rangkarm–The Annual Magazine of IPTA Raigarh* (2006).

Jolie Kaul, "YCI: Smriti." *Bohurupi*, Nabanna Smarak Shankha (1964).

Kathleen, Stewart. "Nostalgia – A Polemic," *Cultural Anthropology*. Vol. 3, No. 3, (Aug. 1988).

Kathryn, Hansen. "Languages on Stage: Linguistic pluralism and community formation in 19th century Parsi theatre." *Modern Asian Studies*, Vol. 37, No. 2 (May 2003).

Kaur, Amarjeet. "Vimala Dang – Ek Jibanbyapi Shangrami," *Cholar Pothey*, Vol. 2 (June 2009).

Kelly, Duncan. "Carl Schmitt's Political theory of Representation," *Journal of the History of Ideas*, Vol. 65, No. 1 (Jan., 2004): 113-134.

Novetzke, Christian Lee. "Bhakti and its public." *International Journal of Hindu Studies*, Vol. 11, No. 3 (December 2007): 255-272.

Manujendra, Kundu. "The dramatic performances act of 1876: reactions of the Bengali establishment to its introduction." *History and Sociology of South Asia* 7(I), Jamia Millia Islamia, Sage Publications (2013): 79-93.

Mitra, Amal. "The English stage in Calcutta circa 1750." *Sangeet Natak*,

Sangeet Natak Akademi, New Delhi, Number 88 (April-June 1988).

Mitter, Partha. "The Early British Port Cities of India: Their Planning and Architecture Circa 1640-1757." *Journal of the Society of Architectural Historians.* Vol. 45, No. 2 (June, 1986): 95-114.

Murdoch, Iris. "Nostalgia for the Particular." *Proceedings of the Aristotelian Society*. New Series, Vol. 52, (1951-1952).

Pandit, Maya. Vohra, Kinnari, Mangai, A. Basu, Dilip Kumar. Thankamma, Catharine and Banerjee, Paramita. 'Women that men created.' *Theatre India: National School of Drama's Theatre Journal*. No. 2 (Nov. 2000).

Pradhan, Sudhi. "Bharater Marxbadi Sanskriti Andolaner Prothom Joog." *Gananatya* (Dec 1989).

____. "Gananatya sangho o Uday Shankar." *Gananatya* (October 1977).

Roychoudhury, Sajal. "Chollish doshoker Gananatya Andolaner Mahila Shilpi." *Group Theatre* (April 1988).

Sahni, Balraj, "IPTA Central Dance Troupe's Programme and Tour." *People's Age* (Sunday, Jan 13, 1946).

Sarkar, Sumit. "Kaliyuga', 'Chakri' and 'Bhakti': Ramakrishna and His Times." *Economic and Political Weekly*, Vol. 27, No. 29 (Jul. 18, 1992).

Sarkar, Tanika. "Birth of a Goddess: 'Vande Mataram', Anandamath, and Hindu Nationhood" *Economic and Political Weekly*, Vol. 41, No. 37, (Sep. 16-22, 2006).

Schechner, Richard. "From Ritual to theatre and back: the structure/ process of the efficacy- entertainment dyad." *Educational Theatre Journal*. 26:4 (1974): 455-81.

Sen, Niranjan. "Bharatiya Gananatya Sangher Itihash." *Epic Theatre* (April-May 1978 to January 1979).

____. "Bharatiya Gananatya Shangher Itihas." *Epic Theatre* (August 1978).

Senelick, Laurence. "Russian Enterprise, Bengali Theatre, and the Machinations of the East India Company." *New Theatre Quarterly*, Vol. 28, Issue 01 (February 2012): 20-29.

Shaw, Denis. "Esther Leach, 'The Mrs Siddons of Bengal'." Vol. 10, No. 4 (Dec., 1958): 304-310.

Solomon, Rakesh H. "Culture, Imperialism, and Nationalist Resistance: Performance in Colonial India." *Theatre Journal*. Colonial/ Postcolonial Theatre, Vol. 46, No. 3 (Oct., 1994): 323-347.

Srinivasan, Amrit. "Reform and revival: the devadasi and her dance." *Economic and Political Weekly* (1985).

Struc-Oppenberg, "Ursula Friedrich Schlegel and the history of Sanskrit Philology and Comparative Studies" *Canadian Review of Comparative Literature* (Autumn 1980).

Tanvir, Habib. "Theatre is in the villages." *Social Scientist*, Vol. 2, No. 10 (May, 1974): 32-41.

The Calcutta Christian Observer, Vol. 1, Baptist Mission Press, Calcutta (June to December 1832).

The Gazetteer Bombay City and Island, Vol. III, Times Press, Bombay (1910).

Paper presented at colloquium and conference

Choudhury, Soumyabrata. "Political Sociability and theatre in the subcontinent: The poverty of appearance, appearance of poverty...". Paper presented at Warwick–JNU Colloquium (March 31 to April 2, 2010).

Rehman, Ram, "Sunil Janah, Photographer and P.C. Joshi: the Making of a Progressive Culture". Paper presented at 14th P.C. Joshi Memorial Lecture, 2010.

Manuscripts and archival material from -

The British Library, London.

West Bengal State Archives, Kolkata.

Natya Shodh Sansthan, Kolkata.

Maharashtra State Archives, Mumbai.

National Archives, New Delhi.

Nehru Memorial Museum & Library, New Delhi.

Interviews

Dina Pathak interviewed by Pratibha Agarwal at Natyashodh, Kolkata, 14 January, 1988.

P.C. Joshi (junior) interviewed by the author in New Delhi, May 13, 2010.

Pratibha Agarwal interviewed by the author at Natyashodh, Kolkata, August 14, 2009.

Preeti Banerjee interviewed by the author at Kolkata, 4th May 4, 2010 and March 15, 2009.

*Reba Roychoudhury interviewed by Khaled Choudhury at Natyashodh Kolkata,(date not provided)

*Rekha Jain interviewed by Pratibha Agarwal, 4 October, 1986.

*Santa Gandhi interviewed by Pratibha Agarwal on at Natyashodh, Kolkata, 28 August, 1984.

Sova Sen interviewed by the author at Kolkata, March, 2009.

Vidya Munshi and Sunil Munshi interviewed by the author at Kolkata, August 14, 2009.

*interviews courtesy Natya Shodh Sansthan, Kolkata.

Websites

http://www.aryasamaj.org/newsite/node/721 Last accessed March 6, 2017.

http://www.harmonyindia.org/hportal/VirtualPageView.jsp?page_id=4975.

http://www.lacan.com/essays/?page_id=126 Last accessed March 6, 2017.

http://www.thehindu.com/todays-paper/tp-in-school/modis-push-for-hindi-irks-regional-parties/article6134455.ece Last accessed March 6, 2017.

http://www.thehindu.com/opinion/editorial/preserve-the-idea-of-india/article6017266.ece Last accessed March 6, 2017.

http://dsal.uchicago.edu/books/artsandideas/text.html?objectid=HN681.S597_23-24_091.gif Last accessed March 6, 2017.

Index